T0021020

"A brilliantly readable exploration of the difficulties and the necessity of class analysis for any imaginably successful left politics."

WALTER BENN MICHAELS, AUTHOR OF
THE BEAUTY OF A SOCIAL PROBLEM

"A fascinating and accessible account of a social class that is too often neglected or misunderstood."

TOM MILLS, AUTHOR OF *THE BBC*

"An incisive, erudite and provocative analysis of the changing class composition and dynamics in Britain. *A Nation of Shopkeepers* will be central to future debates on class in Britain and further afield."

PAUL O'CONNELL, CENTRE FOR HUMAN RIGHTS LAW, SOAS

"A vivid and passionate account of the renewal of class divisions in British society and the visceral forms they take. Anyone who doubts the relevance of contemporary class divides is encouraged to read this book."

MIKE SAVAGE, AUTHOR OF *THE RETURN OF INEQUALITY*

"Does a terrific job of helping us break out of classic class schemas that are either too abstract to help practical political interventions or have not kept up to date with the evolving and complex developments in the formation of classes in Britain."

MIKE WAYNE, AUTHOR OF *ENGLAND'S DISCONTENTS*

"For those serious about making sense of class and the potential for transforming society today, *A Nation of Shopkeepers* makes an important contribution."

JAMIE WOODCOCK, AUTHOR OF *MARX AT THE ARCADE*

A NATION OF SHOPKEEPERS

A NATION OF SHOPKEEPERS

THE UNSTOPPABLE RISE OF THE PETTY BOURGEOISIE

Dan Evans

Published by Repeater Books

An imprint of Watkins Media Ltd

Unit 11 Shepperton House

89-93 Shepperton Road

London

N1 3DF

United Kingdom

www.repeaterbooks.com

A Repeater Books paperback original 2023

1

Distributed in the United States by Random House, Inc., New York.

Copyright © Dan Evans 2023

Dan Evans asserts the moral right to be identified as the author of this work.

ISBN: 9781913462697

Ebook ISBN: 9781913462925

Printed and bound in the United Kingdom by TJ Books Limited

MIX
Paper from
responsible sources
FSC
www.fsc.org   FSC® C013056

To Mabli

CONTENTS

PREFACE

I have always been obsessed with class. If you are reading this book, then there's a chance that you are too.

Like many people, this obsession is rooted in my own personal history and background. My mum comes from a solidly middle-class family of school teachers. Her parents — my grandparents — both went to university, which would have been unusual in the 1950s. My dad's life was very different. He was a PE teacher, but before that a bricklayer. His dad, my grandad, was a miner and steelworker. He didn't go to school, let alone university.

I grew up with a foot in both camps — half working-class culture, half middle-class. Different sides of the family had different norms, accents, politics, leisure habits and even different life expectancies because of their class background. Having to straddle two worlds was confusing in a way that people who grow up in either straightforwardly working-class or middle-class households perhaps don't experience.

This was all heightened by where I grew up. Porthcawl is a small seaside town half way between Cardiff and Swansea in the borough of Bridgend. Porthcawl is widely considered to be "posh" by the standards of the area, an oasis within a solidly working-class, post-industrial region, and has historically voted Tory while the surrounding areas were — until 2019 — firmly Labour.

It is a town built on aspiration and social mobility — historically, it has been where people from the south Wales valleys have a caravan, and then move or retire to if they can afford it. One old woman told me that people who own

1

chip shops in the Welsh valleys move to Porthcawl "like the Jews move to Israel". It was the consensus that once people moved to Porthcawl, "their noses went up in the air"; they started to think they were better than everyone else, forgot their roots and started voting Tory. Most of the people I grew up with, like me, had working-class parents from elsewhere.

I am a product of social mobility. Like many people raised under the welfare state, the Evanses from Port Talbot were upwardly mobile. Within three generations we'd gone from mining and a council estate to university to the suburbs. However, it's safe to say my life hasn't worked out like I planned it. The social mobility journey my family has been on since the 1930s is stalling with me. After I graduated, I spent a few years kicking around working in call centres and bars, and then stupidly went back to university to do a PhD. For about fifteen years now, my life has been a cycle of low-paid service work interspersed with stints in academia, moving back and forth between Porthcawl and Cardiff.

When I moved back to Porthcawl, first during my PhD and then later after being made redundant from yet another fixed-term academic contract, I found myself once again working behind the same bar that I had worked at during school and my PhD. Here, I came into contact with lots of my old school friends, many of whom were now very successful self-employed tradesmen. Others were salesmen, cops, soldiers. They were married to nurses, beauticians, hairdressers.

They had lots of money, or at least a lot compared to me. They had attractive girlfriends and wives, nice cars, and almost always owned their own house. Sometimes they'd come into the bar still in their work clothes and covered in paint, paying for drinks with wads of cash — they never ever used card.

Everyone was sympathetic and confused about my lowly state. "What the fuck are you doing back here, I thought you were a doctor, butt, aren't doctors well paid?", and so on. Despite being the same age, they felt a lot older. More like men, more like our dads. They had entered manhood — job, wife, children — nearly as soon as they finished school and about a decade earlier than me.

The girls I worked with, who had also grown up in this social milieu, were similarly perplexed: "Why don't you have a *house*? Why don't you have a *wife*?" In Porthcawl, these were the things I was expected to have by the age of thirty. I inspired genuine pity.

During the 2017 and 2019 elections, I put pro-Corbyn posts up on Facebook and got hammered for it. People didn't like him, they liked Boris. As I understood it then, I was the stereotypical middle-class lefty, they were working-class Tories.

Many people in Porthcawl fetishize graft — hard work, making money, working out, being flash, having a fit Mrs and nice house as a result of all the above. Do nights, take on extra shifts. Putting the work in, doing as many hours as humanly possible, was celebrated as a virtue. Despite the warmth and love in interpersonal relationships in the town, whenever "politics" came up I noticed there was often a hardness to people's views. I work my bollocks off (true) and I have done OK, so if someone is poor, it's because they are lazy. They often seemed to dislike anyone they saw as idle, anyone who was perceived having something for nothing: students, immigrants, people on the dole.

For years I didn't really understand any of this. My previous framework for understanding class had been a working class/middle class binary that was primarily defined through culture, consumption practices and income. My understanding growing up that Porthcawl was "middle class" was primarily based on the assumption that people in Porthcawl simply had more money than people in the former mining villages that surrounded the town. This made them middle class. Yet now I had been to university, I'd also seen the people above me: *actual* posh people. People who'd been to private school, who would become army officers, lawyers, bankers, managers, politicians. The category of "middle class" no longer seemed to fit. While the people in Porthcawl were certainly more affluent than many other parts of south Wales, they were certainly not "posh", no matter how hard they tried. "Proper" middle-class people, as a rule, did not work in construction, did not pay for meals using cash, and ultimately did not try as hard as people in Porthcawl did to show everyone that they were rich and respectable.

Nor were the people in Porthcawl really working class. They often owned their own businesses, most owned their own houses, some even had multiple houses that they rented out. They were "culturally" working class but economically more affluent.

Equally, I was increasingly confused about my own class. I'd thought of myself as "middle class" because my parents were teachers and I'd been to university, while the people I was serving in the bar were working class, because they did manual jobs. Later, however, when I moved back to Cardiff, my experience of downward social mobility began to change how I thought of myself. Yes, I've been to university, but I'm also renting my house and permanently skint? I began to think that I was part of a new working class because of my increasing precarity.

The working class/middle class binary was unhelpful for understanding the class position of both myself and my hometown.

This experience is not unique or even that unusual. The British left — and indeed left movements around the world — are today predominantly drawn from what the Great

British Class Survey brands the "emergent service class": young people from suburban regional backgrounds who have done well in school, gone to university and accrued a significant amount of cultural capital, but who now find themselves working in low-paid, precarious work, with no savings, their social mobility journey stalled. Significant numbers of this class have stayed in the cities where they went to university, renting a room in a house — one of the biggest internal flows of people in the UK is now young adults from small towns moving to large cities, particularly London. Others will have, like me, moved back in with their parents in their regional towns. While they are back in their small towns, they will come across their "less academic" friends from school, many of whom left school at sixteen to get a trade and who have since built a relatively comfortable life for themselves, owning their own houses, maybe even renting some out. They are what the Great British Class Survey call the "new affluent workers" — people from working-class backgrounds who didn't go to university, but who've nonetheless managed to do well for themselves.

The problem with the Great British Class Survey, however, is that it confuses cultural and regional variations within the same class for separate classes. I am not an "emergent service worker", my school friends are not "new affluent workers". Nor am I "middle class" or "working class".

What I realise now is that I and my school mates who have done very well are both members of the same class: *the petty bourgeoisie*. We are both members of a very specific, historical and powerful class that has grown and grown to the extent that it now constitutes at least a third of the British population.

While this may seem confusing, throughout its history the petty bourgeoisie has been a class that is bifurcated, containing two strands or "fractions", which together constitute the whole. I, and most of the young people on the left, are a part of the *new* petty bourgeoisie, while my school friends back in my home town (and in suburbs and towns across the UK) are the *old* petty bourgeoisie.

Even if they are not correctly labelled or understood as being part of the petty bourgeoisie, the experiences of the section of the new petty bourgeoisie that today constitutes the base of the modern left are well known. The modern, young left is motivated by fizzing anger and frustration at blocked social mobility. Everything is shit. I can't get a house, a steady job. Nothing is ever going to get better. "Our generation" has been screwed over by selfish boomers and Tory homeowners. Addressing housing and student debt — while statistically minority causes for the wider population, who tend to have houses and haven't been to university — have become central to the demands made on modern social democratic parties.

However, the experiences of the other fraction of the petty bourgeoisie — the old petty bourgeoisie — are not. This is because our values, beliefs, our expectations and ways of being and understanding the world are shaped in a large part by our socialization and lives in a particular place. While the narrative of "metropolitan elites" has been cynically deployed by the right, the agglomeration of certain industries and jobs in urban areas – universities, the media and culture industry, the political bureaucracy, the civil service and so on — means that the "progressive classes", which includes both the professional managerial classes and the elements of the new petty bourgeoisie that populate the modern left, *are* overwhelmingly clustered in the cities. And because certain classes become clustered in particular places, people of these classes then also move to these places, so people eventually end up hanging round with and dating "people like them" in these places. This inevitably creates a feedback loop, a solipsism that *our* life, *our* social world, *our* experiences, values and desires are the norm. This is particularly acute in the UK because of the extent of uneven regional development and the concentration of the aforementioned industries in the south east. We increasingly live in hermetically sealed worlds, which are often like oil and water.

As I moved to Cardiff to work in the university, gradually my social world changed. In my new social circle, I no longer knew any tradesmen, cops, squaddies, nurses and salesmen. My world became comprised of declassed graduates, academics, young professionals, arty types. "Lefties", as my old friends would call them.

After spending years on the left and in "progressive circles", I've come to realize that the life experiences, norms, values and even aesthetics of places like Porthcawl just don't register. If they do, they are seen as alien. During the Brexit referendum, for example, I was working at Cardiff University. Based on Facebook, pretty much everyone I knew back home would be voting leave. Yet in the rarefied world of academia, the thought of voting leave was horrifying. The EU was an unambiguous good. It allowed us to go travelling or work in universities across Europe. More and more, looking at social media, it became clear that most of the "progressive" people I knew, either young lefties or middle-aged liberals, were not just horrified by the referendum result, they literally didn't know anyone who voted for Brexit.

This insularity increasingly means that most political phenomena can't be grasped. Who the hell keeps voting for Boris? Why didn't Corbyn win? This disbelief has increasingly led to a despairing narrative that the UK is irredeemably reactionary or uniquely grim (often captured on "left twitter" by the term "rainy fascist island"): the UK is controlled by pensioners, baby boomers hate us, and so on. These are perspectives born of isolation.

I believe that much of the modern left — precisely by virtue of its removal from these communities and experiences — is affected by a romantic view of society — particularly the "working class" — that is largely totally abstract. Stuck in the cities, in university, it's easy to develop a romantic image of society "out there" as black and white: terraced houses, people working down the mines or in factories. I certainly did. But the world of work has changed, the class structure has changed, people's lives have changed. What about new-build Britain? The suburbs? The self-employed?

The petty bourgeoisie now makes up a huge section of the population, and the ideology and working conditions of the petty bourgeoisie has now spread way beyond the class's actual boundaries in a way which has shaped much contemporary politics.

This, in my view, hasn't been appreciated. We on the left do not understand the changing class structure, nor our place within it, and this is one of the main reasons why we continue to lose.

For many years, I have been immersed in both the old petty bourgeoisie and the new petty bourgeoisie, indeed moving between them as I go through a cycle of redundancies, shorthold tenancies and my old bedroom. These are the worlds I know best. I like to think I've got an intimate understanding of both, the similarities and differences, and the divides between the petty bourgeoisie and the working class. While the different fractions of the petty bourgeoisie are ostensibly different in many ways, as this book will show, we also share many similarities. Almost all of my own concerns were individualistic and aspirational, just like my old school friends were. We both wanted housing, we both wanted security and status. While they marked themselves off from the working class through flashing the cash, I marked myself off via cultural and educational capital. The main difference, which had split us politically, was that my lofty expectations had clashed with reality, but theirs hadn't. I was downwardly mobile, they were upwardly mobile. My life was shit, so I was desperate for change. Their lives were pretty good, and they wanted to hold onto that thank you very much.

This book introduces the petty bourgeoisie as a class. It tries to make sense of the changing class structure and the petty bourgeoisie's place within it. It is not the final word but the start: I hope it can help catalyse a wider conversation about class on the left, because the left needs to understand class and its own position in order to have a chance of winning. And while the point of the book is not to think in terms of one's class position as an *individual*, I nonetheless hope it resonates with those of you stuck in your old bedrooms, renting your flat or working in call centres, and helps you understand your own position, as it helped me understand mine.

INTRODUCTION

The death of the petty bourgeoisie — the class miserably sandwiched between the proletariat and the bourgeoisie — has been repeatedly proclaimed. Marx and Engels believed that the petty bourgeoisie would inevitably sink into the ranks of the proletariat as the rise of monopoly capitalism destroyed the power of small artisans. It was branded a "transitional" class: a hangover from pre-industrial times, a living anachronism that had somehow persisted into industrial capitalism but which would gradually and quietly die out.

This did not happen. Far from dying out, the petty bourgeoisie survived. It has played a major role in every revolution and counter-revolution throughout the last few centuries and was central to the creation of both social democracy and fascism.

As the class structure in advanced capitalist democracies has evolved following deindustrialization and the transition to neoliberalism, this class has actually *grown*. The petty bourgeoisie is now one of the most powerful political forces in the world. Today, it is the major driving force behind the major political movements of our time. In the US and UK, different fractions of the petty bourgeoisie have driven Trumpism and Sanders, both Corbynism and Brexit, as well as underpinning ostensibly permanent Tory hegemony. It has been the major social base of Podemos in Spain, Syriza in Greece, the Arab Spring, as well as being a key social base of the reactionary politics of Bolsonaro in Brazil, Erdoğan in Turkey, Jobbik in Hungary, Law and Justice in Poland, as well as newly emerging anti-globalisation movements such as the yellow vests in France, the "freedom convoy" trucker protest in Canada and fuel protesters in the UK.

Across the world, politics on the right and left is moulded by both the petty bourgeoisie and petty bourgeois ideology, despite the class having very little formal political representation in world parliaments.

Yet despite the influence and scale of this class, it is rarely talked about in left political discourse. Of course, unlike the elite or the proletariat, the petty bourgeoisie is not a romantic cause. It does not command empathy, or the heroic images that the working class does. Arno Mayer, a Marxist from the ranks of the petty bourgeoisie, notes that "the petite bourgeoisie has had a harder time commanding scholarly attention than either the power elite or the proletariat: it has no patronage to dispense, it is not seen as a revolutionary threat, and it lacks the romance of utter wretchedness, once removed, that commands empathetic scrutiny."

One of the only times the term is used at all is simply as a pejorative (like fascism) that leftists use to label anything they don't like: a nebulous way of being that is never really explained but which is nonetheless to be distanced from — "this is petty bourgeois", "that is petty bourgeois" — a catch-all term for anything deemed to be "reactionary". Very often, people see what they feel to be "bad politics" and work backwards — "this [the Canadian trucker convoy, the yellow vests, etc.] *must* be driven by the petty bourgeoisie" because, of course, it's easier to blame the petty bourgeoisie than to deal with the idea that the working class don't have the right politics.

Not appreciating the increasing complexity of the class structure and the growth of the petty bourgeoisie in particular leaves the left unable to explain much of what is happening in modern politics. More gravely, not appreciating the distinctiveness of the petty bourgeoisie, its specific interests and values, and its political instability, has historically contributed to the class becoming receptive to reactionary political solutions.

The Death and Resurrection of Class Analysis

The main reason that the petty bourgeoisie is not widely understood or even talked about is because the left no longer has a good understanding of class in general, let alone the annoying classes that cannot be easily categorised as straightforwardly working class or bourgeois.

Class was submerged during the era of progressive neoliberalism. In the UK, Thatcher believed class was a Marxist concept and did her very best to destroy the concept itself, and for a large period she was successful in doing this.

But it wasn't just politicians who dismissed class analysis. The left, too, abandoned class during this period. It was bad enough that Thatcher and Reagan crushed the organized working class, but perhaps even worse — and to the horror of many left intellectuals — large swathes of the working class had ostensibly embraced neoliberalism and abandoned the social democratic movements that were meant to represent them

As A. Sivanandan observed, the new left's post-mortem into what went wrong concluded that the left's problem had been its "economism", which had left it ill-equipped to understand the appeal of neoliberalism and its ability to co-opt large swathes of the population through ideological and cultural manipulation. In response, the "crude" focus on the "base" — the means of production, political economy and class — was replaced by a "cultural turn": a new focus on the superstructure and all the things that "orthodox" Marxism had apparently neglected, including, *inter alia*, "consciousness", ideology, language, images, the media and so on.

In the face of its defeat, it seemed clear that the organized working class was no longer the motor of history. In panic, and disregarding the warnings of theorists like Sivanandan and Robert Brenner, many leftists threw themselves into sectional "progressive" causes, mainly because this was all that was left. The working class — and indeed class in general — slowly disappeared as the main subject of leftist thought. It was replaced by a focus on identity groups and "social movements". Relatedly, the very concept of the collective itself — studying classes and broad societal and historical trends — was replaced by an epistemological focus on the "personal" (i.e., the individual or "the subject") as the site of politics, the inevitable adjunct of a theorisation of power, which moved away from "structures" and was instead everywhere, in human relationships and in our souls themselves.

The trends identified by Sivanandan in 1990 continued unabated. Rather than class, for years the left has been dominated by work on policing, sexuality and gender, racism, social movements, many of which detail the author's heroic involvement in x or y movement and the "radical" potential for "resistance". Rather than classes having competing interests, different fractions and being exploited, society is now widely interpreted as a big web of discrimination (which is not the same as exploitation) in which we all "oppress" each other. When class *is* now reluctantly discussed within this dominant ideological framework, it is not as the determining, structuring force within capitalist society, but merely as one form of discrimination or "oppression" among many others- tagged on at the end of "intersectionality" discourse, which as Walter Benn Michaels argues is in reality just a new way of not taking class seriously.

The excision of class and materialism and the relentless focus on individuals, coupled with the shift in the understanding of power, paved the way for the left to be subsumed wholesale by not just identity politics, but by the infantile liberal view of the world in which people are no longer moulded by structural forces beyond their control, but are now essentially innately good or bad, either reactionary or progressive — particularly racist or non-racist. As Sivanadan argued despairingly, "by personalising power, 'the personal is the political' personalises the enemy: the enemy of the black is the white as the enemy of the woman is the man. And all whites are racist like all men are sexist."

It is now common for the left to have a binary view of the world as divided into good or bad people, which neatly translates into Democrat/Republican or Tory/Labour. Thus, people in Trump's heartlands are racist, far-right authoritarians, despite also often voting for Obama or wanting to vote for Sanders (not the Clinton they were left with). In the UK, people in Labour's mythical "red wall" (a homogenous place occupied by the "white working class") voted for Brexit because they were racist, angry and stupid, despite also voting for Jeremy Corbyn a year later.

However, in some parts of the left the focus is slowly shifting back to class. Following the 2008 crash, a small global capitalist elite has pulled away from everyone else. Today, approximately two thousand billionaires own more wealth than over half the world's population combined. The COVID-19 pandemic brutally highlighted the myriad ways in which the rich profit from crisis and leave the rest of us to fend for ourselves. During the pandemic, this caste has seen its wealth increase more than any other time in the last fourteen years.

Society has returned to a situation resembling feudal times, and class divides are now glaring in a way they were perhaps not under the last days of progressive neoliberalism: people use foodbanks and sleep on the street in obscene numbers, and even those who were previously insulated from the worst excesses of austerity are becoming immiserated. Many of the middle classes have also seen their hopes and dreams of a stable, happy life disappear.

Since the crash, the discourse of "the 99%" (versus the 1%) understandably rapidly proliferated across left movements globally (see also "for the many, not the few"). This narrative has been a powerful tool and, for large periods, seemed to be quite effective, mobilizing loose coalitions of students, trade unionists and immiserated professional people.

The idea of society as increasingly polarised into two camps — the global capitalist elite on the one hand, and everyone else on the other — has been, and remains, central to the left's belated return to class. The middle classes, if they are thought about or engaged with at all, are assumed to be being "proletarianized": stable professions have seen wages cut, and have lost status and prestige. For those poor souls who are experiencing this, it certainly feels that, just as Marx predicted, they are being sucked down the social ladder, forming a new part of a growing working class. The boundary of the working class has been moved upward, submerging these newly poor, educated people below it.

The Communist Manifesto's famous aphorism that class divisions are becoming simplified, and that "society as a whole is more and more splitting up into two great hostile camps, into two great classes directly facing each other — Bourgeoisie and Proletariat", seems to accurately describe this state of affairs.

However, there is a direct tension between the left's narrative about proletarianization and the homogenization of everyone outside "the elite" and the class structure as it actually exists. During the left's "wilderness years" (when it was not focused on class), it became axiomatic among the sociologists who *had* continued to think about class that the class structure in the advanced West had fundamentally changed. Rather than simplifying or neatly polarizing into an elite and everyone else, it had actually become more complex. In particular, they noted the enormous growth of the sprawling "intermediary classes" (i.e., those classes who didn't easily fit into the category of bourgeoisie or proletariat) of managers, professionals, associate professionals, supervisors and so on, as capitalism matured and as state bureaucracy grew. The working class had actually *shrunk*, not grown.

In other words, the situation is more complex and messy than the discourse of elites versus the rest of us maintains. And of course, we don't see global billionaires at all, but we *do* see our neighbours, supervisors and managers. While the narrative of the 99% speaks to an objective truth — that the middle classes and working classes face the same struggles, are both immiserated and have the same interest in a socialist society — class divides and antagonisms between subordinate classes are nonetheless present in everyday life. Class conflict and class boundaries are lived and understood in hundreds of daily interactions at work, in the job centre, in schools, between different communities, over planning permission, which community gets their community centre closed and which keeps it open, home owners campaigning against social housing being built in their area and so on. Class divides are expressed spatially in the areas we live in, socially in the people we know and hang around with, culturally in the things we buy and our tastes, and these divides and boundaries have political and ideological ramifications that split us off from one another.

Although we are undoubtedly living in a period of increased polarization and misery, society is emphatically *not* neatly polarized into two classes. Indeed, at no stage throughout history has society been neatly polarized in this way: Marx spoke of polarisation as a *tendency*, rather than as an existing reality.

Moreover, as the class structure has grown more complex, so has the relationship between politics and class. The last few decades have witnessed a staggering class *dealignment* in politics. Professionals, managers and university graduates now comprise the bulk of the "progressive" forces in society, while the lower middle classes and working classes have been sucked into the orbit of right populist movements — that is, inexplicably siding with movements and politicians that make them poorer. This is an almost total reversal of the picture of society fifty or so years ago, where classes tended to vote simply for their economic interest: the working classes tended to vote for left-wing parties (which were generally comprised of and led by the working classes) and the middle classes and the more affluent sectors of society tended to vote for liberal or conservative parties.

The left has not, in my view, engaged with or understood the increased complexity of the class structure, the reality of dealignment or the reasons behind it. In particular, as the left has belatedly returned to class and class analysis and the relationship between class and politics, it is not armed with a theory of the middle classes, let alone the specificity of the petty bourgeoisie. It is constrained by a dualist view of class, which splits society neatly into two polarized classes, and in which the intermediate classes are an afterthought; or in which it is assumed that the middle classes will inexorably and simply sink into the ranks of the working class.

Even in some of the admirable returns to class in the wake of the defeat of Corbynism, the narrative is that Labour was too "middle class", and it neglected Labour's "heartlands" and core vote, which are portrayed as homogenously working-class places, which is simply not true. The petty bourgeoisie, which now comprises a significant (and growing) chunk of the population in these places, still does not feature at all.

A Very British Problem

There are also problems with understanding class that are culturally and nationally specific to each context. For a nation that is obsessed with class, it often seems that no one in the UK knows what class is, and the British treatment of class is riven with paradoxes. Overwhelmingly, since the shift away from industry, class in the UK is seen as a *cultural* phenomenon — something defined almost exclusively by accent, behaviours or consumption practices: whether you eat avocado or whether you eat pies, whether you like football or boxing or rugby, or the type of clothes you wear, the way you decorate your house, the music you listen to or the TV you watch. This is middle class, that is working class.

Or your class is an *identity*. If you say you are something, then that is it. And your class can never change. It is in the genes and is inherited like the football club you support, regardless of your actual class position. That's why, in the UK, we have "working-class millionaires", "working-class politicians" in the House of Lords, etc. This cuts right across British society. In a recent study, Sam Friedman found that the overwhelming majority of British people consider themselves to be working class. He interviewed people who had been to private school, who worked in the city, who lived very comfortable lives, all of whom claimed to be working class, because their great-grandparent had worked down the mines.

In the UK, unlike the United States, where most people want to be middle class, being working class is great, it's something to be proud of. And because class is about culture and consumption — understood as being not about what job you do or what school you went to, but rather about what you eat, or your affectations or accent — it is easy to demonstrate your working-class-ness. This frequently manifests itself in the phenomenon described by Joe Kennedy as "authentocracy", where New Labour politicians in particular participate in an increasingly absurd, undignified arms race to outdo one another in their quest to be perceived as "authentically" working class. Thus we had millionaire Pfizer lobbyist Owen Smith claiming to not know what a cappuccino was; Andy Burnham tweeting disgustedly about coffee (coffee is a recurring enemy of the proletariat).

Appeals to an "authentic" working class unsurprisingly intensified as candidates like Jeremy Corbyn and Bernie Sanders emerged, advocating policies that would objectively benefit working-class people. It becomes even more important for the defenders of the status quo to appeal to an "authentic", abstract working class in order to discredit anyone who might upset their gravy train by showing how out of touch these left-wingers are, how they lack a grasp of the working class, who instead want war and nationalism, not free broadband and a public health service.

In the rarefied world of the British media, class is chaotic. During the 2019 general election, a range of strange incidents occurred. *Guardian* journalist Helen Pidd travelled to Leigh, a brick in the "red wall", where she interviewed "working class artisan pizza restaurant owner" Andrew Twentyman (who owned three pizza restaurants), who said he was voting Tory. Well, no shit — this was the dictionary definition of a member of the petty bourgeoisie. Not a "working-class Tory", but a literal small business owner, the backbone of the Tory party for a century, but here taken as a natural Labour voter because he lived in "the red wall" and had a "working-class" accent.

When the ludicrousness of this position was pointed out to Pidd on Twitter, she doubled down, claiming "you can be working class and run a restaurant — or indeed be a property developer. Ask Andrew Twentyman how much money he makes from the pizzeria: minimum wage. The Guardian interviews UC claimants all the time — I'm sure I will do so in Leigh before long too."

Class here was again determined purely by accent and geography — sounding a bit common — rather than their economic relationship to capital, their social position and function in the class structure, their political ideology and so on. And because "working class" means anyone who eats chips and has an accent (which of course can be anyone), "middle class" has similarly become an almost totally useless term to describe a set of nebulous behaviours and "posh" consumption practices which can include anyone from the petty bourgeoisie, to comfortable professionals, right the way up to the actual Royal family.

The overwhelming focus on culture, consumption, accent and identity has rendered the petty bourgeoisie — which sits in the grey area between the working class and middle class — invisible. The deeply unhelpful media construction of the "red wall" has led to the mass misidentification of entire swathes of the UK as homogenously working-class regions, in particular submerging the petty bourgeoisie — who make up a central plank of the diverse class structure in these places — as part of the "working class".

The reduction of class to culture and an identity is not just confined to liberal journalists and New Labour politicians,but infects the left commentariat — including academics — too. Owen Jones' *Chavs*, for example — in many ways an excellent, vital book — implies that the real problem in British society is not exploitation, but snobbery

— being looked down on. Class here is again reduced to culture, an identity that the working class has and that they should be proud of.

Class as identity is in many ways an understandable reaction to the exhausting experience of trying to negotiate fields in which a working-class habitus is a hindrance and you feel hopelessly out of place. Faced with the relentless weaponization of other identities by middle-class elites, and the total invisibility of working-class people in politics (particularly left politics), academia and popular culture, for the few working-class people that have found themselves marooned in these milieus it is perhaps natural that class becomes central to their sense of self. Moreover, beyond these isolated individuals stuck in middle-class professions, the institutions which used to be the conduit for working-class life and culture have been decimated and largely disappeared, so one might well argue that class as an identity has emerged precisely because there is nothing else left.

However, there is a more sinister (and predictable) outcome of the absorption of class as another category within identity politics. Calculating that people's justified hatred of the professional managerial classes can be harnessed for a backlash, certain elements in society have increasingly weaponised "working-class identity" — chiefly the misleading idea of the "white working class" — for their own ends. Among the leading intellectual proponents of this strategy in the UK is the "Blue Labour" movement, which repeatedly argues that any reactionary position which can be linked to "the (implicitly white) working class" — at least by the army of focus group consultants employed by the Labour leadership — is what the people want and must be respected, and in turn pulling the Labour Party into even more reactionary positions. Of course, the proponents of Blue Labour are in reality just as divorced from the working class as the more progressive elements of the Labour Party — their whole movement is in fact a cynical ventriloquism, a way of using the working classes to launder, legitimize and mainstream the right-wing positions they hold. It is simply one fraction of the ruling class attempting to use the working class as a wedge to beat another fraction of the ruling class.

The Petty Bourgeoisie, the Professional-Managerial Classes and the Fractured "Working Class"

This book argues that rather than fading away, the "middle" or intermediary classes have stayed put and have in fact grown. The middle cannot be understood by breaking it up into endless strata or by cramming it down into the ranks of the proletariat, or by using the by-now useless term "middle class", or by treating it as an afterthought as a transitional class that will fade away.

The sprawling mass of "normal" people, sometimes referred to as the "C2s", "Essex Man", "Motorway Man", "Mondeo Man", or more commonly the "lower middle classes", can best be understood and explained as *the petty bourgeoisie*. It is a distinct, historic class that cannot be understood purely in relation to the fundamental classes above and below it, but which must be studied on its own terms. As Arno Mayer argues, the class has its own distinct inner structure and lifeworld, its own distinct culture, values and habitus. It has a distinct family structure and patterns of marriage, it has its own social and associational life, and distinct politics and political tendencies.

The modern petty bourgeoisie is split into two fractions. There is an *"old" petty bourgeoisie*, comprised largely of solo, self-employed people — not just the eponymous shopkeepers, but tradesmen (i.e., builders, electricians, plumbers, etc.), publicans, small landlords, freelancers, farmers, hairdressers and many more besides. This fraction is comprised of between four and five million people. Then there is a *"new" petty bourgeoisie*, comprised of "white collar" service workers, including declassed graduates, call centre workers, teachers and teaching assistants, salesmen, estate agents, nurses, firemen, public sector workers and more. They are clustered in the lower end of the public sector bureaucracy and in bullshit jobs in the private sector; those who perform policing or disciplinary functions, either directly or indirectly, and whether on behalf of the state or private capital — the police, prison guards, DWP workers, parking wardens, security guards, human resources; associate professionals and the lower boundary of the professional classes. As a shorthand, we can say the petty bourgeoisie – the new and old combined — constitutes at least a third of the working population. Both fractions are split off from the proletariat and the bourgeoisie in various ways, and both share significant commonalities despite often possessing significant cultural differences.

The book is not just about the internal life of the petty bourgeois class or how it has changed. While this class *has* grown objectively and subjectively, perhaps even more important is that its ideology — and indeed its way of life — has spread way beyond it as a class. Neoliberalism is a project of class war by the rich against the poor, but many of the ills now associated with neoliberalism, particularly the individualism that is all pervasive in modern society, are rooted in the experiences and ideology of the petty bourgeoisie specifically. Thatcherism, the British variant of neoliberalism and one of its most virulent strains worldwide, cannot be understood without understanding the petty bourgeois values and background of its architect, who was very open about her loyalties to this class and her desire to replicate and make universal the experiences and worldview of the petty bourgeoisie that she herself had grown up with. While Thatcherism was certainly a revolution, its goal was *restoration*: to change the class structure and turn the UK *back* into "a nation of shopkeepers", to return to an imagined past that existed before the proletariat had emerged to ruin people's peace and quiet.

However, the petty bourgeoisie does not constitute the entirety of the intermediate classes. The class structure is now very complex and the intermediary classes are huge. Nicos Poulantzas, the Greek-French Marxist sociologist who largely inspired this book, essentially included everyone, from nurses to secretaries to doctors, top professionals and engineers, in the new petty bourgeoisie. I do not agree with this approach. In my view, and as I argue in Chapter 3, the "upper" part of the middle, which is next to and blurs into the bourgeoisie, is best captured by Barbara and John Ehrenreich's concept of the professional-managerial classes. In this sense, "the middle" is split economically, culturally and ideologically.

I had originally aimed to not talk about the professional-managerial classes, but as my investigation into the petty bourgeoisie and its role in British society wore on, engaging with the classes above and below the petty bourgeoisie became unavoidable. As Chapter 3 shows, the upper boundary of the new petty bourgeoisie — for example, teachers and proletarianized academics — share a porous, blurred border with the professional-managerial classes, culturally, educationally and socially. Most obviously, the professional-managerial classes and new petty bourgeoisie together make up the key constituency within "progressive" politics, so anyone interested in exploring the social composition of the left cannot avoid dealing with it or running into it. The enormous cultural gulf between this small, closed-off, socially liberal group and basically everyone else in society, both in terms of values and behaviours, often make it seem homogenous from the outside.[1] Yet while there are similarities between the professional-managerial classes and the new petty bourgeois elements of the left, there are also important differences.

It is unclear whether the professional-managerial class constitutes a distinct class, as the Ehrenreichs argued, or merely a "progressive" fraction or cultural group within the bourgeoisie, as Poulantzas claimed. The trajectory and behaviour of the professional-managerial class — its entaglement with the EU and centrism — certainly does not suggest a class that is in any way "anti-capitalistic", as the Ehrenreichs claimed. As Paul O'Connell has argued, the professional-managerial class's messianic belief in technical expertise and the superiority of their own progressive values appears to be leading them to increasingly authoritarian positions, particularly towards the subordinate classes that are not sufficiently deferential to "experts". They increasingly exhibit a hostility to democracy whenever it produces outcomes that it feels are "irrational", or if it empowers or advantages those they perceive to be uneducated. However, that is another book. What *is* clear though is that the professional-managerial class has expanded enormously, and its distinct culture, ideology and cadence have taken a central role in liberal politics, in fact becoming partly hegemonic in the upper echelons of Western politics and society, dominating higher education, the third sector and, of course, "progressive" politics, exemplified by New Labour, the current Labour leader

---

1 Such is the social and cultural distinctiveness of the group of people most involved in progressive politics, particularly its roots in higher education, that Thomas Piketty has recently attempted to conceptualize it as the "Brahmin left" (Brahmin referring to a particular caste within Indian society).

Keir Starmer, and most Labour MPs, although the class is present across all the major parties. It is now a core part of the ruling class, which is now far more complex and diverse than the old combination of aristocrats and industrialists, and modern liberal politics and capitalist hegemony cannot be understood without understanding this group. Not only do liberal policies — such as the fetishization of the EU — emanate from the professional-managerial class's ideology and interests, the anger and alienation that defines working-class and petty-bourgeois politics is driven at least in part by a justifiable hatred of this class and everything that it stands for. The professional-managerial class is now a key protagonist in British politics, just like the petty bourgeoisie, although it is not as large.

Unlike the US, however, where the concept is routinely engaged with by the left, in the UK the concept is barely engaged with at all. Although the discussion of the professional-managerial class in this book is quite brief, it is a concept that is very useful and deserves more attention in the UK going forward.

The professional-managerial class is referred to throughout the rest of the book as it is a significant political and cultural force in its own right, but it is not the focus of the book and hence is mainly used as a foil for the boundaries of the new petty bourgeoisie. Neither are the working class or bourgeoisie engaged with in any level of detail and are similarly used primarily as reference points for the petty bourgeoisie, although while I am on the topic of the class structure as a whole, it is worth briefly mentioning developments regarding the working class that are significant and influence this account.

The working class used to be defined not just by its relationship to the means of production (it did not own anything, it had to work or starve, it had to sell its labour, it had no autonomy), but also by its distinct intellectual and civic life, institutions and social organizations. These gave birth to its distinct culture and habitus and helped reproduce collectivist values and ideology. What is significant in the modern era is these things, these communities, like the old forms of work that helped produce collectivism, have been destroyed. In other words, while a habitus and worldview definitely endures that is distinct and noticeable, *culturally* the working class has now been forced into the same associational and social life as the petty bourgeoisie, which is to say, a life that has historically had very little or no engagement with collective organizations or institutions (such as trade unions), and which is atomized and individualistic. Thus, in many ways, the boundaries between the working class and the petty bourgeoisie have blurred, both outside work and inside. This has also been helped by increasing fractures within the working class itself — along various lines, which are too numerous to get into here — but one of the most significant is the emergence of a visible underclass or *lumpenproletariat* — an entrenched, marginalized percentage of the population locked out of the job market, forced into poor housing and at risk of homelessness, poor health, engaged with the criminal justice system, not engaged with education or lacking educational qualifications and so on.

This reserve army of labour under neoliberalism is rarely described these days as a *lumpen* group, but this remains a very useful concept for understanding the modern class structure. It is relevant because I believe the effect this split has had is to push a higher element of the working class (traditionally called the "respectable" working class) closer to the petty bourgeoisie culturally, socially and ideologically.

The Left within the Class Structure

As I have already intimated, an ignorance of class is a major problem for the left. One of the major consequences of not engaging with the theory of the middle classes and the petty bourgeoisie is that the left does not understand its own class composition or place in the class structure, and hence its relationship to other classes (or "normal people"). The jarring and all-consuming horror of downward or blocked social mobility currently being experienced by many leftists seems to have warped their understanding of class. Many seem to now genuinely believe that the working class is "anyone who works"; that beneath the elite we *are* all essentially the same because we don't own the means of production. Thus, temporarily impoverished graduates are called the new working class. Striking professors sing "three cheers for the working class" (i.e., themselves) on UCU picket lines. And after all, isn't this the case? We work, therefore we are the working class. We wield union banners, we go on strike, just like the working class have always done.

Some of this stems from a genuine but mistaken reading of Marx's theory of class: that "the working class" is literally or "technically" everyone who does not own the means of production and the bourgeoisie are only those that own it, and beyond that it doesn't matter. Another generous interpretation would be that the young leftists who believe themselves to be a new working class are rooted in a student milieu in which people have simply yet to experience the world of work — they just haven't experienced the complexity of the class structure under modern neoliberalism. A more cynical interpretation would be that it is a way for the professional managerial classes that dominate the Labour Party and left commentariat to genuinely kid themselves and others that they are the same class as me or you. In a country where many prominent leftists are — and always have been — from the upper classes, there is maybe a vested interest in keeping the discussion about class narrowly oriented to questions of who owns the means of production, avoiding the role of culture or a discussion about the influence of the professional managerial classes. After all, who wants to admit to having "privilege" in this day and age?

Of course, if we are all the same class (i.e., all the working class, the 99%), there is no need to work to build class alliances. There is no need to understand the different allied classes, class fractions and so on; their specific values, ideology and why they act or vote as they do. There is no need to engage seriously with the petty bourgeoisie. There is no need to reflect about the failures of the left and socialism; we can just assume everyone is brainwashed or has "internalized" neoliberal beliefs. There is no need to wonder why managers are now on picket lines with their subordinates, or what the implications of this are politically; no need to worry about the fact that, in universities, the academics are the radical ones, always on strike, while the low-paid janitors, security guards and cleaners are not involved; no need to worry that trade unionism — and the labour movement in general — is overwhelmingly concentrated in the public sector and among highly educated graduates and managers; no need to worry that the majority of people are increasingly working in isolated, individualized workplaces in which we are all encouraged to compete with one another or to take on supervisory roles and so on. There are no antagonisms, we are all working class, everything is fine. This misrecognition of our own position has had disastrous consequences.

As C. Wright Mills and others pointed out in previous generations, becoming proletarianized "economically" (i.e., getting poorer or struggling) does not mean that one's class will change (or even that one's class consciousness will actually change), not least because class is emphatically not about how much you earn, or about whether you have to work for a living. It is urgent to understand that class divides are absolutely glaring — painfully so — particularly between the left activists and the "normal" people they try to persuade to socialism every four years. This is a class divide that many on the right see (and weaponize), but which the left remains oblivious to, even in the face of repeated defeats and failures. As with so many issues, the biggest problem is that people don't seem to think there is a problem at all. If you don't see how your values, ideology, behaviours, way of doing politics, interests and policies are increasingly alien to most of the country, then what is there to be done?

"The left" across the world, insofar as it still even exists, is a combination of classes. The left at the upper echelons are often the professional-managerial classes. This can range from lawyers like Keir Starmer to lobbyists and journalists like Owen Smith, but also at the local level, retired social workers, teachers, academics, probation officers — "lefty" or "caring" occupations that have been degraded and are now on the border between the new petty bourgeoisie and the professional-managerial class — whereas most of the "far-left" activists and new union members are made up of elements of the new petty bourgeoisie- downwardly mobile graduates, often with humanities or arts degrees, often based in cities or university towns, stuck in dead-end jobs despite being the "smart kids" from school. Then there remains a rump of far smaller elements of the working class.

I don't want this book to facilitate graduates insulting other graduates. As Ehrenreich herself noted, calling someone a member of the professional-managerial class is not meant to be a slur. We have to stop personalizing politics. The point is merely to be aware that there are class boundaries between the classes that comprise the left and the working class and the traditional petty bourgeoisie.

What is Class?

So if class is not an identity and not about culture, then what is it?

The first thing to say is that whether we like them or not, and whether we identify with them or not, in a capitalist society classes exist "objectively", because capitalism requires a class-divided society. In other words, there's no wishing away class. It exists. Beyond this basic, fundamental law, however, class is more open to debate.

Rather than providing an absolutist definition of what class is, it's better to think about the things we have to consider when we talk about class. Class is an economic, social, political and cultural phenomenon, and we have to think about all of them to make sense of it.

Firstly, we have to think about where classes come from. Class is "economic" in the sense that classes are formed by changes to the economy, by "the relations of production". Changes to the economy bring classes into being (or, as this book argues, change the balance of the class structure). The obvious example is the role of the Industrial Revolution in creating the proletariat and the bourgeoisie. These classes did not exist in the feudal economy. Under feudalism, the social structure was comprised of a gentry or aristocracy, a small class of artisans (more to come about them and this later) and peasants (and later agricultural labourers) who were tied to the land in a relation of serfdom. As the Industrial Revolution and technological innovation changed the economy, workers from the countryside increasingly moved into the new towns and cities to labour first in iron and cotton works, and later mines. As they settled in the towns and lived in new forms of accommodation, and worked in new workplaces, they eventually formed a new class — the proletariat.

Similarly, class is also "social" in that it is relational. As Erik Olin Wright describes them, classes only exist in so far as they are defined against other classes; they have antagonistic interests with other classes, hence "class struggle". This gets at the dynamism of Marxist class analysis: in social stratification analyses, which talk about myriad class fractions put together like a rock formation, classes are simply there, lying side by side peacefully. There is little discussion of how they got there, their relationship to one another or where they are going. Yet Marxists argue that the proletarian is poor precisely because the bourgeoisie is rich; the proletarian owns no land or property because the bourgeoisie owns it all — they have directly competing class interests. While it is feasible to imagine a scenario in which racial and sexual disparities and discrimination were eliminated under capitalism, it is impossible to eliminate class antagonisms because these are built into the capitalist system.

And because classes exist in relation with one another, it means this relationship contains both objective and subjective aspects. Thus, the bourgeoisie objectively exists in an exploitative relationship with the proletariat — they get rich and rule through their domination of the proletariat, extracting wealth from them. The proletariat thus have objectively antagonistic interests with the bourgeoisie. But as Wright argues, class analysis must also incorporate class formation. We have to think about both class "in itself" (objective or 'on paper') and class "for itself" (subjective, social) — not just how class is created, but how and why classes act in certain ways, how people come to think of themselves as belonging to a class in everyday life and understand their interest as a class. That is, the proletariat were not just magicked into being; they became the proletariat when they became conscious and aware of their own power as a collective. As E.P. Thompson famously put it, "class *happens* when some men, as a result of common experiences (inherited or shared), feel and articulate the identity of their interests as between themselves, and as against other men whose interests are different from (and usually opposed to) theirs."

And just as class is social, it is ideological and political. Marx's political writings detail how particular classes possess particular ideologies or a particular outlook on life as a result of their position in the productive process and their relationship to other classes. They also (in theory) come to understand what their interests are and think in terms of how politics can benefit their class as a collective. However, this is a complex process and we cannot simply assume or read off ideology from someone's position in the class structure. As we have already seen, there is now no simple alignment between politics and class, and politics does not simply reflect "class interest" as is sometimes implied. The ruling class manipulates subordinate classes and attempts to organize the "common sense" of society in a way that produces consensus and stability; they deliberately attempt to prevent the subordinate classes becoming conscious of their class interest and coming together. The attempt to influence and mould social consciousness is done in myriad ways, through academia, the press, religion, the education system, popular culture and so on. Classes and class interests are also influenced by political parties and movements. These things do not create classes, but parties and movements mobilise different classes and class fractions; they seek to co-opt certain classes as part of hegemonic strategies.

Finally, if we wish to understand how classes become conscious agents, we need to also, in my view, incorporate an analysis of "culture" — of everyday life and things like consumption and aesthetics. We should not throw out the baby with the bathwater because of the overemphasis on culture, consumption, accent and so on in the media. People become conscious of class and capitalism because of their work, because they sense differentials of power and control over their lives. But they also feel and identify themselves as belonging to a class through other things: dispositions, ways of talking, walking, eating, accent, the houses they live in, the food they eat, the things they watch on TV and the way they dress. Just as class is relational in terms of objective economic interests between classes, this relationality is lived and felt in everyday life through other means as well as economic — when we feel out of place somewhere, for example, or whether we feel confident writing a book, or giving a lecture, or going for a certain job and so on

For E.P. Thompson, class consciousness was "cultural", but here, in making reference to culture, he did not mean whether someone ate avocado or liked coffee or whether they liked classical music or rock music, but rather how common class interests and common experiences at work translated into shared values, traditions, ideas and institutions — i.e., culture in the "ordinary" sense that Raymond Williams talks about: the whole range of human experiences, our daily lives and traditions. Thus the transition from class "on paper" to something that is lived and felt and understood in everyday life through "culture", behaviour and institutions is a vital component of understanding class, and for this reason culture and everyday life are vital in understanding class "for itself".

Because culture and everyday life is important, the work of the French sociologist Pierre Bourdieu can greatly help us understand how class consciousness is arrived at and how class is reproduced from generation to generation.

Bourdieu disagreed with the assumption, inherent in much orthodox Marxism, that "classes on paper", (or "classes in themselves"), inexorably become "actual classes" (i.e. "class for itself'") in the sense of a conscious, subjective group mobilized for struggle. For Bourdieu, "top-down" analyses of class and class identity treat people as "things" or "objects" which simply "have" class. People are separated into sketched "probable" classes: working class, middle class and so on, based on "objective" things like occupation. It is then assumed that these people "automatically" identify as working class, middle class, upper class and so on. For Bourdieu, this approach is more suited to "zoologists and botanists" than to human beings. This approach does not acknowledge the role of the individual, the complexity of class or how people actually understand class in everyday life — if, indeed, people *do* actually classify themselves as belonging to particular classes. He therefore called explicitly for a micro-level analysis of class in everyday life as a way of understanding how people became aware of their own class, and how class divides and boundaries worked in everyday life through our behaviours, cultural consumption, aesthetics and so on (see Glossary). Bourdieu is also of significance because he was himself from the petty bourgeoisie and experienced the dislocation and shock of social mobility and the sensation of feeling out of place that is disproportionately experienced by this class. He was thus more sensitive to the changes and influences that this class experiences than those who focus on the fixed classes, and is therefore particularly well placed to help describe it.

While Bourdieu is sometimes dismissed as being overly concerned with the minutiae of class divides in everyday life, it is important to appreciate that his analysis and concepts relating to class "culture" are conceived of as a system of social control. That is, he is not analysing how people behave, what people wear and what they eat in and for themselves, but because it is through these everyday things that the class system and hierarchy is held in place. Taken together, these subtle forms of domination which reproduce the class structure (e.g., people feeling unwelcome in certain places, not suited to certain professions, stigmatising certain classes and so on) are described as "symbolic violence": a low-intensity class war — understood by both sides — which happens in daily life. It is perhaps difficult for those who rarely feel out of place in a field to appreciate the centrality of things like habitus, culture, accent and aesthetics.

Ultimately, different theories of class correspond to different levels of analysis and different epistemological orders (i.e., forms of knowledge). Those who favour what C. Wright Mills called "grand theory" — formal, abstract concepts and broad brushstrokes — will generally not be sympathetic to or particularly concerned with analyses of everyday life. Equally, sociologists who are focused on everyday life and get caught up in the minutiae of interaction are frequently hostile to the domination of sociology by "dry" large-scale quantitative analyses, which gloss over the complexities of everyday life. Yet the macro and micro are not mutually exclusive, but complementary. Without understanding the macro level — in this case, the "grand theory" of how classes are produced and how they act generally as large-scale collectives — studying everyday interaction is useless. As Michael Burawoy notes, we have to look at everyday life armed with theory and an understanding of large, general trends. Theory helps us to understand everyday life and make sense of the interactions and things we see around us every day. Theory is necessary, in this respect, otherwise all we are doing is merely describing things we see, which is no different from journalism. Equally, everyday life can help us understand grand theory because it helps us test and improve theories by applying them to everyday life, before then reflecting on whether they actually fit, whether they tally with the things we see with our own eyes. We have to then approach class from above and below — in general, sweeping terms of objective classes, and also how class works in everyday life. We need both to understand capitalist society.

The Specific Problem of the Petty Bourgeoisie Within Class Analysis

The petty bourgeoisie is undoubtedly complex and heterogeneous, and as I have found to my inconvenience, does not make for easy reading or analysis. It is easy to tie oneself in knots trying to pin it down, and once one pulls one thread to interrogate it, the whole thing unravels and reveals complex, never-ending questions about class itself, as well as other related classes: what makes a class, what counts as a class boundary and so on.

The *new* petty bourgeois fraction in particular is problematic precisely because it shifts class away from traditional models of class based on ownership. While the old petty bourgeoisie's separation from the proletariat — based on owning its own means of production — is relatively straightforward, the new petty bourgeoisie, like the proletariat, do not own their own means of production (or indeed anything) — they are forced to work, lack autonomy at work and so on. In short, they seem, "on paper", to tick all the boxes of the proletariat, yet they are repeatedly placed outside the proletariat (and not just by Poulantzas) for social, cultural and ideological differences rather than economic ones. It is understandable that this is uncomfortable or unacceptable for many. Understanding the distinctiveness of the new petty bourgeoisie — and why we are not the working class, however some of us might like to be — depends on a flexible approach to class in general.

It specifically means moving beyond an analysis of class that is purely economic and based narrowly on ownership of the means of production (i.e., "if you work for someone else, you are working class", "anyone who does not own the means of production is working class") — a conception of class in which the professor and junior academic, manager and worker, are the same class. It depends on a conception of class that is social, relational and rooted in work, power and everyday human interaction.

In order to make sense of the bloated middle classes, we have to return to socialist theories of the intermediate classes put forward in earlier eras, particularly the work of Poulantzas, but also theorists like Wright Mills, Carchedi, Braverman, Gorz, Ehrenreich, Olin Wright and many more, all of whom — unlike the modern left — took very seriously the changing class structure and the growth of the intermediate classes in particular. All paid great attention to the *workplace* and the growing hierarchies and methods of control within the labour process as being central to the changes to class relations and to defining the intermediary classes. All attempted to bridge the gap between grand theory and everyday life, the objective and the subjective aspects of class and to square the intractable difficulties of theorising this class while staying "true" to Marxism or "what Marx said", something which frequently proved to be nigh on impossible.

I hope this book will help people understand the middle, allowing them to better interpret everyday class divides, in particular the divide between the left and the working class, and why people act in certain ways.

The point of this book is to re-introduce the petty bourgeoisie into modern political discourse. Beyond the class specifically, this book is about how society has changed. By talking about the petty bourgeoisie, I hope it makes people think about the class structure more broadly, how class works in everyday life, and catalyses a discussion about class more generally. The point of this book is *not* to provide a checklist (*x* is petty bourgeois, *y* is working class, *z* is professional-managerial class and so on), or a definitive, hard and fast guide to the petty bourgeoisie or even class itself. A particularly important approach to the problem of the intermediary classes (and class in general) is that found in the work of Erik Olin Wright. In opposition to Poulantzas's approach of creating a new "definitive" class (the new petty bourgeoisie), Wright put forward the idea of "contradictory class locations" to help understand the intermediate strata of society. Quite simply, he argued that "not all positions in the social structure can be seen as firmly rooted in a single class: some positions occupy objectively contradictory locations between classes", and that people often have contradictory needs and interests. Wright therefore allows for proletarians to temporarily take up petty bourgeois positions, for the petty bourgeoisie to temporarily take up proletarian interests and so on. He argues that some people simply occupy the grey areas on the boundaries between classes and may therefore have elements of the interests (and ideologies) of both classes. Thus some people may occupy the border between the proletariat and the petty bourgeoisie (for example, foremen), some between the petty bourgeoisie and the bourgeoisie (technicians and managers) and so on. This is not so different to Marx's conception of the petty bourgeoisie as being "cut up into two" and caught between the capitalist and the proletariat. For Wright, it is not necessary to create entirely new classes or frameworks (i.e., the new petty bourgeoisie, the professional-managerial class) to describe the new, complex class structure and the emergence of the intermediate classes that defy easy categorization; it is enough to simply approach classes with flexibility and fluidity. Moreover, Wright argues for the permeability of class boundaries, arguing that people are not fixed in one place over the course of their life, but can and do move up and down between class positions over the course of their lifetime. Similarly, the Ehrenreichs, using the example of nursing, argue that different agents within the same profession can occupy different classes, based on the amount of autonomy they have at work, their level of education and the route they took into nursing, whether they supervised other workers, whether they are incorporated into the management structure and so on.

Class is very complex — particularly the petty bourgeoisie, which moves up and down, that absorbs influences from classes above and below it — and this is the sort of flexibility that we need to understand it, particularly in an epoch where people are changing class more and more as the economy changes so quickly.

Structure of the Book

Chapter 1 is a potted history of the petty bourgeoisie. It explores its evolution, how it has been continually renewed and replenished from epoch to epoch and its political tendencies. The next chapters then explore the different fractions of the class separately. Chapter 2 looks at the "traditional" fraction (today exemplified by the solo self-employed), its historical social experience and how it has evolved and changed in the modern era and how the social condition of the petty bourgeoisie has become widespread. Chapter 3 then explores the *new* petty-bourgeois fraction, how it re-emerged as the class structure evolved under neoliberalism, and the myriad ways in which this fraction is split off from the working class and other classes. Chapter 4 then looks at the role of education in the class structure and its specific role in splitting off the new petty bourgeoisie from the working class socially and ideologically. Chapter 5 explores the role of housing in the class structure and how the marketization of housing has been one of the prime delivery systems for spreading the individualism of the petty bourgeoisie beyond the boundaries of the class itself and into wider society. Chapter 6 then concludes with a discussion of the role of the petty bourgeoisie in modern politics and how the trajectory and many of the failures of modern leftism can be explained by its roots in the petty bourgeoisie and its chaotic political tendencies.

CHAPTER ONE
THE HISTORY OF A CLASS

Part One: Feudalism to Industrialisation

The petty bourgeoisie played a key role in the story of the creation of capitalism, the modern democratic state and labour movements across the world. It has played a key stabilising role within capitalist society as well as — paradoxically — frequently emerging as a key actor during revolutionary periods of capitalist crisis. Far from disappearing, as Marx predicted, it is a constant, resilient presence that developed alongside and in symbiosis with the bourgeoisie and the proletariat.

Throughout its history, the petty bourgeoisie has evolved and taken different forms in different periods based on the changing economy, and has been continually replenished with new recruits in each epoch. Thus, the petty bourgeoisie of pre-industrial capitalism was of a different nature to the petty bourgeoisie of industrial capitalism, and, as the rest of the book argues, the petty bourgeoisie has continued to evolve and expand with the later stages of capitalism.

It is important to trace the evolution and transition of this amorphous class from period to period. As Arno Mayer argues, "the mentalities, attitudes, and values of the petty bourgeoisie retain greater vitality than the economic and social conditions that originally shaped them". Class ideology and habitus is rooted in the collective historical experience of a class, and endures even when the material conditions that forged these values and attitudes no longer hold. By exploring its history, evolution and social world, we can understand not just how the petty-bourgeois class came into being, but also how certain social, ideological, political and cultural traits began to be associated with this class, and endured like muscle memory from epoch to epoch, regardless of the form taken by the petty bourgeoisie in each.

****

The Petty Bourgeoisie and the Origins of Capitalism

Capitalism was born in the countryside. "Solving the land question" — i.e., introducing capitalism and getting rid of pre-capitalist social relations in the countryside — was a precondition for sweeping away feudalism and transitioning to a bourgeois capitalist society.

Numerous Marxist theoreticians give the petty bourgeoisie a starring role in the birth of capitalism. One school of thought argues that capitalism, like some deadly virus, was *already immanent* in the small producer making something in his workshop or the small farmer who owned his smallholding. This thesis argues that, once the retarding influence of feudalism was removed, capitalism developed organically, blossoming outward from the small-scale production of the artisan and the small farmer into a system that spread across the world. To use a contemporary analogy, in this story the petty bourgeoisie are the "patient zero" of capitalism.

Others, such as Ellen Meiksins Wood, argue instead that capitalism was a *rupture*: something entirely new, rather than something that was already lurking in the soul of the petty bourgeoisie. The alternative hypothesis is that capitalism began with the enforced transformation of land — via the nascent English state — from something held in common and tended according to traditional collective values and techniques into a commodity that had to make a profit for the individual. The capitalist imperative (or "logic") spread like wildfire and totally transformed social relations and the old way of life. Peasants were cleared from their land in order to make way for new landed estates owned by a new class of enlightened men who were willing to develop land for profit.

Whether or not these small farmers and artisans were in fact the first "true capitalists", it is generally accepted that the new capitalist social relations that emerged produced a class structure of "landlords living on capitalist ground rent, capitalist tenants living on profit, and labourers living on wages" as the core of the new capitalist agrarian society. Thus, a "middle" or intermediary class clearly existed right at the birth of capitalism, rapidly internalized its ruthless logic, and was key to perpetuating the new agrarian capitalism (quite simply because capitalism came into being before a mass proletariat existed).

Wood argues that, while this middling, ultra-productive strata was the unwitting backbone of agrarian capitalism, it was also, paradoxically, the first to be affected and eventually decimated by it. As pressures grew, more and more of these small farmers were dispossessed and pauperised, losing their small holding farm — the one thing they owned — and joining the ranks of landless wage labourers, the class that would make its way into the new urban areas and later become the proletariat.

Yet the roots of the petty bourgeoisie are not purely rural. While these changes were transforming the class structure of the formerly feudal countryside, there was also a parallel lower middle class within the early towns and cities that had expanded rapidly as the newly dispossessed rural poor migrated to them. Early towns were oases within the rural, feudal landscape, based on trade and manufacture rather than raising crops and livestock. Within these towns, Mayer argues that the lower middle class of artisans, craftsmen and small tradesmen in fact constituted the bulk of the population.

Theirs was a mode of production with a very limited social division of labour: a small independent craftsman in his workshop, using his own tools, with maybe a few apprentices working under him. This was not a way of working that was conducive to large-scale production and mass profit, and just as in the countryside small farmers got decimated by the introduction of capitalism, the urban petty bourgeoisie was a class that was very soon turned into an economic anachronism by the emergence of industrial capitalism and larger-scale manufacturing.

Marx argued that this small handicraft production was inherently conservative *vis à vis* the development of large-scale industrial capitalism. The type of work and entire way of life that the artisans did was threatened by the development of capitalism and it resisted this change fiercely. The artisans used their institutions — craft guilds, forerunners of craft trade unions — precisely for this end: to defend their skilled trade and preserve their way of life and relatively privileged position in the social structure against large-scale production.

The urban petty bourgeoisie was therefore a class on the defensive from the very formation of capitalism, precisely because of its precarity within the evolving capitalist system. Even at this early stage, Mayer argues that this class had already developed a distinct culture and way of life:

This bent toward tight economic preclusiveness by the petty burghers was coupled with an unpliant and hidebound personal as well as social morality, a localist mental set, a rudimentary literacy, and a factitious sense of status.

Members of the "guilded" lower middle class may never have had more than a moderate income, a comfortable life, and a low drive for infinite self-enrichment. Even so, they felt themselves superior not only to unguilded artisans but, above all, to the much larger pool of menial workers in the urban labour force whose existence was impoverished (not to say destitute), benighted, and insecure.

The class was intensely familial, careful to ensure that skills and guild membership passed through to their sons, who they employed in their workshops. There was a clear tendency towards defensiveness in their politics and worldview. This was not something that was just in the water, but rather a worldview and habitus that emanated from the precarious position of small, skilled handicraft production caught up in the transition to large-scale industrial capitalism, which threatened to deskill and undermine their autonomy.

While the class was innately precarious and defensive, it nonetheless frequently helped shore up the status quo and worked to ensure political and social stability, existing in a symbiotic and paternal relationship with the big bourgeoisie in the towns. The petty bourgeoisie depended on the large merchants for credit, contracts and other forms of protection. In return, it could be relied upon by the large merchants in the city to act as the backbone of local militia, enforcing the law against the roaming underclasses of landless serfs and peasants who descended on the cities seeking work. For this reason, it was kept onside by the big merchants and given political and economic protection. The petty bourgeoisie therefore ironically acted as a key pillar of support for the evolving capitalist order that would eventually send so many of its members to the wall.

Revolution and Change: The Petty Bourgeoisie Emerges as a Political Actor

The gradual transition to industrial capitalism saw the creation of a new class, as the large merchants evolved and became the bourgeoisie. This change was resented by both the landed aristocracy, who faced the loss of political and economic dominance, and the peasant and the small artisans, who now faced extinction. As Marx predicted, the small handicraftsman and peasant who owned their own means of production now seemed to face two possible fates during the transition to large-scale manufacturing: either grow and be transformed into a bigger capitalist, or suffer ruin and be sucked into the ranks of the proletariat.

The transition to modern capitalism and democracy and the simultaneous struggle to hold back the march of history manifested in a series of revolutions in Europe, a long period that Hobsbawm calls a "dual revolution", centred in particular on the French revolution of 1789 (i.e., a political revolution) and the Industrial Revolution in England (an economic revolution).

As these revolutions reverberated around Europe and the new world, the petty bourgeoisie was at the centre of the action. In *Age of Revolution*, Hobsbawm argues that "the discontented petty-bourgeoisie of independent artisans, shopkeepers, farmers and the like who (together with a mass of skilled workers) *probably formed the main corps of Radicalism in Western Europe... As little men they sympathized with the poor against the rich, as men of small property with the rich against the poor."

The rural and urban petty bourgeoisie were placed in a contradictory position by these upheavals. The petty bourgeoisie was inspired, and had much to gain politically, by the prospect of property-owning democracy; yet its way of life and economic position was simultaneously threatened by the transition to industrialization. It was thus pulled in both directions, and Hobsbawm argues that these "divided sympathies" led to its political participation in these revolutions — which was nonetheless very consistent — being defined by fatal hesitancy and doubt. This position — being pulled in both directions — would mould the political activity of the petty bourgeoisie for centuries to come.

Before the dual revolutions, however, was the often overlooked English revolution (1640-1660). This was a period of revolution and counter-revolution in which the monarchy and feudal system was replaced by an interregnum of bourgeois parliamentary democracy following the English Civil War, only for there then to be a counter-revolution culminating with the restoration of the absolute monarchy in 1660 (although the restoration continued the direction of travel of nascent capitalism).

It was also the first real political engagement that the petty bourgeoisie participated in. Christopher Hill argues that the English Civil War and revolution constituted a class war between the Royals and landlords on the one hand, and an alliance of big burghers, progressive independent gentry (personified by Oliver Cromwell) and the rural and urban petty bourgeoisie on the other. The aims of the petty bourgeoisie, both rural and urban, were personified by the Levellers, a movement that represented the small producers and which was well represented within Cromwell's own new model army.[2] The radical aims of the Levellers represented the early democratic spirit

---

2 Today the Levellers are often held up by some on the left as one of the symbols of English radicalism that a new "progressive patriotism" could be based upon, so it is interesting that they were petty bourgeois in composition.

that accompanied the radical break with feudalism that capitalism was producing: agitating for the freedom of small producers from monopolies, the security of small property, as well as a republic with full political suffrage.

Predictably, however, the independent gentry such as Cromwell, whom the Levellers had put their faith in, had no such aims. While getting rid of the divine right of kings was obviously radical, the overthrow of the monarchy saw the property rights and privileges that had previously been the preserve of the Royals and aristocracy simply passed to the new bourgeoisie. The Levellers, feeling betrayed by this, rebelled and were put down.

Crucially, Hill argues that the political failure of the Levellers was ultimately rooted in the movement's social base in the nascent petty bourgeoisie, and that the contradictory political position of this class was again rooted in their contradictory economic position. They wanted revolution and change but as small capitalists were also dependent on the big bourgeoisie, and so ultimately acted as the troops of the bourgeoisie. Despite their militancy and desperation for political change, they were never actually an independent political or social force. Moreover, the class was split economically and hence politically: some bigger producers soon began to side with the gentry, while the smaller producers who were facing ruin sided with the radicals. The class was too heterogeneous and divided and therefore had a tendency to be unreliable and splinter based on economic position, thus preventing unity and dramatically weakening the movement as a whole.

France, meanwhile, had been more resistant to the transition to industrial capitalism than England, and thus the rural rich peasant was more numerous there. Unsurprisingly, therefore, the petty bourgeoisie then played a key role in the first French revolution of 1789, where Mayer argues it was the "main social base and popular force that the liberals and democrats used to stage their initial assault" and was prominent in the Jacobin movement.

As Lenin argues, broadly speaking, the first French Revolution was about the bourgeoisie overthrowing the absolutist monarchy and landed nobility. Then, in February 1848, came a second brief revolution in Paris, which set off a huge chain of revolutions across the continent. For Marx, this was first time the proletariat emerged on the historical stage.

Marx's analysis of the second French revolution — *The 18th Brumaire of Luis Bonaparte* — constitutes one of the most famous analyses of the political instincts of the petty bourgeoisie during this period. While it had played a decisive role in the earlier revolution, in the 1848 revolution it was caught between the emergent proletariat and the bourgeoisie, and consequently played a schizoid, unstable role. The French petty bourgeoisie oscillated between siding first with the bourgeois against the workers, but then, after not being rewarded for their loyalty in the latter stages of the revolution, it splintered, with large swathes coming to side with the workers against the bourgeoisie.

This coalition of the lower petty bourgeoisie and workers in the latter stages of 1848 eventually came to form the social democratic party (*La Montagne*). Indeed, Marx claims that social democracy *as a concept* was born out of the fusion of the petty bourgeoisie and the working class in this period, and he is very clear that it is the influence of the petty bourgeoisie specifically that gave social democracy its "peculiar" reformist character and its refusal to push to overthrow capitalism. He argues that in the course of its development, social democracy "changed with the class that it represented", and agitated for "the transformation of society in a democratic way, but a transformation within the bounds of the petty bourgeoisie". Marx argued that while the petty bourgeoisie was angry and desperately wanted change, it could not accept that there was an inherent antagonism between capital and labour — and hence the need for revolutionary class struggle — instead believing *all* classes could be helped by democratic reform which simply attempted to weaken the inherent antagonism between capital and labour and "transform it into harmony" — which has arguably been the core of social democracy ever since.

Thus, for Marx, it was the petty bourgeoisie that retarded the development of the social democratic party and blunted the radicalism of the proletariat in France. Lenin later put it more bluntly: "In 1848 it was a question of the proletariat overthrowing the bourgeoisie. The proletariat was unable to win over the petty bourgeoisie, whose treachery led to the defeat of the revolution."

In the German revolution of 1849, the petty bourgeoisie again played a leading role. At this time, the petty bourgeoisie was the leading class in the small towns of Germany, and the leadership of the insurrection and the provisional governments that arose amidst the revolution were dominated by the petty bourgeoisie. In *Revolution and Counter-Revolution in Germany*, Engels wrote that "this class of petty tradesmen, the great importance and influence of which we have already several times adverted to, may be considered as the leading class of the insurrection of May, 1849". Yet Engels contemptuously places the blame for the failure of the insurrection squarely at their feet. He bitterly claims that having worked itself into a frenzy with its fiery rhetoric, at the moment of the revolution, which the working class threw itself into with full force, at the last minute the petty bourgeoisie got cold feet and essentially sabotaged the revolution through their hesitation and weakness. Having called for a revolution, once it had begun the petty bourgeoisie was horrified by the realization that the proletarians that they had mobilized might actually seize power and that the petty bourgeoisie might end up losing their property and status within the local social structure. Sensing this possibility, "they actually did everything in their power to take the sting out of the movement, to unman, to destroy it".

Engels thus concludes that the petty bourgeoisie was "capable... of nothing but ruining any movement that entrusts itself to its hands". Despite attacking big business and the state, they could not countenance a true revolution that also threatened their own privileges. Unlike the proletariat, who of course had "nothing to lose but their chains", the petty bourgeoisie *did* have something to lose — their property and their status over the proletariat — and it was this which held it back and which limited its political goals. Indeed, Marx and Engels' famous axiom and insistence about the revolutionary nature of the proletariat is perhaps more understandable or tangible when it is directly contrasted with the petty bourgeoisie. The proletariat would overthrow society because it was the only class that had nothing invested in the system.

Both Marx and Engels paint a deeply unflattering picture of a class that, unlike the proletariat, was chaotic and dangerously unreliable. Whilst the petty bourgeoisie wanted change, Marx argued that they would never see the need for class struggle and the overthrow of capitalism because they believe themselves to be "the people": neither the lazy aristocrats or the troublesome workers. In other words, they believed they were above class antagonisms, and relatedly did not recognise that the state was the representative of ruling-class interests but rather something that was simply there to help society maintain order. They both deemed the petty bourgeoisie incapable of carrying out revolutionary change because of the limitations of its ideological framework, which was rooted in its interstitial economic situation. Engels also alleged that the small-scale nature of the form of capitalism that the petty bourgeoisie engaged in inexorably produced a small-mindedness in general, which carried over into the petty bourgeoisie's political horizons.

Yet both theorists also repeatedly acknowledged the scale of the petty bourgeoisie and its huge potential power and influence as a kingmaker class — and relatedly its potential role as a powerful and important ally of the proletariat — noting repeatedly that the petty bourgeoisie was needed to buttress bourgeois rule and that, without it, the bourgeoisie would struggle to maintain consensus.

Towards Industrialisation

Despite seeing them as a powerful force in society, Marx nonetheless saw the petty bourgeoisie as a "transitional class". He believed they were a relic of pre-industrial capitalism but which, like the aristocracy in the UK, persisted in a residual form in a new era. He stated clearly that the tendency within capitalism would be for the petty bourgeoisie to be made extinct as their form of small-scale production was usurped and rendered obsolete by the transition to large-scale manufacturing.

Marx's prediction about the disappearance of the traditional petty bourgeois was entirely logical, given the rise of machinery that would surely put an end to small manufacturing and the social division of labour that produced the small artisan. He was here, as in many other instances, speaking of a tendency rather than an iron law. In reality, change is never linear, and there are always countervailing tendencies.

The changes wrought by industrialization did not happen overnight but were piecemeal and uneven, impacting on different areas and industries in different ways and allowing the petty bourgeoisie to survive for far longer than anyone could have predicted. In *The Making of the English Working Class*, for example, E.P. Thompson shows the extent to which small artisan workshops persisted way into the industrial nineteenth century, particularly in Birmingham.

Nonetheless, small artisan production *did* decline (although not on the scale that was expected), but while the opportunities for small production gradually decreased, the Industrial Revolution and the influx of workers into the new cities also dramatically increased the potential for other commercial activities outside of (but also dependent on) the new industries, including shopkeeping (which included things like bakeries as well as general haberdasheries) and petty landlordism; but also money lenders, accountants, those involved in transporting goods and so on. Thus the Industrial Revolution marginalized the small producer, but rather than dying out, as Marx predicted, the petty bourgeoisie simply evolved into new forms. It is well known that the Industrial Revolution created the proletariat, but it also created the modern petty bourgeoisie alongside them.

While these small traders and intermediaries were focused on service and pure profit rather than skill, they shared key commonalities with the artisans in terms of their isolated work situation. As Bechhofer and Elliot put it, "the work situations remained as they had always been, small in scale, highly personalised, lacking the opportunities for sharing work experiences with large numbers of others and equally innocent of any sophisticated distribution of authority".

So while the class structure during the Industrial Revolution is very often thought of as being starkly divided into a huge working class and a small class of bosses, in reality there was a sizeable middle class — the petty bourgeoisie — who played an important role in the class-divided society. John Foster's magisterial *Class Struggle and the Industrial Revolution,* for example, paints a picture of a large, influential class of shopkeepers and artisans, who took great pains to differentiate themselves from the workers socially and culturally. This was often achieved through religion, which was used as an everyday class divide. The class also consciously reproduced itself and its culture through marriage, which was essential for the preservation of property and assets from one generation to the next.

During the early industrial period, the petty bourgeoisie also emerged as a significant *political* force in Britain. During the early years of the Industrial Revolution, the petty bourgeoisie had attempted to maintain political neutrality. There were good reasons for this — siding with the bosses against the majority of your customers would be bad for business. This was not about being boycotted or politely shunned: there was a very real threat of working-class violence against shopkeepers and other traders who sided with the bosses over their patrons. In repeated instances, the small shopkeeper — as the local face of capital — was the scapegoat of the angry, impotent working class. Overnight, a pillar of the community could very easily become seen as one of "them".

Yet the petty bourgeoisie gradually emerged as political leaders of the nascent working-class movement. During this period, numerous socialist and liberal political leaders were drawn from the ranks of the petty bourgeoisie, including Owenite socialists and many of the founding Chartists.[3]

It was perhaps not that surprising that the shopkeepers became politically active. Like the workers, they were extremely vulnerable to economic crisis. As Foster argues, despite their ongoing attempts to distinguish themselves

---

3 Marx and Engels later argued that weaknesses and reformist tendencies of the Chartist movement were rooted in the petty bourgeois origins of many of their leaders.

from the ordinary workers in a social and cultural sense, they were nonetheless economically close enough to the working class to see, understand and themselves experience real hardship. Like the workers, their lives were deeply precarious, and they were often in debt. Moreover, working-class poverty ate into their profits: during such periods they could not sell goods and instead had to give credit to the community.

But the early radicalism and polarization towards the working class did not last as the petty bourgeoisie again demonstrated their political incoherence. Foster illustrates how, even at the peak of its radicalism, the petty bourgeoisie oscillated in its politics, becoming more or less polarized towards the classes above and below them, based on specific circumstances and conjunctures. As in the 1848 uprising in France, the petty bourgeoisie emerged as unreliable and schizoid, with a notable tendency towards violence. Its complex economic position sandwiched between the proletariat and the bourgeoisie — as simultaneously capitalist and worker — meant that, politically, it inevitably ended up "facing both ways", often espousing radical demands and then, during key moments, either brokering compromises or siding with employers and Tories against the workers at the last minute.[4]

As in the French, American, German and English revolutions, the ideology of these early petty-bourgeois radicals was ultimately rooted in a Painean defence of small property rights and independent businesses against the state and big businesses — all highly individualistic, libertarian ideas that naturally resonated with the small producer. Their ideology was thus often furiously anti-

---

4 The most horrific example occurred at Peterloo, when the region's lower middle classes allegedly comprised the majority of yeomen who perpetrated the massacre.

establishment and anti-monopoly, and for the time certainly radical, but certainly not anti-capitalist or even socialistic.

As the working class and its political movement — which was by now more openly rooted in collectivism and class politics — massively expanded, the social and political lines between the petty bourgeoisie and the working class grew sharper instead of diminishing. Increasingly "squeezed" between the professionals and working class, they rapidly shed their early radicalism and increasingly adopted a defensive, reactionary political posture, intensely disliking the powerful working class and labour movement beneath it, but also resenting the growth of big business and the state bureaucracy and the new caste of managers and professionals above it. While they never regained their leading role in politics, they remained politically significant in municipal politics in towns and cities across the UK. In the late nineteenth century, the Liberal Party best represented its libertarian individualism, but this soon changed to the Tories.

The Twentieth Century: Expansion, Stabilisation, Crisis, War, Revolution

As the nineteenth century turned into the twentieth, the petty bourgeoisie continued to grow, not decline. There was still no neat, two-class society. In *A Class Society at War*, Bernard Waites notes the complex class structure in the UK in the period just before the First World War. Outside the homogenous, closed worlds and cultures of heavy industries like mining (which has generated much of the heroic imagery and analysis of the working class within labourist hagiography, and which *did* have a clear polarization between worker and owner), small ownership and subcontracting in traditional working-class industries like construction was widespread, with the main class antagonism being between these small employers and labourers. Moreover, many skilled workers also employed wage labour in small workshops on the side.

On top of the blurred class boundaries within manual work was the emergence, once again, of new recruits to the petty bourgeoisie. Whilst shopkeepers, small traders and artisans remained — although they were increasingly struggling to keep their heads above water and politically marginalized — the start of the twentieth century produced, then as now, a huge new strata of white-collar workers, which soon engulfed and overshadowed the "old" petty bourgeoisie: clerks, accountants, shop workers, servants — a new class of people who "serviced" capital. Moreover, the state bureaucracy also massively expanded (schools, government departments, hospitals and the like), which in turn created small functionaries, teachers, nurses, police, soldiers and so on. Just as the petty bourgeoisie was replenished and changed form in the early nineteenth century with the emergence of shopkeepers, it again changed form at the turn of the century. Thus, this period saw the creation of another "new" petty bourgeoisie.

This new white-collar class of petty functionaries and administrators that emerged in the early twentieth century was huge. In *Age of Empires*, Hobsbawm argues that, by 1900 in the USA, it *was already larger than the actual working class* (although this was exceptional); similarly, in pre-First World War Germany, the petty bourgeoisie was a hugely significant class. Mayer describes the composition of the class structure in Germany and the ever-increasing size of the white-collar petty bourgeoisie and the expansion of the small shopkeeper:

> there were some 13 million industrial workers in Germany, although ... many labor aristocrats in big industry and

workers in small enterprises were of petit bourgeois disposition. In any event, clearly separated from this vast proletariat in the labour force were 2 million white-collar employees, 2 million lower and middle civil servants, 1.5 million traditional craftsmen and artisans (of whom close to 500,000 still were guild members), 700,000 retailers, and around 2 million small peasants.

The proletariat were still the largest class, but the petty bourgeoisie were also a highly significant force.

Moreover, the development of services within capitalism meant that the white-collar class was already at this stage in the ascendency numerically:

by the turn of the century, Germany's white-collar sector was expanding rapidly: between 1883 and 1925 the number of white-collars increased more than fivefold while the number of industrial workers less than doubled. There was now one employee for every five workers. But perhaps it should also be noted that, at this same time, the number of small retailers, which is so often assumed to have declined significantly, actually grew faster than either the population or the national product. During the first quarter of the twentieth century the number of retail stores rose from roughly 700,000 to 850,000, an increase of some 20 percent. By the time of the big crash in 1929 the small retail sector had expanded by an additional 3 percent.

There was also a gender dimension to this strata, as females comprised a significant proportion of this new workforce for the first time.

While on the surface they seemed very different to the old petty bourgeoisie of shopkeepers and artisans, like the old fraction of the petty bourgeoisie they also consciously separated themselves from the working class ideologically, culturally and socially. Waites argues that this new class of clerks, despite often earning less than the skilled worker, "felt himself to be middle class", despite often having humble origins. Their physical proximity to management placed them, unlike the worker, in a servile personal relationship with their employer. It was widely believed that they were, unlike the skilled industrial worker, fixated on social mobility and *individual* betterment, rather than collective. For all these reasons, a clear social, cultural and ideological divide opened up between the clerks and the workers, and the clerks became increasingly hostile to trade unionism and associated with the bosses. During a period of intense trade union organizing and labour disputes, the emergence of a new, low-paid strata that refused to unionise, and which was often actively hostile to organizing efforts, created intense mutual suspicion between the new white-collar strata and the industrial workers. The clerks and other white-collar workers were widely thought to be "deferentials" by the union hierarchy, and indeed Hobsbawm argues that the cultural and social divide between the new white-collar, non-manual workers and the manual workers was far more intense than previous differences between the old petty bourgeoisie and the workers, who, for all their differences, had at least shared the common experience of "toil" and working by hand.

The new white-collar recruits to the petty bourgeoisie soon began to reproduce socially and culturally. Socially, their quest for upward mobility often involved delaying marriage, practicing contraception and deliberately having smaller families than the workers. They also continued to expand *geographically*, moving into the new suburbs on the edge of cities in a further attempt to differentiate themselves from the working class crammed into inner-city areas.

But as the petty bourgeoisie increasingly climbed the social ladder and consumed, aspiring to the middle class, they were in turn looked down upon by the established middle classes, who viewed them as unwelcome upstarts. This was also highly gendered, and began an ongoing trope about petty-bourgeois women dominating their households, and the lower middle class as being uniquely emasculated in their new suburban surroundings.

Crisis

The British picture of the petty bourgeois as a mild-mannered, emasculated figure belied the chaotic situation that was simmering across Europe and the central role the "*Mittelstand*" were playing in it. At the beginning of the twentieth century, industrialized, mechanized capitalism had become turbo-charged — a global interlocking system that spanned the globe via a web of huge empires, many of which remained politically conservative and led by aristocrats. As with the transition from feudalism, then away from handicraft and manufacturing, and then again at the start of industrialization, the new productive forces of capitalism were creating a new way of life and were attempting to "burst asunder" the social relations of the old society on which they existed.

For Mayer, the irreconcilable contradiction between advanced, connected global economies on the one hand, with conservative national political administrations led by the remnants of feudal-era aristocrats on the other, catalysed a new epoch of political crisis defined by war, revolution and counter-revolution. As in the dual revolutions, there were classes and interests who sought to gain from this change, and those who sought to prevent change bursting through. As the crisis between capital and labour simmered dangerously, across mainland Europe the petty bourgeoisie's sense of strength and importance began to grow. It began to gain class consciousness, seeing itself as a buffer class, a pillar of social stability that could prevent the looming conflict between the workers and the rich. As Geoffrey Crossick argues, it saw itself as the moral core of the nation, representing moderation, tradition, stability, honour.

The First World War temporarily postponed this crisis, as the labour movement and the working class across Europe were infected with national chauvinism, with large sections of the socialist movement throwing themselves behind their national ruling class and supporting the war. The lower middle classes also threw themselves into the war, with many finding in the military a fantastic avenue for social mobility, being commissioned as officers (known as "temporary gentlemen") because of a shortage of the aristocrats who normally comprised the officer class. Indeed, some historians argue that the *majority* of First World War officers came from outside the traditional officer class, with the largest single element coming from the new suburban white-collar workers. Female domestic workers (i.e., servants and maids) were moved to work in munitions factories, where they thrived. While the war is often seen to have been a great social leveller, being the first time that aristocrats and workers had mixed on the same side, it also had a particular importance for the standing and sense of status of the new petty bourgeoisie.

Because new production techniques for mass production for the war economy marginalized the need for skilled labour, the First World War also catalysed a period of homogenization within the working class in which the labour aristocracy declined in significance, both in terms of its wage and social standing. This in turn led to the decline of elitist craft unions and the rise of larger, more militant mass unions. Moreover, during this period, clerks

— who had begun to get used to being officer material — increasingly became proletarianized as their work too became increasingly deskilled and rationalized, more closely resembling factory work than previously. While before the war, clerks had been loath to join trade unions, the period immediately following the war witnessed a huge surge in white-collar unionisation and a shedding of the deference that had previously characterized their profession, perhaps because of their experience of leadership in the war. Similarly, the female domestic servants were highly reluctant to return to their old domestic jobs after their wartime experience working in factories because their experience of collective work and life had extinguished their deference. The petty bourgeoisie in the UK therefore briefly moved towards a cultural and political alliance with the working class, after losing its previously privileged status. However, this did not last.

In the UK, the First World War led to the incorporation of the official trade union movement (if not the rank and file) into the state and a weakening of the radical left through the growth of labourism. As Ross McKibbin notes, with the exception of the general strike in 1926, the UK in the post-war period was relatively stable. Although this is often absent from left hagiographies, in the face of a militant working class the Tory party's hegemony between the wars became impregnable. It created a narrative of "labour versus the public", and forged a coalition of essentially everyone outside the unionized working class. This coalition in fact included much of the working class, who were united by a fear of the great unwashed and the belief (later used by Thatcher) that inflation was caused by greedy workers rather than the government. Central to this electoral coalition were an estimated ten million petty bourgeois, the "constitutional class", believing themselves to be the backbone of the nation. They supported the government firmly during the general strike and formed the majority of the strike-breakers.

However, stability during this period was unique to Britain, which arguably exported much of its internal contradictions to the empire. In other countries, most noticeably Russia, the disastrous experience of war catalysed revolutions.

Russia's industrial underdevelopment meant that the proletariat were not a majority there. For this reason, class alliances under the leadership of the revolutionary proletariat were a central pillar of Bolshevik strategy, and hence Lenin paid incredibly close attention to the class composition of Russia and the specificity of the other subaltern classes: the peasantry and the petty bourgeoisie.

The petty bourgeoisie in Russia was large, and Lenin saw it as a particularly important class within the social structure. Like Marx's analysis of their role in the French revolution, Lenin believed that the petty bourgeoisie were an oppressed class and a potential ally of the proletariat because of their common exploitation by capital. But because of the nature of their social conditions — their isolation from others in their work — their role within the revolutionary milieu was chaotic and unstable. He associated them with individualism, and regarded them suspiciously:

Marxist theory has established — and the experience of all European revolutions and revolutionary movements has fully confirmed — that the petty proprietor, the small master (a social type existing on a very extensive and even mass scale in many European countries), who, under capitalism, always suffers oppression and very frequently a most acute and rapid deterioration in his conditions of life, and even ruin, easily goes to revolutionary extremes, but is incapable of perseverance, organisation, discipline and steadfastness. *A petty bourgeois driven to frenzy by the horrors of capitalism is a social phenomenon which, like anarchism, is characteristic of all capitalist countries.* The instability of such revolutionism, its barrenness, and its tendency to turn rapidly into submission, apathy, phantasms, and even a frenzied infatuation with one bourgeois fad or another — all this is common knowledge.

After the revolution, rather than diminishing, the petty bourgeoisie remained vast, "surrounding the proletariat on every side". Lenin bitterly complained that the physical presence, ideology and whole way of life of the petty bourgeoisie represented a residual feature of the old reactionary, capitalist society that refused to go away, and which infected and corrupted the proletariat with individualism. Yet he also understood that the sheer size of the petty bourgeoisie and the influence of its ideology meant that it could not be conquered by force. "The force of habit in millions and tens of millions is a most formidable force", he wrote:

> It is a thousand times easier to vanquish the centralised big bourgeoisie than to "vanquish" the millions upon millions of petty proprietors; however, through their ordinary, everyday, imperceptible, elusive and demoralising activities, they produce the very results which the bourgeoisie need and which tend to restore the bourgeoisie.

Thus, he concluded wearily, "they cannot be ousted, or crushed; we must learn to live with them. They can (and must) be transformed and re-educated only by means of very prolonged, slow, and cautious organisational work." Winning the petty bourgeoisie over to socialism was crucial.

In Germany, unlike Russia, the socialist revolution of 1918-1919 failed, and again the petty bourgeoisie, which constituted a huge proportion of the German population, played a decisive role. Following the failure, Rosa Luxemburg, like Engels nearly a century earlier, took aim at the petty bourgeoisie, claiming that they stood behind the counter-revolution led by the SPD leadership.

Fascism and the Petty Bourgeoisie

Following the Russian and German revolutions, the "crisis of the old regime" continued unabated. In the midst of economic depression and unemployment, working-class movements grew in strength, communist parties grew, strikes and occupations occurred in every country. The organized working-class movement was looked upon in horror by ruling elites across Europe, who feared for the stability of bourgeois capitalist society. As the crisis deepened, elites across the continent consciously began to patronise the new middle classes as they attempted to calculate the size of a reliable, anti-socialist political base that they could rely on when push came to shove.

Gradually, these ruling capitalist interests — both big business and the national ruling classes — lost faith in parliamentary democracy to create consensus, and decided to enlist reactionary, undemocratic movements as their helpers to crush the organized working classes. The petty bourgeoisie across Europe had been proletarianized during the crisis and were by this stage, in Trotsky's words, "frenzied" with rage and frustration. This made them the perfect fodder for the bourgeoisie, who, sensing their rage and impotence, consciously began to split the subordinate classes off from one another and prevent an alliance forming between the petty bourgeoisie and the working class. The bourgeoisie sought to enlist the petty bourgeoisie as its foot soldiers in their war against the proletarian movement, which was relentlessly portrayed as a threat to the national interest and to "the public". The petty bourgeoisie thus came to form the main social base of the fascist movement in Europe.

While it is today often used as a catch-all synonym for "intolerance" or "bigotry", fascism at its inception was, at its core, a counter-revolutionary, anti-communist movement that sought to defend private property from the threat of peasants and the proletariat. Despite their own immiseration, the petty bourgeoisie were themselves often small property owners who were terrified of losing their own small property and meagre status. It was this slender advantage that allowed them to be split from the other subordinate classes and mobilized by the big landowners and industrialists as shock troops to defend private property against the red threat. In Italy, Gramsci argued that fascism's defining characteristic was that it was the first political movement that had succeeded in mobilizing the petty bourgeoisie, a class which had previously been too chaotic and heterogeneous to organize:

> [T]he characteristic feature of fascism consists in the fact that it has succeeded in creating a mass organization of the petty bourgeoisie. It is the first time in history that this has happened. The originality of fascism consists in having found the right form of organization for a social class which has always been incapable of having any cohesion or unitary ideology...
>
> The petit bourgeoisie, even in this last political incarnation of "fascism," has definitively shown itself in its true nature of servant of capitalism and of landed property, of agent of counter-revolution.

Yet Gramsci was clear that fascism was a genuinely popular movement which infected all classes, lest we believe that it is only the petty bourgeoisie that can succumb to its allure.

In the 1930s, surveying the rise of fascism in Europe, Trotsky was similarly explicit in his analysis of the class basis of the rise of fascism. He wrote that

> the genuine basis [for fascism] is the petty bourgeoisie. In Italy, it has a very large base — the petty bourgeoisie of the towns and cities, and the peasantry. In Germany, likewise, there is a large base for fascism [because of the aforementioned huge white-collar and shop-owner class, and] the fascists find their human material mainly in the petty bourgeoisie. The latter has been entirely ruined by big capital. There is no way out for it in the present social order, but it knows of no other. Its dissatisfaction, indignation, and despair are diverted by the fascists away from big capital and against the workers. It may be said that fascism is the act of placing the petty bourgeoisie at the disposal of its most bitter enemies. In this way, big capital ruins the middle classes and then, with the help of hired fascist demagogues, incites the despairing petty bourgeoisie against the worker. The bourgeois regime can be preserved only by such murderous means as these...

The petty bourgeoisie was thus the "battering ram" for fascism, which crushed the working-class movement during periods of crisis. During previous epochs, the anger of the petty bourgeoisie had led it to oscillate during times of unrest, siding with both the workers and the bourgeois. What was different now was there was no siding with the workers at all. The tendencies identified by Marx in *The Eighteenth Brumaire of Louis Bonaparte* had come to a horrifying conclusion. The cruel irony, of course, was that the petty bourgeoisie did not lead the fascist movement in any country, but was rather used by capital to crush the working-class movement and to gain power, before then being abandoned.

As Trotsky predicted, in Germany the petty bourgeoisie or *Mittelstand* became a key social base of Nazism, which was at its core a popular anti-communist doctrine. It is important to understand the appeal of Nazism with reference to the specific historic and social conditions that enabled it, including the class structure of Germany, rather than exceptionalizing it as an anomalous moment of collective madness, or the idea that the Germans were somehow genetically inclined to authoritarianism.

In Germany, the interwar period was a bleak time for white-collar workers. For the first time they experienced unemployment, making up 10% of Germany's total unemployed population. Their experience of proletarianization led to the birth of the expression "panic in the *Mittelstand*" (which referred to both white-collar workers and the old petty bourgeoisie of artisans and shopkeepers) being coined in the 1930s. The link between the petty bourgeoisie and Nazism has been overstated, but both fractions of the class nonetheless remained over-represented within the NSDAP, with the new white-collar clerks and the old petty bourgeoisie of artisans, craftsmen and mechanics forming a huge chunk of its support.

Nazism in Germany originated in the cities, but its growth was temporarily checked by strong left organizations. Forced outwards, it thus began its real growth in protestant rural areas among the local petty bourgeoisie who ran middle-sized family farms, who were firm in their belief in themselves as the moral backbone of the nation, and who were deeply worried about red revolution and the potential threat to their property. The Nazis preyed on fears about the destruction of the rural way of life and the threat to small farms posed by big capital and industrialization on the one hand, and the reds on the other. Opposition to "statism" — bureaucrats — in particular was exploited by the Nazis. Although the Nazis were corporatist and backed by big business, they nonetheless targeted policies specifically at this strata, passing laws that helped families to own farms in order to appeal to the rural petty bourgeoisie, and taxed big department stores in order to appeal to the small urban petty bourgeoisie. And of course, the persecution of Jews — who were often small business owners — removed the local competition for many of the petty bourgeoisie.

Despite being one of the main social bases of fascism, it is important to realise that the petty bourgeoisie was not innately fascistic, but rather its unsocialised anger made it ripe for radicalization towards the right at this particular moment in time. As Trotsky repeatedly noted, the anger of the petty bourgeoisie and whether it was polarized towards the left or the right was contingent on specific national circumstances but particularly the strength and ability of socialist movements to lead it. The uncomfortable reality is that both fascism in Italy and Nazism in Germany were cross-class, with large working-class support. It would be obviously unreasonable to infer from this that the working class are also innately prone to fascism, yet this is commonly done with the petty bourgeoisie. It is important to remember, given the polemics against the petty bourgeoisie by Marxists, that in other countries (the UK and the US, for example) the petty bourgeoisie did *not* surge to fascism.

Part Two: The Welfare State to the Modern Day

In the interwar period, the self-employed fraction of the petty bourgeoisie in the UK remained relatively large, rising to nearly 12% of all employed people (similar levels to today). The Beveridge report of 1942, which underpinned the welfare state, recognized the extent of "independent workers" (i.e., the self-employed) within British society ("small shopkeepers, crofters, fishermen, hawkers, outworkers... small farmers") and, moreover, recognized their precarity within the system: "Many independent workers... are poorer than many of those employed under contract of service and are as much dependent on good health for their earnings". The report subsequently recognized the need for these workers to be covered by the new system of social insurance.

However, the post-war reordering of the economy was in some ways a zero-sum game. The working class gained and the traditional fraction of the petty bourgeoisie — the self-employed — lost out. The introduction of welfare capitalism in the US and Europe — and nationalized industries in particular — squeezed the small specialized ancillary firms (small workshops) that had been run by artisans. The introduction of minimum wages and strengthened trade unions were resisted by smaller firms and the self-employed, just as the welfare state was resisted by big capital. Paradoxically, however, the emergence of a newly affluent working class with disposable income for commodities also meant that small shops were able to be kept going.

As a rule, however, small businesses — the traditional fraction of a petty bourgeoisie of shopkeepers and artisans — shrunk in the West under the unprecedented period of welfare capitalism, and its political influence similarly waned. In terms of the traditional fraction of the petty bourgeoisie, the basis for petty capitalism increasingly shifted away from production (artisans) to service (shopkeepers). Yet while the traditional fraction declined, the new white-collar element increased. There was now a massive welfare bureaucracy to run, which required both professionals (civil servants, teachers, doctors and nurses) and an army of low-paid clerical and administrative workers. As in previous epochs, the class had been replenished.

A notable exception to the decline of the traditional petty bourgeoisie was France, where the country's distinct historical economic development meant that the self-employed remained a significant force even at the start of welfare capitalism. Small shops had grown dramatically in France during the war and by the 1950s numbered over 1.3 million small businesses with nearly 2.5 million employees. Post-war France witnessed the rise of the "Poujadist" movement (named after its leader Pierre Poujade), one of the first (and last) openly and explicitly petty-bourgeois movements.

Poujadism, based around "the union for the defence of artisans", emerged as a reaction against government bureaucracy and big capital, which was felt to be threatening a traditional way of life in the countryside. The Poujadists focused on lowering tax, successfully drawing together a base of small farmers, peasants, wine growers, bakers and shopkeepers, who were all united in their hostility to modernity ("*la France du Coca-Cola*"), representing France's first anti-globalisation movement. It was comfortable using violence — smashing things up — and was detested by France's metropolitan professionals as symbolising obdurate conservatism. Although Poujadism soon faded away, it accelerated the crisis of the Fourth Republic and left a significant legacy in modern French politics, representing a social base and values that are still very visible and vocal in the country today.

In Eastern Europe, the petty bourgeoisie, which had been disproportionately comprised of Jews, was almost totally wiped out by the Holocaust, leaving an economy where small shopkeepers and artisans were a tiny minority. Moreover, while in the West the self-employed petty bourgeoisie declined "naturally" under welfare capitalism, in the socialist states of the new Soviet bloc small business was officially and actively marginalized and discouraged as it was viewed suspiciously as an unhealthy capitalist, Western residue. Despite this, however, self-employment remained attractive to many people, even within a centralized socialist economy, and was eventually begrudgingly accepted and tolerated by the Soviet authorities.

The class structure, of course, is global. Different countries have different class structures based on different stages of economic development. For example, countries with large industrial bases have larger proletariats, while those with underdeveloped or mainly rural economies have a small proletariat and larger petty bourgeoisies and peasantry. While the traditional petty bourgeoisie was marginalized in the developed and industrialized West, the petty bourgeoisie remained a very powerful force on a global level. The underdeveloped semi-rural character of economies in the Global South meant that the industrial proletariat in these countries was relatively small. Indeed, on a global scale, the peasantry and petty bourgeoisie were possibly larger than the proletariat in the post-war period. In the Third World, as in earlier epochs, it was the petty bourgeoisie — *not* the proletariat — that emerged as a revolutionary class, playing a leading and often progressive role in anti-colonial struggles in Africa and Latin America.

Thatcher's Foot Soldiers and the Rise of Right Authoritarianism

Whilst they had been relatively small in size and politically dormant throughout the welfare state era, the death of the welfare state and the subsequent transition to neoliberalism changed the global class structure and brought the petty bourgeoisie centre-stage politically once more. In the UK, this was catalysed by the accession of Margaret Thatcher, a petty bourgeois herself (once branded "a Poujadiste female with ideas above her station" by Christopher Hitchens). Thatcherism was a social and cultural revolution that changed the common sense of society as a whole, but while Thatcherism was to some extent a popular movement that also appealed to large sections of the working class, it is important to understand the specific origins of Thatcherism's ideology and social base in the petty bourgeoisie.

Before Thatcher, small businesses and the traditional petty bourgeoisie were a minor element within the British economy and state, both objectively small in number and, accordingly, politically insignificant; often the mainstay of the local Tory Party and prominent on local councils, but hardly important to the party of monopoly capitalism. Much like Labour's post-industrial heartlands, this was a constituency that, pre-Thatcher, the Tories could (and did) essentially afford to take for granted.

Yet despite renouncing class as a concept, Thatcher had a keen awareness of class and how it operated in everyday life. Unlike the Labour Party, which neither recognised or responded to the seismic changes to the class structure that were occurring under their feet, Thatcher understood the changing class structure and saw an opportunity to peel off layers of subordinate classes and incorporate them into the ruling bloc. She honed in on the petty bourgeoisie specifically, identifying it as a pillar of a wider hegemonic strategy, arguably for the first time since fascism.

As the daughter of a greengrocer that grew up in a market town, Thatcher understood this class and its values, desires and insecurities intimately. The petty bourgeoisie were her people, and her hegemonic strategy was both targeted at the petty bourgeoisie and rooted in its values. She articulated an ideological vision of society that explicitly spoke to the tenets of traditional petty bourgeois ideology and drove a clear wedge between the petty bourgeoisie and the working class. This was done firstly by crushing the organized working class and the simultaneous gutting of employment rights, but also by the articulation of a political ideology that was composite, comprised of different strands that were skilfully wound into a whole. Thatcherism as an ideology had a *negative* component that mobilized people against an enemy Other. Most famously, this was based around a "Churchillian" British nationalism that whipped up hatred of foreigners, but it also honed in on an enemy *within* — the lazy and idle, the shirkers and parasites. Crucially, this Other could be both those on welfare (and Thatcher genuinely *did* hate the working class) and state bureaucrats and professionals, therefore appealing to the petty bourgeoisie's dislike of the working class below them *and* the professional managerial class above them. Trade unions were alleged to be responsible for rising unemployment and portrayed as an enemy to the nation, stoking long-held fears that socialists would take people's property. Much like today, inflation was also portrayed as the result of irresponsible fiscal policy, which directly appealed to petty bourgeois notions of thrift and responsibility and looking after every penny.

But Thatcherism also had a *positive* component — a narrative of aspiration and social mobility, the defence of small property, traditionalism, free enterprise, family and entrepreneurialism, all of which appealed instinctively to petty bourgeois sensibilities. She also appealed to the petty bourgeoisie through concrete material concessions. Most obviously, this was the right-to-buy policy, which, as Chapter 5 shows, split the working class and created huge numbers of working-class Tories. But she also devoted a huge amount of effort to wooing and promoting small businesses (Chapter 2) and creating a culture of "enterprise" and "entrepreneurialism". Through these strategies, she ensured that the Conservatives, the party of big business, were able to bind to the ruling bloc the section of society that historically had been most hostile to big capital.

Thatcherism was emphatically not a *broad* "middle-class" movement, but one which mobilized the petty bourgeoisie — the lower middle class — specifically. As Savage notes, while the petty bourgeoisie specifically became the most ardent Thatcherites, the middle class *as a whole* was actually now less likely to vote Tory. The rapidly growing "professional managerial classes" (i.e., the Keir Starmers, teachers and social workers of this world) were socially very liberal, and were horrified by Thatcher's (and the entire lower order's) perceived social conservatism. Thus, while she gained one section of the "middle class", she lost another. Under Thatcher, the professional managerial class began to move away from conservatism and towards the Labour Party, particularly as it had at this stage begun to abandon any pretence of socialism that might actually economically impact the status of this class.

New Labour

Thatcher's political and cultural revolution was followed by Blair's passive revolution. New Labour continued and often deepened Thatcher's neoliberal economic policies, but these were also supplemented with a veneer of social liberalism and limited elements of redistribution (such as child tax credits), facilitated by the mini-economic boom that New Labour inherited.

While Blairism is often felt to be a straightforward continuation of Thatcherism, Blair's British iteration of "progressive neoliberalism" left its own distinct imprint on the class structure and the political and ideological landscape of British society. Blairism, like Thatcherism, had a class character and a specific social base. Whilst Thatcher embodied, emboldened and mobilized the petty bourgeoisie, Blair personified the professional managerial class, and New Labour heralded the entrenchment of professional-managerial-class ideology — and its strange blend of paternalism and disgust towards the working class — in the body politic. New Labour's economic focus on the "knowledge economy" helped dramatically grow the professional strata that was to become their base, while manufacturing — which had sustained the traditional base of Labour's vote — went into freefall (no government since the Seventies oversaw such a dramatic drop-off in productive work).

As Chapter 3 explores in more detail, the working class now began to shrink, as the amount of people engaged in unproductive, white-collar work expanded. The massification of higher education also created a new mass of young, skilled recruits for the new knowledge economy, who would later become the new petty bourgeoisie. Of course, these changes were already occurring, but they were, whether consciously or not, accelerated by New Labour.

Under Blair, the "C2s" (i.e., lower middle classes) certainly came back to Labour (where they had been in the mid-Seventies before Thatcherism), but this was not the major realignment of the era. What defined the New Labour era, in terms of the relationship between class and politics, was its mass capture of progressive professionals — the professional managerial class — followed by the inevitable mass abandonment of Labour by the working classes. In 1974, just 19% of "middle-class" votes went to Labour (although polling does not distinguish between the different facets of the middle class). By 1997, however, this had risen to 31% — an almost unthinkable realignment.

Under Thatcher, the class composition of the Tory Party begun to change. Older, more conciliatory one-nation Tory figures, who had a paternalistic attitude towards the working class, were joined (if not totally supplanted) by new — often petty bourgeois — Thatcherites, hell-bent on aspiration and the free market. This shift prompted a sea change towards more ruthless individualism within the party and a policy shift towards more free-market ideas. Similarly, under New Labour, the composition of the Labour Party also dramatically changed. Labour MPs, once a mixed bag of old trade unionists and social workers, morphed almost overnight into a new cohort of slimy professional politicians. As late as the 1980s, professional politicians had formed only a tenth of the parliamentary Labour Party, but under Blair they became the dominant demographic.

The new class composition of the upper strata of the party inevitably changed the policy focus, away from even the modest attempts at redistribution of the early New Labour era, and squarely onto the pet topics of the professional managerial class — progressive forms of social liberalism and representation.

In response to the capture of the labour movement by the professional managerial strata, the working class deserted it. This was an entirely rational response to the Labour Party openly ignoring it. While Peter Mandelson could confidently say that the Labour Party could now afford to ignore the working class as they had nowhere to go, what happened instead was the working classes simply abandoned politics and voting. In the UK, this shift was a direct result of New Labour's policies and image, but this realignment and abandonment has happened across the globe (sometimes called "Pasokification") as social democratic parties abandoned their traditional base.

Following the deserved collapse of social democratic parties, there is now no automatic link between the working class, working-class "ideology" and the Labour Party and labour movement as there once was, simply because the Labour Party is no longer a working-class party or movement.

While Blair did not pay specific attention to the petty bourgeoisie like Thatcher did, New Labour nonetheless significantly contributed to the deepening of class divides and the promotion of petty bourgeois ideology in two key ways. Firstly, by continuing Thatcher's ideological division between "hard-working families" on the one hand and the "underclass" (single mothers, benefit frauds, "ASBOs" and Muslims) on the other, it entrenched the boundaries between "us" and "them" in the minds of the petty bourgeoisie and within the working class itself. Second, and relatedly, it helped spread the individualism that was previously only narrowly associated with the petty bourgeoisie through their overwhelming focus on the ideology of *social mobility*, which, during the New Labour period, became the main ideological pillar of the party (rather than collective class advancement). To this end, policies that systematically promoted social mobility — in particular, the enormous expansion of higher education — were massively expanded. As an ideology, social mobility became embedded as a universal good within British society. This was a new, *respectable* form of individualism — as opposed to Thatcherism's get-rich-quick kind — which was necessary for neoliberalism to become hegemonic and accepted.

Towards Authoritarian Neoliberalism

Across the world, the global crisis of capitalism, which progressive neoliberalism attempted to offset, is bursting through. In the face of increasing ecological crisis, the death of social democratic parties, the increasing rate of exploitation and far more visible negative consequences of capitalism (e.g., starvation and homelessness in the Global

North), the progressive neoliberal era and its shibboleths are collapsing.

In the UK, David Cameron's coalition government represented a continuation of progressive neoliberalism, but it also abandoned the limited crumbs of redistribution of the New Labour era, replacing them with austerity measures. In the US, Barack Obama similarly failed to tame the contradictions simmering beneath the surface and was replaced by Donald Trump.

Politics is increasingly polarizing away from the centre — both left and right — and within this interregnum the petty bourgeoisie has emerged once again as a significant political force. Its different fractions — the traditional self-employed and the new, white-collar petty bourgeoisie — are increasingly polarized towards radically different political positions.

In the US in particular, analysis of the rise of right-wing authoritarianism has belatedly grown more sophisticated than caricaturing it as "a working-class revolt", or "traditional versus metropolitan", or as the liberal dichotomy of progressives versus racists. The traditional petty bourgeoisie, i.e., the small self-employed, rather than the working class, have increasingly been identified as a core pillar of Trump's support.

In *Dissent* magazine, for example, Melinda Cooper argues convincingly that Trumpism was a "reaction of small family capital against big capital" (which as we have seen has happened throughout history), which had its roots in the Tea Party movement:

> The Trump diehards who cut their teeth in the Tea Party were not wage workers, nor even misclassified independent contractors, but small businesspeople concentrated in the blue-collar residential construction sector and its white-collar satellite professions of homeware retail, real-estate

services, mortgage brokerage, and accounting. It was the meteoric rise and fall of the small business sector — not the long saga of deindustrialization — that gave birth to the current cycle of far-right populism.

In the UK, the self-employed have become a pillar of conservative politics and are far more likely to vote for UKIP and the Brexit Party. This is the case across the world. The "old" petty bourgeoisie are now a key base of the AKP in Turkey, Le Pen in France (38% of Le Pen's southern vote are self-employed), Bolsonaro in Brazil and more.

The rise of right authoritarianism is at least partially explained by the changing class structure and the re-emergence of the petty bourgeoisie as a political force, coupled with the spread of petty bourgeois ideology beyond the class proper and the death of strong socialist parties, which could have won the petty bourgeoisie over to the left. While the working class is now a popular scapegoat for the rise of the right, the reality is that the defining political characteristic of the working class is not right populism but non-engagement. It has not returned to politics since being sold-out by the social democratic parties.

While the traditional self-employed have ostensibly broken to the right, the new petty bourgeois strata — which emerged with the transition to a service or knowledge economy — has broken "left" towards social democratic parties. Promised a future of upward social mobility under progressive neoliberalism, it has been confronted with the reality of an economy that has little use for them, as the supply of graduates has massively outstripped demand and the "skilled" "knowledge" jobs they have trained for have been devalued and deskilled. The new class has therefore been proletarianized as its labour has been devalued, getting poorer and more miserable. As a consequence of having its upward trajectory blocked, in many countries (although not all) it has become politically polarized towards the left, and with the professional managerial class, has now largely replaced the working class as the electoral base of social democratic and progressive parties such as Labour in the UK and the Democrats in the US. These two classes sit in a frequently uneasy coalition within social democratic movements across the world.

Conclusion

As this chapter has shown, society has never been neatly polarized into two classes. Despite Marx's early predictions, the petty bourgeoisie never disappeared: it has always been there, from the beginning of capitalism to the present day.

The petty bourgeoisie has proven to be remarkably resilient, and as capitalism has evolved so too have they, continually changing form, "being made and remade" from epoch to epoch, being replenished by new recruits. While its objective size and strength ebbed and flowed, it remained a constant feature of capitalist society, as well as a powerful and dangerous global political force with schizoid political tendencies, which have remained consistent throughout its history. Originally comprised of the artisan and small farmer, during the Industrial Revolution the artisan was gradually replaced by the shopkeeper as small handicraft production was marginalized by monopoly capitalism and the petty bourgeoisie moved away from small handicraft work and towards service/ownership. In turn, the shopkeeper was supplemented in the early twentieth century by a new army of white-collar clerical workers, created to manage the new form of capitalism and to work in the state bureaucracy. With the transition to neoliberalism, the petty bourgeoisie has grown, and has been replenished yet again as a new fraction of the petty bourgeoisie has emerged of deskilled, proletarianized "white-collar" service workers. Although in the popular imagination it is often associated with conservatism and reaction, it has at different periods and contexts been drawn to both progressive and reactionary politics.

If the twentieth century "belonged to the proletariat", as Göran Therborn claimed, the twenty-first century so far has belonged to the petty bourgeoisie. The class is larger than it has ever been, and as well as being a huge political force, its ideology has now also spread far beyond the borders of the class proper.

It is therefore impossible to understand modern life under neoliberalism without understanding the nature of the petty bourgeoisie. The rest of this book is dedicated to improving our understanding of both fractions of this class, new and old.

CHAPTER TWO
SUPERSTAR TRADESMEN: THE RETURN OF THE TRADITIONAL PETTY BOURGEOISIE

Superstar tradesman, stand at the bar
Get a trade son, you will go far
You'll have a house in the ferry, and a new guitar
That's never been played before and it never will

The View were a Libertines-adjacent landfill indie band from Dundee with a few hit singles. Although music buffs will no doubt recoil in horror here, their hit single, "Superstar Tradesman", really resonated with me. The band themselves were working as apprentices in the building trade when they took off, and the song was about the very familiar tale of small-town (in their case, council estate) young men being repeatedly encouraged to get a trade and make some money. The song addresses the conflict between this conventional path and the perceived rewards, values and worldview it represented on the one hand, and the creative, upwardly mobile and more worldly path of the new petty bourgeoisie on the other.

The implication in the lyrics is that the hard-nosed view of the world expressed by tradesmen essentially precluded an appreciation of culture — you'll be able to afford an expensive guitar but, unlike the sophisticated new petty bourgeoisie, you'll never play it or understand it. The traditional petty bourgeoisie's utilitarian view of culture — get an expensive guitar purely to show it off rather than play it because you've got money — is in fact repeatedly referred to in Bourdieu's analysis of the class's ostentatious consumption habits that members use to distinguish themselves from the working class.

The song came out when I was away at university, struggling being away from my family and mates and once again wondering what I was doing with my life. I liked it because the tension between the two worlds in the song is one I remember well. Go to any football or rugby club in any small town across the UK on a Saturday afternoon and the car parks will be full of the vans of self-employed tradesmen. And like the song said, in many small towns the tradesmen really *are* superstars: they were locally famous because, in a working-class or lower-middle-class town, they very often make lots of money and have nice cars. People want to be like them and for good reason: they personify a particular view of the world, a particular set of values and aspirations.

For many lower-middle-class kids growing up in these towns, there are two paths that confront you: stay local and get a trade, or leave home, go to university, and try and make it in the world in a different way, based on the assumption — instilled in you through the education system — that you are somehow different to those who stay. I've been fixated on self-employment ever since, firstly because it's what I grew up around, but also because it represents the path-not-taken, a sort of counter-factual history of my own life.

Yet there are multiple forms of self-employment. One of the other incidents that inspired this book occurred when I campaigned — briefly — for the Labour Party in my home constituency of Bridgend.

While out canvassing, we had a bizarre engagement with a female parcel courier who kept doing deliveries on the same street as us. She would helpfully tell us which houses were in and which ones weren't. One of my colleagues began talking to her and asked if she would be voting. She said yes, for Boris, and that she didn't like Corbyn. When my colleague probed further, she said she had three jobs, all of which were zero hours. My friend told her Labour would work to ban zero-hour contracts. She said she was self-employed, actually, and was doing just fine.

No job security, no trade union representation, no rights. Yet here she was saying she was self-employed and would therefore be voting Tory, as naturally as if she was a traditional small business owner. Her non-traditional — and bogus — form of "self-employment" had inculcated the views of the traditional petty bourgeoisie — the rugged individualism and fetish for hard work that the tradesmen had, except this had none of the "superstar" glamour of skill, autonomy, strength or masculinity that they did. This woman wasn't making big money.

I began thinking about the different forms of work, about self-employment, and the connections and similarities between these ostensibly different paths. As I got older, more and more people in Porthcawl seemed to be going it alone, but increasingly moving beyond the traditional forms of self-employment in ways that were influenced by their class. On top of the builders, self-employment now included the working-class mums from school selling Herbalife or some other Ponzi scheme on Facebook, or other lads doing increasingly small-scale handyman work. At the other end of the spectrum, other people I knew from university started becoming consultants or contractors in the world of finance. Then, when Covid came along, there was a flurry of middle-class people setting up bakeries and other services from home.

***

As the previous chapter made clear, the petty bourgeoisie is split into two fractions. The old or traditional petty bourgeoisie, which is defined in the class structure by its ownership of its own means of production; and a new petty bourgeoisie, which, while it does not own its own means of production, is nonetheless split off from the proletariat and placed in the ranks of the petty bourgeoisie for myriad other reasons. This chapter explores the traditional petty bourgeoisie, while the new petty bourgeoisie are explored in more detail the next chapter.

In talking about the changing class structure and the emergence of a new, mass petty bourgeoisie, as well as the spread of petty bourgeois ideology, it would be easy to get caught up in the legions of beleaguered call centre workers with Masters degrees — precisely because this is the experience that is closer to "us" on the left — and overlook the simultaneous huge growth of the traditional (or old) fraction of the petty bourgeoisie — the small, self-employed worker who owns his own means of production. The need to explore the traditional petty bourgeoisie is becoming more and more urgent given that, as Chapter 1 outlined, the self-employed are once again becoming increasingly associated with authoritarianism and right-wing politics, although *why* this might be the case — if indeed it *is* the case — is rarely explored.

Are my school friends *really* fascistic? Is your plumber a secret Blackshirt? What might it be about the lives and values of the traditional petty bourgeoisie that makes them authoritarian, if indeed they are? Is the class still fixed, an anachronism, as it was in the nineteenth century, or has it evolved and diversified? These are urgent questions.

While Poulantzas and others argued that the traditional petty bourgeoisie would remain small and be replenished by the new petty bourgeoisie, what has in fact happened is that *both* the old *and* new fractions of the petty bourgeoisie have grown exponentially because of changes to the economy. While it sounds hard to believe, there are now nearly as many people classified as self-employed in the UK as there are employed in the entire public sector (5.6 million people). Before being disproportionately decimated by Covid-19, in 2019 self-employment in the UK peaked at *5.1 million* people. At the time of writing, there are still many more than four million self-employed workers. Thus, the traditional fraction of the petty bourgeoisie constitutes a significant chunk of the working population, and because solo-self-employment tends to be a family affair, more people still will be related to or deeply influenced by the experiences of this petty-bourgeois way of life.

Indeed, along with the explosion of professionals and managers, the growth of self-employment is arguably the single biggest story in the British economy in recent years. According to a recent IFS report, in 1945 just 7% of the population were self-employed; in 1975, at the twilight of the welfare state, it was still only 8% of the British population. By 2019, however, this had increased to over 14% of the workforce, a huge swathe of people, with the main rise occurring since the 2008 financial crisis. Crucially, this rise has been driven almost entirely by "*solo* self-employment", i.e., own-account workers *without* employees, who comprise the absolute majority of the total self-employed. This is a huge change: in 1975, nearly half of the self-employed had employees. According to the IFS, solo self-employment has accounted for over a third of all employment growth since the financial crisis, while the self-employed who actually employ other people has fallen from 4% to around 2% of the total self-employed workforce.

In other words, the majority of "small business people" today do not employ others. This, of course, is the dictionary definition of the traditional petty bourgeoisie: people who own their own means of production but who do not employ wage labour. Thus the traditional fraction of the petty bourgeoisie alone in the UK (not the new) comprises *at least four million people*. By way of contrast, the NHS employs 1.3 million people, there are approximately half a million teachers, 145,000 armed forces personnel, 135,000 police, 240,000 railway workers and 430,000 civil service personnel.

The growth of the traditional petty bourgeoisie is not limited to the UK either — solo self-employment has risen in the majority of the OECD countries, and in Greece and Chile the solo self-employed constitute nearly 25% of the total workforce, although it is far lower in advanced welfare capitalist states: Germany, Denmark, Japan, Norway and Switzerland all have far lower rates of self-employment than the UK.

Within this vague category of "solo self-employed" also lie an estimated 1.1 million people employed in the British "gig economy", where people access short-term, task-based contract work (hence "gigs") through digital platforms that allow people to do both highly localised jobs, like being a bicycle courier or an Uber driver, as well as high-tech "cloudwork" roles like online freelancing, where workers complete online tasks remotely. These platforms allow people to register as self-employed contractors, meaning that people working for these platforms are often denied basic employment rights, not allowed to claim the national minimum wage and so on. In other words, this "self-employment" is widely seen as bogus: it is simply beneficial to the bosses to categorize employees in this way so as to cut costs and maximize profit.

The fight against this bogus self-employment has led to a wave of union and legal battles. Whereas workers once fought to be free of wage labour or to get higher wages, the battle here is simply to be classed as a worker. That these are the new frontlines of the labour struggle shows how far society has drifted into a new dystopian state. In the UK, after a huge campaign, Uber drivers won their case and are legally now classed as employed and can now enjoy their right to be exploited in the same way as everyone else, but with access to the minimum wage and paid holidays.

The Persistence of Small Business

Before assessing the nature of self-employment and why it is important for the left, it is first necessary to consider the relationship between big and small capital and the persistence of petty or small-scale capitalism during the era of monopolies, as this is the wider context within which the traditional petty bourgeoisie has persisted and now grown.

It is well understood that we live in an era of oligarchic capitalism — huge multinational firms dominate the world. The interests of international and large capital also clearly dominate our politics, with parliaments across the world being stuffed with their representatives. Conflict within the domestic and global system, such as Brexit, never-ending rifts within the Tory Party, and between the Democrats and Republicans in the US, is frequently driven by conflict between factions of big capital — national versus international, finance versus productive — and so on. It is logical, then, that international and large national capital are the main target of socialist analysis and organizing. Although small businessmen remain prominent in local politics, normally as Tories, small capital is ostensibly not a significant political force at the national level in the UK insofar as it has hardly any political representatives. Small to medium capital does not therefore seem politically interesting or relevant, despite being a central part of the global and local economy.

Yet small, local capital (small businesses) persists and is a key part of the global capitalist mosaic.[5] Although larger firms — those with 250+ employees; your Walmarts, Amazons, Volkswagons, McDonalds, etc. — employ the absolute majority of workers, particularly in countries like Germany and Japan with strong manufacturing bases, across the world, micro-businesses, with between one and nine people employed, comprise the majority of all private businesses. In 2021, in the EU, there were twenty-one million micro-businesses, making up 93% of all companies within the bloc, employing over eighty million people. In the UK, 96% of all businesses are micro-businesses, and 76% of all businesses have no employees. And although politicians love to bribe large businesses to come and set up in their backyard to provide loads of shitty, fleeting, low-paid jobs, it is *small* firms that account for the majority of new jobs created in the British economy.

How, then, is petty capitalism so resilient in a world of oligarchic capitalism?

---

5 It is very important, as Poulantzas reminds us, to distinguish between "small capital" and the petty bourgeoisie, and not to conflate non-monopoly capital with small capital, or medium with small, and so on. Small capital is not "everyone outside big monopoly capital". By small capital, I mean microbusinesses with 1-9 employees, whereas the petty bourgeois are those solo-self-employed who employ no one. There is a clear and important difference between those who employ themselves, or maybe family members, and those who employ others. The petty bourgeoisie were defined by self-exploitation and the particular social isolation and circumstances generated by solo-self-employment. It is *solo* self-employment that has historically driven the centrality of the family to the petty-bourgeois experience, as well as the particular patriarchal social relations and worldview that emerge from this particular situation.

There are a multitude of explanations for the persistence of small production and self-employment. Mainstream economists would argue that, within the global system of monopoly capitalism, small firms have simply continued to harmoniously co-exist with big capital in a mutually beneficial relationship. Small, specialised firms focus on the niches of the economy not yet colonised by big capital, often in time-consuming, high-skilled sectors that big capital simply doesn't have the time or interest to invest in. And when the small business is involved in an industry or field that is dominated by huge corporations, this *still* doesn't mean the end for them. Instead, when the small firms make specialized products in a big industry, they exist in a symbiotic, big-brother-little-brother relationship with big firms. While some large firms manufacture parts in-house, many more outsource and subcontract parts of the supply chain and production process to smaller specialized firms with high skills — so the large firm makes the big parts and assembles them while small manufacturers make the very high-tech components at their own site, which then get sent to the big factories to be assembled, in a modern version of the putting-out system. Indeed, 77% of small firms in UK are part of supply chains. A traditional example of this is looking at how cars get from factory to person — they get manufactured and assembled in huge plants, but many of the smaller individual components are made by small companies before being delivered to the factory for assembly. In the UK, over 90% of auto-component suppliers are small and medium-sized enterprises. Moreover, cars are generally sold to the public by small businesses. This is not just the case in manufacturing. Small family-owned retail stores survive next to large supermarkets because they may sell specialist goods, offer a particular service or by having different opening hours.

More broadly, and outside the direct supply chain, many regional economies have become — or always have been — entirely dependent on extremely large global businesses (for example, Ford in Bridgend, Nissan in Sunderland, Airbus in Broughton and so on). In these places, the large business underpins the entire local economic ecosystem as a huge variety of smaller businesses and self-employed people depend on it: employees and their dependents use the local services — cafes and bars, hair salons, gyms, schools and so on. Those who provide small personal services are very often dependent on a large business for their custom, either directly or indirectly.

On a global level, the uneven nature of capitalist development means that industrialization is often awkwardly superimposed on underdeveloped rural economies, creating a situation where traditional forms of self-employment persist alongside and are dependent upon more recently arrived larger capital.

Yet far from a harmonious ecosystem where everyone benefits, the *real* reason that small capitalism has survived against the odds is simply because it benefits the capitalist political system to have a reservoir of small, desperate, dependent capital. The increased fragmentation of the economy into smaller units and the lengthening of the supply chain is, on the face of it, irrational, but it is always at base about maximizing profits.

Construction is the field where solo self-employment is most prominent and is therefore a useful example of the persistence of small capital, and why it benefits big capital to integrate it into supply chains and the capitalist ecosystem. It is a field that is famously fragmented, and subcontracting is central to the industry. On any large-scale building site, there will be a number of different crews of small self-employed builders, with up to seventy sub-contractors working on any large site; moreover, the contracts on these sites tend to be short-term, relatively low-paid and specialized. Employers would argue this is because buildings themselves are complex and have different parts — on top of the bricks and mortar (brickies, scaffolders, plasterers), there is plumbing, electrics, air conditioning, alarms, glazing and so on — therefore requiring lots of different specialized skills that smaller firms specialize in, and it would be impossible and undesirable for one large firm to cater for all these specialisms.

The real reason, however, is that subcontracting ultimately allows lower costs and avoids unionisation — something the construction industry's big firms are notoriously hostile towards. In 1972, there was a highly effective construction workers' strike, a remarkable achievement given the fragmentation of the industry (for which Ricky Tomlinson and others were jailed). Big construction companies reacted to this militancy by attempting to minimise the amount of workers that they directly employed. While having a plethora of small businesses working at the same site may seem illogical, this system prevents the emergence of a large, unified, socialized and potentially unionized workforce. So not only do smaller firms cost less, they are almost never unionized. Smaller construction firms that rely on subcontracts are also frequently subject to late payments or get paid less than they were promised, and as a result many fall into debt. A majority of small firms also have no administration functions, have no say over the terms and conditions of their contract and are often unable to say anything because they are scared of losing the work. This sums up the condition of small capital: it is *dependent* — it needs big capital to survive but is also at its mercy.

Subcontracting ultimately allows big firms to pass costs and risks down the system to the little men at the bottom, and there's nothing the small firms can do about it because they are totally dependent on big capital for contracts. This is a deeply unequal power relationship, which benefits one side far more than the other.

In every industry, and particularly within a febrile economic climate, managers of large firms have frequently found it safer to subcontract work out in order to avoid taking on permanent staff that they would then struggle to get rid of when the economy slumps again. Why take someone on full-time if you won't need them after this job is done and they will become a liability? Far better to subcontract someone in for a specific job and then get rid of them. Across nearly every industry, subcontracting has risen enormously, and the number of small firms and self-employed contractors has risen in turn. This is also, of course, the ultimate driver behind the gig economy's bogus form of self-employment — it allows employers to pass off costs and risks to the employee whilst not having to pay them a proper wage or provide them with any benefits. What is now being discussed as a new development in the gig economy has arguably been common practice and normal for the self-employed for decades.

Moreover, at the broader societal and political level, during times of crisis small businesses create jobs far more than larger firms, and in a massively overqualified knowledge economy, small firms are importantly more likely to hire those without formal educational qualifications, relying on informal hiring practices and disproportionately allowing the working class to work in small towns across the UK. They are thus a "shock absorber" for the entire capitalist system, preventing unemployment reaching levels that are too high during times of crisis and allowing economies to recover after periodic crises by taking people on.

Lastly, small business and the self-employed are also useful ideologically. First, they personify and help promote and embed the spirit of capitalist individualism and entrepreneurialism throughout the whole of society, particularly during periods of crisis. Second, they can also serve to obscure the interests and controlling role of big capital within society: hence, in anti-gentrification activism, it is common for anarchists and the like to target small "hipster" businesses — often the face of gentrification — whilst ignoring the large landowners and property developers that actually drive this process. This has also historically been the case in working-class race riots, which target petty-bourgeois shop-owners — often drawn from minority ethnic groups — "fall guys" for the entire unfair capitalist system.

For all these reasons, small business lobbies have actually frequently been funded and encouraged by *large* businesses who understand the political and social benefit to capitalism of small business and small capital. Small capital has therefore not persisted "naturally" "against all odds", but precisely because its dependence makes it useful for large capital and the modern capitalist system overall. It is very useful to have a sector of small businesses, which are always in threat of collapsing, that you can bring in on a short-term basis, that you don't have to pay much, that will create jobs and stop the unemployment levels from getting too high, that will keep trade unionism low. The thrust for the growth of self-employment and the persistence of small capital from the ruling class is always self-interested. As Colin Ward notes, the idea that the government would actually encourage small firms and normal people to have *genuine* control over any aspect of the economic process or supply chain is ludicrous.

The Rise of Self-Employment in the UK: Thatcher to the Present Day

Although the UK was allegedly labelled "a nation of shopkeepers" by Napoleon, historically shopkeeping — and the traditional petty bourgeoisie more generally — was far bigger in France, Germany and the US. Napoleon perhaps looked at the conservatism and stability of the UK and worked backwards.

Like many things, however, this changed with Thatcher. As the global economic crisis gripped the UK in the Seventies, the petty bourgeoisie was feeling the pinch, and she sensed that this "silent majority" were ripe to be radicalized, mobilized and incorporated into her bloc. In 1975, shortly after being elected Tory leader, she gave an impromptu speech to the National Chamber of Trade, the body representing 350,000 small business owners. She told the conference:

> People feel the big battalions win all the time, so it is nice to be able to support small traders...we used to be famous for two things—as a nation of shopkeepers and as the workshop of the world. One is trade, the other is industry. We must get back our reputation.

She then spoke of her own background working in a shop and her allegiance to the values of the small shopkeeper:

> I knew full well during my first 18 years—spent over a shop—of the tremendous number of hours that went into earning your keep. I knew the woman of the house often had to put in a great deal of work in the shop, too....I knew father and mother could probably never go away on holiday together because they could not leave the shop at the same time. And I knew what it was when the rates went up.

Right from the start of her tenure she begun to create a narrative between the national economy and household spending, about tightening belts, stopping inflation and cutting public spending. These tropes are now mainstays of neoliberalism, but here at their inception they were explicitly linked to and justified by reference to the norms and values of the shopkeeper.

Her tenure helped cement the link in the popular imagination between small business and self-employment, "enterprise" and Toryism. Thatcher's "Essex man", the popular archetype of her upwardly mobile, culturally working-class base, is often felt to be a nebulous, "median voter" or "C2": a skilled working-class man, or the brash young man working in the city. In fact, Essex man was conceived as the modern incantation of the East End barrow boy, i.e., the small self-employed trader, the traditional petty bourgeois.

Simon Heffer, the person who coined the term "Essex man", states that under Thatcher, Essex became a county of small businesses, and it was this small businessperson's instinctive hostility to collectivism and socialism that became the essence of popular Thatcherism and which defined her new aspirational geographic bases like Basildon.

Under Thatcher, the Tory Party — while remaining the party of oligarchic capitalism — began to consciously promote the interests of small capital, and essentially became an unofficial sponsor of small business, forming backbench committees and a small business bureau. In turn, the small business lobby began to grow and form institutions, which were often promoted by right-wing elements in Thatcher's cabinet who believed small entrepreneurs personified the spirit of capitalism and believed that the self-employed could help spread the ideology of neoliberalism throughout society.

They also realized the political utility of fostering small business as they sought to break the backs of the trade unions. In the same way that the Tories promoted nuclear power to break dependence on coal and hence weaken the National Union of Mineworkers, growing the amount of small businesses and the amount of people employed by them was similarly a general tactic for weakening the union movement. Growing the amount of self-employed people and smaller firms was a calculated policy to kill off socialism and entrench Tory hegemony.

As well as creating a culture of "enterprise" and "entrepreneurialism", Thatcher deployed a dual policy towards the new legions of unemployed: first, she aimed to make unemployment uncomfortable and untenable in the long term; and second, she encouraged the unemployed to become self-employed, i.e. to actually *grow* the petty bourgeoisie as a class.

And self-employment *did* grow significantly under Thatcherism. In 1980, there were 1.9 million self-employed people, which was then nearly 8% of the employed workforce. By March 1989, however, that had grown to 3.1 million, approximately 12% of the workforce. This was, ostensibly at least, down to the encouragement of a so-called "enterprise culture". According to slavish press coverage at the time, Thatcher's efforts to promote self-employment "helped transform Britain from a nation of heavily unionised coal miners and steelworkers back into a nation of shopkeepers (and taxi drivers and window cleaners)".

While the working class *mainly* stayed true to labour, Thatcher's efforts peeled off large swathes of the "C2 — skilled manual worker", and many of these were self-employed tradesmen. Many "self-made men" like Alan Sugar and Charlie Mullins made their fortunes during this period, and accordingly still worship Thatcher.

Thatcher's creation of "enterprise" culture, now often called "entrepreneurialism", was continued wholesale by New Labour and has become a mainstay of economic policy across the UK. While not as skilled at talking the language of class as Thatcher — and as Chapter 1 noted, very much dedicated to his base in the professional managerial class, — Blair, of course, had his own version of Essex man: "Mondeo man". Again — significantly when we talk about swing voters or "middle England" — Blair's Mondeo man was actually a self-employed electrician (i.e., the traditional petty bourgeoisie), who Blair met on the campaign trail and whose views — switching from Labour to Tory because he'd moved up in the world and wanted to defend his gains — inspired him to build "getting on", that is, individual social mobility — the essence of petty-bourgeois ideology but inimical to socialism with its strong collectivist bent — into the very fabric of the modern Labour Party.

New Labour's "new deal" explicitly encouraged self-employment and Blair, albeit less consciously than Thatcher, certainly courted the self-employed, and repeatedly stated he wanted the self-employed to expand. Significantly, Blair's policies also made being unemployed uncomfortable as well as introducing new public management regimes into the public sector.

In order to encourage the spirit of capitalism, "business" entered the school curriculum where it has remained a central pillar, as "entrepreneurship" — a nebulous spirit of rugged capitalist innovation — has become widely seen to be an engine of a successful capitalist economy by consecutive Labour and Tory governments (and, indeed, by governments across the world). If the economy is sluggish, entrepreneurs can save us and pull us out. Repeatedly during economic crises, the small businessman is invoked as the saviour of capitalism and the economy. Accordingly, under the Tory-Lib Dem coalition government that took office amidst a crisis, self-employment was encouraged as the driver of economic recovery. Cameron hailed the self-employed as "go-getters", and it was under the coalition in 2014 that self-employment expanded to its highest level in forty years. Like Thatcher, the coalition government formalized self-employment as a route out of *unemployment*, creating numerous initiatives to this end.

Who Are the Traditional Petty Bourgeoisie? Exploring a Class and Its Social World

So, we have seen how and why it has grown in the neoliberal era, but who are the traditional petty bourgeoisie, this class that has grown so much and is now so large? Chapter 1 outlined how they came into being and how they have acted politically throughout history. But broad-brush political polemics don't always tell us who these people are — that is, the internal lifeworld of the class, its values and outlook that flows from this. Many Marxist accounts throughout history have simply taken it for granted who they are — they are reactionaries, that's just how the class is — even though history has proven that their political tendencies are far from uniformly conservative. But even if they were, *why* would they be conservative, what would it be about the petty-bourgeois experience that led to right-wing politics? It is only by exploring the lifeworld of the petty bourgeoisie that we can begin to understand the social, ideological and political effects that emerge from its unique experience of work.

As Chapter 1 illustrated, the roots of the modern petty bourgeoisie lie in small handicraft production — a craftsman making products in his own small workshop, just before the transition to industrial capitalism. One of Marx's most famous observations regarding the petty bourgeoisie emerged during this period:

The independent peasant or handicraftsman is cut up into two persons. As owner of the means of production he is capitalist; as labourer he is his own wage-labourer. As capitalist he therefore pays himself his wages and draws his profit on his capital; that is to say, he exploits himself as wage-labourer, and pays himself, in the surplus-value, the tribute that labour owes to capital.

The petty bourgeoisie is both a worker and a capitalist. Like the worker, they have to work or starve, but like the capitalist, they own their own means of production, which, regardless of how modest this was (shop, tools, workshop, etc.), nonetheless split them off economically and socially from the proletariat. This was — and remains — necessarily a unique, schizoid existence. This torn position influences everything the petty bourgeoisie does and thinks. Its interests are neither purely on the side of labour nor purely on the side of capital. Its ideology and culture contains elements that are sympathetic to the cause of labour, and some which are hostile to the cause of labour and pro-capitalistic. As Chapter 1 illustrated, throughout history this interstitial economic position bled into its political engagement.

It has also similarly been claimed that small handicraft production lent itself to conservativism simply because it was — and is — an economic anachronism, constantly fighting for survival against big capital and modernity. Small forms of isolated, skilled and autonomous production are focused on preserving and defending skill and its way of life and are therefore innately opposed to societal and economic change and bureaucratic or state interference over their lives. It also produced a particular set of values, focused around discipline and skill, that was defined against the unskilled and unvirtuous worker. Institutionally, this was expressed through craft unions or guilds, whose borders they policed militantly.

E.P. Thompson argued that artisans were overwhelmingly libertarian, focused on the right of every man to earn a fair living by working autonomously through "the sweat of his own brow":

> I was a — regular, active, and industrious man, working early and late ... and when out of the workshop never so happy anywhere as at home with my wife and two children. The alehouse I always detested ... I had a notion that a man ... was a fool not to make a right application of every shilling.

This passage is a good example of how habitus — our way of thinking, which structures our dispositions in the world — is rooted in a particular economic and social milieu. As Thompson noted, this was not just an economic category or "a job", as factory work was for the proletariat; this was an entire social world whose values, outlook on life and society — thrift, discipline, piety and so on — flowed from their unique working situation. It is not hard to see how this way of life led to both a dislike of wage labour and giving the profits of your labour to others; but equally how the self-sufficient, autonomous existence also led to a particular set of values that emphasized thrift and scorned the worker for spending his money in the tavern.

Another famous, in-depth portrayal of the traditional petty bourgeoisie and their habitus is provided by C. Wright Mills, who contrasted the ruined self-employed small businessman with the emergent class of white-collar workers in America in the post-war period. This was a class of self-employed business people that employed no wage labour other than their own family, a class which spanned the rural and urban, and which were characterized by their marginal, precarious existence just above the breadline.

Mills paints a portrait of a brutal, unforgiving existence. A class of "midget entrepreneurs" defined by thrift and relentless overwork. A feature of this class was a scorn for formal education and those who pursue it, prioritising instead practical knowledge and "common sense" — often, in fact, to the detriment of their business, as they were unable to adapt to modern technology and more efficient ways of working. Mills notes in particular the centrality of the family unit for the petty bourgeoisie, and this remains an important feature of modern petty-bourgeois life, which is frequently overlooked in contemporary politics. In the first instance, the family unit is important because the petty bourgeoisie needs the family to work in the business, hence the family is exploited all in the name of the business. Children will typically experience the world of work and exploitation from a far younger age than their peers from other classes. From this family business unit grows both a highly patriarchal culture and strict discipline towards the children — justified for both business reasons but also because of the striving for upward family mobility (i.e., the desire for the children to do well at all costs), which distinguishes it from other classes. The children of the petty bourgeoisie have a disproportionately strict petty-bourgeois upbringing because, unlike the working class, the parents almost always attempt to ensure their child experiences upward social mobility, and thus a disproportionate amount of the children of the petty bourgeoisie tend to enter professional occupations or clerical work. Thus, for Mills, the "economic freedom" pursued by the petty bourgeoisie is at the expense of the freedom of the family.

Mills' picture of the petty bourgeoisie — a class he himself came from — is incredibly unflattering to say the least. While previous portrayals of small businesspeople had defined them through stoicism, piety and morality, and the artisans as graceful and skilled, he portrays a class defined by anger and bitterness, eschewing all other considerations in the process of survival. He argues that the insecurity and frenzied permanent worry about their business and declining status begin to bleed into the personality, values and habitus of the petty bourgeoisie, and that this permanent anxiety and bitterness had supplanted their previous strict morality. Their thrift becomes selfishness, meanness, penny-pinching; their obsession with the survival of their business sours their personal relationships as everything is reduced to economic calculations: "the calculation for gain spreads into the whole social life... he thinks of his whole social universe, including the members of his family, as factors in his struggle". In turn, the class becomes consumed with guilt and resentment. The petty bourgeoisie grow to despise the proletariat in particular. Forced into treating them with civility in public as customers, in private they harbour great animosity towards a mass that they both feel superior to, threatened by and often jealous of, and are furious at the lack of deference towards them in modern society.

He concludes that, "from this small scale wretchedness, a fretful assertiveness is fed, human relations are poisoned, and a personality is formed with which it is not pleasant to exchange political greetings". And because the petty bourgeoisie "is scared", they embrace "sordid and narrow" political ideas in their desperation for some prestige. Thus, their reactionary politics flowed from their anxiety and precarity, which is rooted in their conditions of life.

Ethnographic Portrayals of the Petty Bourgeoisie

However, we are not stuck with inferences from historical polemics or Mills' broad brushstrokes, however masterful. The study of the micro-level, of everyday life, is central to understanding the conditions that produce class consciousness. In the late Seventies and Eighties, while Poulantzas was focused on the new petty bourgeoisie in France, a small group of sociologists, led by Frank Bechhofer and Brian Elliot, doggedly pursued the study of the traditional petty bourgeoisie and its curious persistence within modern life. While Poulantzas and others focused on updating Marxism and broad strokes of theory, these sociologists instead pursued empirical ethnographic studies of small farmers, shopkeepers, bakers and small construction workers across the world. These are an excellent companion to historical studies and extremely important given the dearth of empirical research into the class either before or since. The snapshots and insights that these studies provide are absolutely invaluable when thinking about the ever-expanding modern petty bourgeoisie, how it acts and the changes that have occurred to society, class formation and reproduction more generally.

Bechhofer and Elliot's study of Edinburgh shopkeepers captures the private lives of the petty bourgeoisie as well as their social and political attitudes. Like Mills' earlier work, it also paints a picture of a brutal existence where the physicality of the job and the hours worked in the shop were almost always longer than factory work. Again, the price of the "freedom", of "being your own boss" — the most cherished ideal of the shopkeeper — was extremely high. Socially, the shopkeeper — like most small businesses — had no separation between home life and work life. Not only did the business occupy all the time and effort of the entire family, the entire family were also generally employed and exploited in the service of the business. The shopkeepers' mode of work was simple — they detested bureaucracy and technology and preferred traditional ways of doing business.

Ultimately, two hundred years or so after Painite ideas motivated the petty bourgeoisie to participate in democratic revolutions, Bechhofer and Elliot concluded that the small shopkeeper was characterized by a "radical individualism" and concomitant hostility to collectivism, rooted in his autonomous, isolated conditions of work. They were

> the repository of many of the traditional values upon which a capitalist social order was built. The shopkeepers' passionate individualism and the moral evaluation of work emerge clearly enough. So too does the vision of a laissez-faire economy in which men like themselves will prosper. Moreover, their belief that by hard work and wit you can succeed is crucial to the conception of ours as an open society. Thus, the symbolic significance of the stratum resides in the fact that, to many, their lives appear to demonstrate the possibility of individual mobility. Despite the modesty of their origins many have succeeded — succeeded that is, in terms quite fundamental to a capitalist society. They have won, albeit in small measure, property and autonomy.

Unlike the working class, all these respondents had no contact whatsoever with collectivist institutions or collective experiences such as trade unions. As in Mills' analysis, the main social unit was the family and the business, not society as a whole. Even when involved in pragmatic collectives such as local small business associations, the difficulty in rubbing along with one another was palpable.

Politically, the shopkeepers were generally conservatives, but this was not so much motivated by a love of the Tory

Party as much as it was a hatred of the Labour Party and the trade unions, who they believed to be both bureaucratic and meddling, overly militant and corrupt. They also hated the Labour Party for their associations with the working class. As in earlier periods, the relationship between the shopkeeper and the proletarian customer was complex. Formerly of higher status in the community, as the shopkeeper became more marginal and impoverished, they were increasingly required to distinguish themselves from large stores through their better customer service. As the working classes gained more purchasing power, this brought the shopkeeper into contact more with the worker, forcing them to be deferential — through their better customer service — to those that they felt to be their social inferiors. They were also increasingly resentful of the material gains often being won by the working class (the forty-hour week, holidays, etc.).

As the working class grew more affluent during the welfare state, the economic and status divides between the classes became narrower, much to the horror of the shopkeepers. This frequently bubbled over into a deep hatred of those beneath them — the respondents in the study believed the working class to be feckless and lazy, and that the Labour Party was therefore a party that rewarded idleness. Their economic precarity and fear of falling into the working class — status anxiety — far from making them ally with the working class or somehow blend into the working class as the two-class proletarianization hypothesis implies, in fact drove them to increasingly reactionary positions. The closer they got to the class below them economically, the more they tried to differentiate themselves from the lower class socially, culturally and politically.

Newby et al.'s study of small farmers in Norfolk offers a snapshot of the shopkeeper's rural counterpart. Like the shopkeepers, this was a portrait of a libertarian group with significant similarities with the shopkeeper, although there were also important differences. Unlike the shops, many of which had been bought by former wage labourers keen to move up in the world, the small farms had generally been inherited, and hence family played a disproportionate role in the lives of the farmers. This group was also a "clannish" self-contained world: marriage was almost exclusively to other farming families and was central for land transfers and business, and the extended family and social circle was also rooted in farming, ensuring the reproduction of the class. Like the shopkeepers, the small farmer's focus on family informed a highly traditional, patriarchal way of life in which women were expected to provide domestic duties while the males performed the farm labour. As in Mills' study, they eschewed formal education, believing it to be a waste of time, instead emphasizing the importance of practical sense and learning on the job.

And like the shopkeeper, the small farmers were active politically. They were motivated by a deep hatred of taxation on land (and on inheritance), and shared the shopkeeper's hatred of big business, expressing great hostility to industrialization and what they perceived as meddling in rural affairs by outsiders and planners (i.e., the specific rural manifestation of the traditional hatred of bureaucracy). Of particular note was the farmer's "us and them" siege mentality, created by this isolated, precarious existence. They voted Tory but, like the shopkeeper, could not be said to support the status quo or be dyed-in-the-wool Tories. Their precarity meant that they were generally angry at *everything*, and this anger was directed both up and down: "'Us', in this case, was the 'little man' striving to earn an honest living against the predatory demands of 'them': politicians, bureaucrats, trade unions and big business, the urban mass of the population." The petty bourgeoisie were felt to be the backbone of the nation — ordinary, decent, hard-working folk. The working class were disliked precisely because of this fetish for "hard work" — it was strongly believed that the proletariat were lazy and workshy. The unions were hated because they were felt to be a force that could impinge on freedom and cause farm labourers and seasonal workers to become seditious.

Both studies supported Mills' analysis of the brutal, bitter lives of the petty bourgeoisie and the hardness and reactionary politics that resulted from this way of life.

But while the small shopkeeper and small farmer often personify the petty bourgeoisie, there is a danger in assuming they were or indeed *are* representative of the entire class, which has always been more heterogeneous than simply "shopkeepers". Indeed, shopkeepers, the "classic" representatives of the petty bourgeoisie, have always been (and remain) far more likely to employ wage labour than other elements of the petty bourgeoisie, and hence arguably belong to the grey area of the boundary between small capital and the petty bourgeoisie.

Despite the history of artisans as a pillar of the petty bourgeoisie, rarely today are builders and other small tradesmen considered as anything other than a part of the working class (despite being disproportionately self-employed), because in a society whereby manual work has become so rare, they are seen as the epitome of "blue-collar" work, both culturally and socially.

Richard Scase and Robert Goffee's study of self-employed builders paints an alternative, and entirely more flattering, picture of the petty bourgeoisie. They argue that the petty bourgeoisie's interstitial position in the class structure, as owning their own means of production (which splits them from the proletariat), can ecompass small property ownership (small landlords), labour power (artisans, freelancers) and a *mix* of property ownership and labour power (shopkeepers and farmers). Other historical studies overwhelmingly focused on the latter without any focus on those rare elements of the petty bourgeoisie who depend on labour power without always owning small property, such as self-employed artisans, who have in fact always been far more numerous than the shopkeeper. Their means of production are in this interpretation their tools (and normally van) and by their nature the job is somewhat itinerant — not tied to a particular site or location like those who own a shop or a farm — but travelling around as required to apply their skills.

Building and construction is interesting in that it has escaped — although not entirely — some of the automation and deskilling that has degraded most other areas of work. Tradesmen therefore often retain a relatively high degree of skill and individual autonomy at work. Scase and Goffee's study paints a picture of an oasis of relatively non-alienated labour within a modern capitalist economy: while builders don't get to keep the things they make, they have a large degree of autonomy over how they go about it (the labour process).

Like the analysis of the shopkeeper and the farmer, the builders in this study were drawn to self-employment because of a sense of autonomy and "freedom". But unlike the shopkeeper, who often sought respect and status, or the farmer who was born into it, this was often motivated by a dislike of people interfering in their skilled labour process and making money for other people.

Further social features of the builders included a tendency to develop long-term relationships with customers and to price and take jobs based on a sense of mutual obligation. In the course of these long-term relationships they developed a dislike of ruthless capitalistic "cut-throat" practices of competition. This was very different to the shopkeeper's obsession with profit and their antagonistic relationship with their customers described by Mills. Even today, this sharing out of the work in a more collectivist way on a local level is a common practice. In a recent Federation of Small Business study of the self-employed in Wales, the tendency was often towards co-operation at the local level rather than competition, and indeed this is the norm in my own town, where the superstars would pass on work to others if they could not take it on, or encourage their apprentices to set up on their own and subcontract out to them and so on. Next was a reluctance to take on too many employees and a desire not for conspicuous consumption or "respect" or status but to view work in a purely utilitarian way. Many of the builders in the study stated they wanted to make enough money to live on rather than to expand the business or to facilitate social mobility, which was important for the shopkeepers and farmers.

While the shopkeepers and farmers had deeply hostile views of the working class, the builders had the opposite position. Largely because of the type of specific work they did (manual labour), they viewed themselves as belonging to a wider, productive working class (that was defined as those who engaged in productive manual work — i.e., work that produces profit). The builders were keenly aware of the proliferation of unproductive white-collar work and had the perception this work was not useful, and also that the unproductive workers were paid well compared to themselves. They thus drew class boundaries between themselves and the new fraction of the petty bourgeoisie. Despite not being part of an organized working class and outside the union movement, they did not exhibit the same hostility to the organized labour movement as the other studies. Those who exhibited suspicion towards unions did so because they felt the unions to be weak and corrupt, i.e., they believed that unions were not actually concerned with the workers, rather than a general hostility.

Far from a rugged individualism, the tradesmen in fact exhibited a radical politics that was entirely compatible with socialism and saw themselves clearly as allied to the working class. Scase and Goffee argued that this group had a quasi-proletarian relationship to hierarchy, and hence possessed a "class instinct" that Lenin spoke of. Like the other studies, their work was also a relatively isolated experience, and they clearly also had a libertarian view of the world, but of a seemingly different strain, which had different manifestations and consequences. It did not lead to the same reaction or individualism as the other elements. Poulantzas in fact makes the same clear distinction within different elements of the petty bourgeoisie, claiming that "artisans... have always displayed an objectively proletarian polarisation far more than have the small retailers. Artisan production was the cradle of revolutionary syndicalism and its traditions of struggle are still very much alive."

The Traditional Petty Bourgeoisie Today: Modernity, Heterogeneity and Despair

The ethnographies undertaken in the 1980s were snapshots of a class and social milieus that had ostensibly barely changed in hundreds of years. Yet they were also conducted at a period when the petty bourgeoisie was a tiny minority relative to the overall class structure — indeed, so small that it was justifiably treated as a niche sociological concern. This is no longer the case today as it is now a significant (and ever-expanding) chunk of the class structure, and crucially within the modern solo self-employed there is now a huge diversity that simply was not there in previous eras. We therefore have to update our understanding of the class, but this must always be informed by the sociological characteristics of the class throughout history in order to assess the similarities and differences.

Solo self-employment (the traditional petty bourgeoisie) today comprises a huge range of activity — although primarily clustered in services — from tradesmen to management consultants, tutors, childminders, freelancers, graphic designers, hairdressers, personal trainers and so on. They can range from wealthy entrepreneurs to taxi drivers, graduates and people who left school at sixteen. Within this group, people will have different life experiences, be from drastically different social backgrounds, have different educations, social networks, reasons for becoming self-employed and experiences of self-employment. Moreover, whereas the shopkeeper, small farmer and artisans obviously belonged to a traditional, older way of life and hence neatly fitted into small, non-monopoly capitalism that was hostile to big business and to bureaucracy, this is by no means obviously the case for everyone else in the traditional petty bourgeoisie, given the amount of freelance managers and consultants specializing in high technology and management within the bureaucracy today (to take one example). In terms of wages, IFS data shows that the majority of the solo self-employed lie outside the highest and lowest earners, although the largest increases in self-employment in recent years have occurred in the highest and lowest waged sectors of the economy, suggesting that society's "hourglass" shape of low-paid versus high-paid is mirrored amongst the traditional petty bourgeoisie.

The picture that emerges is of a class which is now very heterogeneous as well as being starkly divided between the richer and poorer elements: some at the upper level are clearly on the boundaries of the professional managerial class, while those at the bottom are closer to the proletariat.

Precarity and Push Factors: Forced Self-Employment

What is also interesting when we look at the modern picture of self-employment is that, contrary to the traditional narrative of entrepreneurialism and the "Essex man", a great many solo-self-employed people are really struggling. Thus, for every superstar tradesman making a "wedge", there is another tradesman scraping a living. For every freelancer or management consultant, there is a Deliveroo driver, hairdresser or personal trainer in a chain gym. Whilst much literature on self-employment shows a degree of satisfaction because of "freedom", autonomy and "being my own boss", wages amongst the solo self-employed are on average now 30% lower than employees. Moreover, many of the self-employed, particularly those working in the platform/gig economy, are *under*employed.

Most shockingly of all, in the UK, the IFS report shows that nearly a full quarter of the solo self-employed moved into self-employment from unemployment, and the solo self-employed were nearly 50% more likely to have recently been economically inactive. The report thus concludes that

> relative to employees, the solo self-employed do appear to be an increasingly marginalised group: they were no more likely to have been recently unemployed or inactive than employees in 2000, but by 2019 they were 45% more likely to have been.

This picture of a stressful and unhappy existence is buttressed by Jack Blundell's 2020 investigation of the groups of primarily young, often immigrant men employed in the gig economy, who reported that they simply did not like being self-employed. As the historical sociological studies have shown, this hard existence has always been a defining feature of the petty bourgeoisie, so revelations about the brutality of self-employment are not a departure from the historic condition of the class. However, in historic studies of the petty bourgeoisie, what is striking is that, despite the brutal existence, the class was nonetheless continually replenished by those who aspired to social mobility, who wanted more freedom and status than when they were a wage labourer. The assumption was that, despite the difficult existence, the class was continually replenished because it was ultimately attractive; it was almost a calling.

Studies of the traditional petty bourgeoisie have therefore tended to focus on the *pull* factors — its persistent appeal as a lifestyle choice, its persistence as a cultural phenomenon related to libertarian ideals and so on. Even in Bechhofer and Elliot's ethnography of shopkeepers, despite all the hardship, the internal narrative about freedom (even if it never matched reality) and the perceived status of being your own boss still shone through. Yet the emergent snapshots of the lower strata of the modern self-employed portrays an alternative reality that has perhaps been overlooked by sociological discourse on "self-employment": today, many people *do not want to be self-employed*. They are self-employed because they have no other options, or because their working conditions in employment were poor. Until recently, few have discussed the push factors.

Andrew Henley supports this assumption of "push" factors. In a large-scale quantitative study of self-employment and the reasons people take the plunge to go it alone, he found that this is now generally driven by push factors, specifically the negative experiences of work and the state of the labour market, including

low pay, long hours of work, temporary contracts, absence of workplace representation, as well as lack of employer provided opportunities for training. These appear to lead to reductions in organizational attachment providing "push" towards self-employment entry and offsetting the positive impact of personal characteristics and opportunity drivers.

Self-employment was thus an attempted escape from the end of secure, paid work under neoliberalism. Moreover, Henley also found a positive correlation between the prior experience of working for a small firm and self-employment. This has historically been conceptualized as those who work for small firms simply absorb the spirit of entrepreneurialism and are inspired to go it alone themselves. However, Henley argues it is far more likely to be that, as previously discussed, small firms are far less likely to allow things like flexibility, unionisation and so on. In other words, working for a small firm is more likely to be terrible and more likely to make you want to leave.

Solo self-employment for hundreds of thousands of people has not risen because of a rise in "entrepreneurialism" or the freedom for professionals to work "nimbly" from remote houses — it has risen because of neoliberalism and misery and is very often a result of desperation following the gutting of employment rights, job security and the public sector. The IFS report makes clear that solo self-employment is a "fall back option", and that "the solo self-employed are increasingly those with poor alternative options"; or at the other end, professional people in the public sector who have been burned out by the culture of new public management introduced under New Labour.

Self-employment expanded most during periods of Tory rule: 1980-1995, and then again from 2008 (following the financial crash). It was at its lowest in the post-war period (7% in 1945). It is not a coincidence that countries with strong welfare states and job security have the lowest rates of solo self-employment. Under strong welfare systems and unionised, secure work, there is less of an incentive to try and escape the system. But wherever these things are taken away, the petty bourgeoisie will grow as more and more people try and escape.

Anywhere where there is chaos and instability and the gutting of secure employment sees the rise of self-employment, often on the "grey" or "informal" economy. This is why Greece and Chile, countries destroyed by neoliberalism, have the highest levels of solo self-employment. In *Planet of Slums*, Mike Davis explores how neoliberalism has changed the class structure and class dynamics in the world's most impoverished places. Rather than simply collapsing everyone in these situations into a homogenous, desperate, proletarianized mass, Davis instead outlines the *shrinkage* of the formal proletariat (e.g., people working in mass manufacturing or extractive industries) and the concomitant rise of the "informal petty bourgeoisie" (people running casual small businesses to get by) alongside the "informal proletariat" (comprised of domestic servants and those who work for the aforementioned micro-businesses).

And as in the UK, Davis notes that the hollowing-out of the public sector and the welfare state has led to what he calls this "forced entrepreneurialism" in the grey economy. That is, hustling to get by. Davis focuses on the new — depressing — social relations that neoliberalism has created: rather than increased solidarity, increasingly desperate and poor people are thrown into deep competition with one another. Informal and small-scale formal enterprises ceaselessly war with one another for economic space: street vendors versus small shopkeepers, jitneys versus public transport, and so on.

Permeable Boundaries Between Classes: The New Normal

Within the chaotic informal milieu that Davis describes, and which has been created by modern capitalism, class boundaries are not fixed or static but, as Erik Olin Wright proselytized, permeable. Not only do people occupy the boundaries or grey areas between classes, they frequently switch between them. It is clear that, in particular, the boundaries between the working class and the lower end of the petty bourgeoisie are becoming blurred.

In his ethnographic study of petty entrepreneurialism in Istanbul, for example, Alpkan Birelma details the frequency with which highly skilled workers — including experienced trade union movement leaders — leave mass employment to join the traditional petty bourgeoisie, opening up cafes, market stalls and other small businesses. Birelma's study shows the fluidity of this process and how it unfolded over the life course of the worker and within the same area: after making the leap, many would stay in small business, but others rapidly became disillusioned and returned to the relative security of waged employment. It is therefore always important to bear in mind Danny Dorling and Erik Olin Wright's attention to the *life course* under precarious neoliberalism: we are no longer fixed to one workplace or even one class, but may increasingly move in and out of classes — increasingly the various subordinate classes — as we grow older. An awareness of the fluidity and permeability of class boundaries over time is therefore absolutely essential if we are to make sense of the modern class structure.

Yet the blurred boundaries also occur at the higher end. Sarah Holloway and Helena Pilmott-Wilson's 2021 study of private tutoring suggests that, in professional occupations too, many people's class position is similarly blurred as they dip their toe into self-employment while still employees. Moreover, their work reminds us that people increasingly enter the petty bourgeoisie from different class positions, and these new members of the traditional petty bourgeoisie will increasingly bring with them the residual culture and ideology of their previous class, creating even further diversity within the class.

The Gig Economy: The Petty Bourgeois Experience in the Modern Day

Can gig economy workers really be considered as part of the expanded petty bourgeoisie? It is now commonsensical that low-paid platform workers are the new working class or "the precariat". They are the working class because they work, because they get paid very little and are exploited, and also because they very often deploy the *accoutrements* of the working class — they are in unions; they are militant. Jamie Woodcock persuasively argues that it is ludicrous to label workers in the gig economy as self-employed, and one of the central reasons is the question of what can reasonably be seen to constitute the ownership of the means of production. Small farmers owned farms, shopkeepers owned shops. Can ownership of a car, or even a mountain bike, be classed as ownership of the means of production? This is obviously stretching the term to breaking point. Just because the company calls a worker self-employed so they don't have to give them holiday pay or any other benefits obviously does not make someone self-employed.

Nonetheless, I think we equally have to be careful about simply labelling precarious platform workers as the new working class just because they are in unions and don't get paid much. This brings us to a fundamental point: class is not about money. Being paid very little does not make you working class. A self-employed worker can — and often will — earn less than someone doing the exact same role as an employee. But he will still be part of the petty bourgeoisie, and the worker part of the working class, because class is not about wages but about your social relationship at work and ownership of the means of production. Equally, being exploited doesn't make you working class. The petty bourgeoisie are and always have been exploited, and endure the same awful conditions as the working class (indeed, often far worse). Enduring such does not make you the proletariat. Nor should we work backwards from union membership and radical politics and ascribe class to people based on their radical politics or if they display the accoutrements of the working class.

I am aware that many may feel that it is being overly particular or finicky to obsess over these things, or stretching the term to call a mobile hairdresser or taxi driver petty bourgeois. It is worth restating that the term is not an insult but a specific interstitial condition within the class structure that I want people to start thinking about a bit more. I do not think that our understanding of class is well served by lumping "the poor" or "precarious" together in one undifferentiated mass (e.g., "the precariat"), which takes no interest in the specificity of one's working conditions, relationship to other workers and the ideological ramifications of these conditions, in the same way that the unemployed or lumpenproletariat also have different experiences, interests and ideology to the working class. Being unemployed, for example, is a fundamentally different experience to being exploited at work. It is still shit, but it *is* different.

For what it's worth, my own belief is that platform workers occupy a grey area at the boundaries between the working class and petty bourgeoisie. However, focusing on what constitutes the "means of production", or what class

Deliveroo riders are "technically", is something of a red herring. As I stated in the introduction, this is not about providing a checklist and placing different occupations in different boxes. Far more significant than what class Deliveroo drivers are in is what the gig economy augurs and can tell us about modern capitalist society.

The gig economy and platform capitalism in general essentially relies on inter-worker competition. Callum Cant's powerful study *Riding for Deliveroo* offers an optimistic example of resistance in the gig economy and how workers overcame structural barriers caused by their relative isolation from one another to organize. It is a positive, practical case study of how to organize in non-traditional sectors that big unions would do well to learn from. However, other studies of the sector are less optimistic. An ethnography of gig economy food delivery riders in Australia (Barratt et al., 2020) illustrates how, rather than getting organized collectively as in Cant's study, most workers instead engaged primarily in "individualized expressions of agency which reinforce, rather than test, capital's accumulation". This individualism was not down to any innate personal tendency but was rather moulded by the platform that the workers used. Because the platform placed workers "in market competition with each other", any forms of "resistance" were necessarily also highly individualized. The platforms constrained the forms of agency and resistance available to workers, "resulting in individual expressions of agency — which we characterise as 'entrepreneurial agency' — which aligns individual workers, as labour, with platforms while pitting workers against each other". As a result of the forces they were subject to in this field, many workers' self-understanding shifted from a dependent employee to internalizing the idea that they were "their own boss" or a micro-entrepreneur, and subsequently "their behaviour reflected those of entrepreneurs seeking capital accumulation rather than employees seeking redistribution of profit, and "workers expressed entrepreneurial forms of agency, aligning their personal interests, as labour, with capital in market competition and in opposition to the interests of other workers — that is, over class-based interests".

In practice, this entailed doing things like upgrading their means of production (car, scooter, etc.) or rigging the electronic devices they used in a way that would enable them to take on more work (thereby depriving someone else of a "gig"). Thus Barratt et al conclude that by placing workers in direct competition with one another the gig economy creates new norms and ideologies among the workers who work within it. It inculcates a highly individualized, "entrepreneurial" mindset, leading to the bleak conclusion that in some circumstances, labour does not challenge capital but complies with its imperatives. Similarly, in Holloway and Pilmott-Wilson's article on modern tutoring, the tutors internalized an "entrepreneurial subjectivity" in which they themselves were a "project" to build up (like a brand) and engaged in a wide array of entrepreneurial activities to recruit and retain clients and take on more work, regardless of their actual motivations for being involved in tutoring and regardless of how much money they were making.

The gig economy has attracted so much interest precisely because the conditions that many of the workers are subject to are so horrifying. I find it interesting because there seem to be so many parallels between this modern, high-tech experience, and the historical experiences of the old petty bourgeoisie. In fact, it seems to be replicating it. The aforementioned history of the social and working conditions of the petty bourgeoisie show that what is happening in the gig economy — subcontracting, isolation, precarity, enforced competition — is not actually new, and in both the aforementioned modern ethnographies of platform work, the workers exhibited the traditional individualism of the petty bourgeoisie. While Deliveroo riders and freelance tutors are not traditional, non-bureaucratic — they exist because of high technology — and nor are they a whole culture or way of life like the artisans, shopkeepers or small farmers (i.e., they presumably don't marry other Deliveroo drivers), they nonetheless also share fundamental similarities in their working conditions and lifeworld that are vitally important when it comes to understanding class and modern society in general, particularly the social isolation and individualism that flows from these working conditions. Like the shopkeeper and farmer, they are always working, there is no division between work and home life, they are in competition with one another, and they are dependent on big capital.

Conclusion

From a minor social experience and niche sociological concern, the traditional petty bourgeoisie has massively grown, from a sliver of the workforce under welfare capitalism to a sizeable chunk under neoliberalism. However, this has not been because of enterprise and business schools and an increase in entrepreneurialism, but a response to the desperation brought about by neoliberalism. The hollowing-out of the public sector, and the removal of an effective social safety net, means that many people are being *forced* into solo self-employment as a last resort or as an escape route from the destruction of formerly secure professions like teaching. The growth of solo-self-employment in the UK is thus not a symptom of our predilection to become shopkeepers, but of the consequences of being a laboratory for the worst excesses of neoliberalism that has driven hundreds of thousands of people into an awful existence scraping a living outside wage labour.

Given the sheer extent of the self-employed — and the fact that it will continue to rise as neoliberalism forces more and more people into it — it is vital that we understand the specificity and history of the petty bourgeoisie, its social world and the ideology and values that have traditionally flowed out of its unique interstitial position between wage labour and capitalism.

The traditional petty bourgeoisie has changed massively. Long thought of as a small, homogenous, reactionary group — indeed, one which was defined precisely by its minority experience — the petty bourgeoisie has also changed in its internal composition and is now a large, heterogeneous group. It has expanded beyond its traditional base in shopkeeping, small farming and small tradesmen. It is taxi drivers, personal trainers, marketing consultants, coffee shop owners, and more. It is no longer rooted in small, non-monopoly capital, nor rooted in traditional work practices, but is increasingly engaged with technology. Its history as an anti-modern, anti-bureaucratic, family-central class will also not be the norm, although we still need to pay attention to this. It is also clear that the traditional petty bourgeoisie, like the new petty bourgeoisie, is fractured, split between the rich and poor, and is expanding particularly at the higher and lower ends. The insecurity wrought by neoliberalism means that at the lower end in particular, the boundaries between the petty bourgeoisie and working class are dissolving as self-employment increasingly becomes a last resort, rather than a calling. These new recruits to the petty bourgeoisie no longer enjoy any of the relative prestige that used to demarcate the petty bourgeoisie in the class structure. People are bouncing in between jobs — between low-wage employment and precarious self-employment and back again because there is no security anywhere: every day they tell themselves that they need a change, that x has to be better than this, only to find once they get there that, actually, nowhere is better, nowhere is secure, everything is shit.

Relatedly, ownership of the means of production used to mean relative control over your labour, but in the modern era there has been a separation of ownership from control over your own labour. So, the modern self-employed no longer control their labour, but are often either controlled by an algorithm or are inserted into broader cycles of capital that ultimately subordinate them to large-scale capital — this is as true of certain small companies as individuals; for example, farmers who are entirely dependent upon supermarkets, since a vast number of small groceries have been destroyed, meaning that even large farms cannot control their production. This loss of autonomy is central in the transformation of the petty bourgeoisie in the modern era even when they "technically" possess their means of production.

The specific habitus and culture associated with the traditional petty bourgeoisie was produced and reproduced by its marginal position in society and the relatively closed boundaries of the group. Given the history of tight guilds defending tradesman exclusiveness, and the closed-off social world of the shopkeeper, this permeability is a new development in the history of the class. Because of these permeable boundaries, it is more and more likely that the "classic" experience, culture and habitus of the petty bourgeoisie will become a minority experience within the class, and that it will be harder to speak of a distinct petty-bourgeois habitus. Instead, the upper and lower parts of the class will likely be increasingly influenced by the culture and habitus of the working class or the professional managerial class.

Because of its new heterogeneity and the permeability of class boundaries, the historical and sociological picture of the petty bourgeoisie (and stereotypes of meanness and so on) can no longer be simply imposed on this class and be used as shorthand to describe it. Equally, however, the increased heterogeneity and diversity of the class in the modern era importantly does not mean that the social conditions and historical experiences of the petty bourgeoisie have changed. While the outward face and internal demographics of the petty bourgeoisie have dramatically changed, more recent studies of the new generation of self-employed people reveal certain important continuities and similarities in terms of the working conditions with the petty bourgeoisie of previous epochs — chiefly, precarity, isolation and individualism.

Arguably more important even than the growth of the class itself is the proliferation of technologies and strategies that replicate and proliferate the historic condition of the petty bourgeoisie among the wider population. The gig economy is the most glaring (and well-researched) example of the presence of the historic conditions of the petty bourgeoisie in the modern day. But as Woodcock and others have pointed out, gig economy pioneers like Uber are *pathfinders*, whose working practices and employment relations are revolutionizing and reshaping *all* work for the benefit of capitalism. The gig economy is a harbinger of what is coming and is the most brutal, egregious example of a long-term, ongoing trend that extends way beyond the boundaries of the gig economy itself.

Recreating and replicating the precarious and isolated social world of the petty bourgeoisie seems to have become functional to capital in rearranging production processes right across the board. Thus, even beyond the self-employed and beyond the gig economy, we have seen a huge expansion of disciplinary tools and technologies that attempt to create the isolation, precarity (and hence individualism) of the petty bourgeoisie. While Deliveroo, Amazon and Hermes delivery drivers are timed, tracked on the map and ranked for their performance, academics, teachers and others — pretty much everyone — are now also similarly subject to disciplinary metrics and technologies and frequently placed directly in competition with other workers.

Whether they are self-employed or "technically" the petty bourgeoisie or not, there is now a larger — and continuously growing — proportion of people working on their own, in isolated, non-unionised, non-collectivized environments. The experience of driving a car on your own, in relative isolation, or working in your own house, or working on site on your own or with your son or brother, week in, week out, is a different social experience of work and society to working in a collective, unionised workplace. We know from historical insights into the petty bourgeoisie that these conditions of life and work have often logically produced an individualism that has often been hostile to collectivism, and so this development is therefore highly significant for the left and society more generally.

CHAPTER THREE
THE NEW PETTY BOURGEOISIE AND CLASS ANALYSIS (OR, WHY WE ARE NOT THE WORKING CLASS)

"In the course of the next generation, a 'social class' between lower white-collar and wage-workers will probably be formed, which means, in Weber's terms, that between the two positions there will be a typical job mobility. This will not, of course, involve the professional strata or the higher managerial employees, but it will include the bulk of the workers in salesroom and office."

C Wright Mills, *White Collar* (1951)

One of the key arguments of this book is that the petty bourgeoisie is, and has always been, comprised of two parts or fractions, like a double helix. Chapter 1 demonstrated how the petty bourgeoisie was continually replenished throughout history by new recruits, and that very often the new recruits to the class — new fractions — were, on the face of it, very different. Unlike the old petty bourgeoisie of shopkeepers and artisans, white-collar workers such as clerks and department store workers did not own their own means of production, yet it was nonetheless widely accepted — for example, in the histories of Mayer and Hobsbawm — that they were a part of this same class.

Despite their different "technical" position *vis à vis* the means of production, which placed them *in theory* in the working class, the new white-collar workers were nonetheless split off from the working class and placed in the petty bourgeoisie in a number of ways. Because they were mobile, and because they could potentially fall down the class structure as well as move up, they were, like the old petty bourgeoisie, necessarily highly individualistic and focused on their own personal social mobility rather than the collective. Like the old petty bourgeoisie and unlike the working class, their working conditions were often isolated and in close proximity to their bosses. They often had a higher level of formal education than the working class, and consciously attempted to distinguish themselves from the class below them in terms of their behaviours, cultural and social pastimes, where they lived, how they dressed and so on. They ultimately internalized a belief in hierarchy, and their hopes that they could climb the social ladder produced a servility and deference that made them hostile to the trade union movement and notoriously difficult to organize.

So, even if "on paper" they shared the same economic relationship to capital as the working class, the new petty bourgeoisie were thus split off culturally, socially and ideologically from the working class in everyday life. This was not an abstraction, but was a mutually understood class divide, which frequently came to a head in labour disputes and the union movement. The workers and white-collar workers both knew that the one was not like the other, and class consciousness and identity is very often about defining oneself negatively: we know who we are by what we are *not*.

Today, large swathes of the population — including the person writing, and possibly the person reading, this book — are also best understood not as a vague "middle class", not as "new working class", but as the *new petty bourgeoisie*: a new, distinct fraction of the historic class originally populated by shopkeepers, small farmers and artisans. The majority of the modern left are rooted in this class fraction. As throughout history, while the modern iteration of the new petty bourgeoisie is often culturally distinct from the old petty bourgeoisie, it nonetheless shares certain key characteristics that place it in the petty bourgeoisie as a whole. Specifically, its mobility — and hence precarity — and the individualist ideology that flows from this liminal position.

This focus on the specificity of the petty bourgeoisie, and the emphasis on the differences and boundaries between the subordinate classes more generally, is a break with the dominant left approach that has been to view the middle as an afterthought; or to view the classes beneath the elite as homogenizing because of economic proletarianization of the middle. As stated in the introduction, this has prevented the left from understanding its own class character and its relationship to other classes, particularly the working class.

This is not a new argument. It was put forward in the 1970s by Nicos Poulantzas in his book *Classes in Contemporary Capitalism*. My understanding of the new petty bourgeoisie, and the ways in which this class is split off from the working class, is largely rooted in Poulantzas' work. Understanding the new petty bourgeoisie — and indeed accepting that this class even exists in the first place — depends upon an interpretation of class that moves beyond "economic" considerations of ownership and which instead embraces the social, cultural and ideological dimensions of class. Poulantzas' work is so important because it is not just about how classes are produced "objectively" by changes to the economy, but also about how people actually become aware of their class and their role in society; how their experience of life and work inexorably produce ideology, values, and political tendencies, which in turn defines different classes.

His work is therefore vital for making sense of the modern class structure.

Part One: The Emergence of the Intermediary Classes and How to Interpret Them

Neoliberalism and the Changing Class Structure

Like many other developed nations, the British economy was (speaking very roughly) based on manufacturing and heavy industry such as mining, steel working and shipbuilding from the second industrial period to the second half of the twentieth century. This period was characterized by what we might like to think of as the "classic" imagery of national capitalism: initially, a small number of people owned capital (factories, mines, etc.), then large state-run monopolies in core sectors, with large amounts of workers brought together to make tangible products like cars, or to extract raw materials like steel and coal, with a *relatively* small class of "NCOs" or supervisors. We have plenty of pop-culture depictions of such models, such as the division of labour in Springfield Power Plant in *The Simpsons*. Because of the dominance of these particular forms of industries, with their stark divisions of labour between the workers on the one hand and the bosses/state on the other, the class structure of the UK was relatively simple. Until the 1960s, the majority of households in the UK were proletarian, with the old petty bourgeoisie remaining a persistent minority.

The working class had their own towns, institutions and a distinct culture and civic and intellectual life. There was also a strong sense of working-class identity and class power — this was a class *for itself* — that is, a class that is self-aware — as well as a class that existed objectively. This was evidenced by a strong trade union membership, with both parties forced to recognise the intimidating presence of a working-class majority. In 1946, there were around eight million trade union members, by the late Seventies this had increased to over 13 million.

Yet traditional forms of work such as agriculture, extractive work like mining and construction and manufacturing (which had boomed after the Second World War) went into irreversible decline in the Sixties. Gradually, as a response to the world economic crisis, the basis of the economy changed profoundly and deeply in a relatively short period of time.

While manual work was predominant for the first half of the twentieth century, changes during the Sixties and Seventies saw a huge rise in clerical, administrative and supervisory work as manual professions declined. In 1951, all forms of manual work (skilled and unskilled, and including foremen) constituted nearly three quarters of the entire workforce. By the Eighties, however, more than half of the British workforce was employed in non-manual labour. By 2003, only a third worked in manual professions. This was, as Michael Kitson and Jonathan Mitchie describe it, a "deindustrial revolution".

Next, as manufacturing technology evolved (and workers were increasingly deskilled), there was a sharp rise in technician or supervisory, foreman-style work. John Urry and Nicholas Abercrombie demonstrate how "lower foremen or supervisors" grew from 1.29% in 1911 to over 5% of the male workforce in 1971, while during the same period the amount of workers shrunk. Management similarly grew as a percentage of all male workers, from 3.9% in 1911 to 10.9% in 1971, nearly tripling in size. There was also a huge parallel rise in professional occupations such as lawyers, doctors and accountants. The expansion of the professional class was so significant that Harold Perkin describes this growth as the "third revolution".

These tendencies identified by sociologists writing as the welfare state collapsed have only intensified. In 1955, "services"[6] accounted for 53% of the British economy while manufacturing and so on accounted for 47%. By 1990, however, services in the UK accounted for 72%. In 2016, they accounted for 84%, more than any other country in the G7.

The occupational structure has grown more complex, with a huge array of roles and lifestyles. Stocktakes of the British workforce, such as the Labour Force Survey and the National Census, repeatedly show a total transformation of the type of work people do. During the early and mid-half of the twentieth century, manual labour was dominant and professional and administrative roles were marginal. Now, professionals, administrative, clerical and managerial roles have massively increased, and manual work is marginalized. Today, "straightforwardly" working-class jobs now constitute only around a third of the workforce in total, whereas a relatively short time ago they constituted an absolute majority. Trade union density, a crude marker of class consciousness and class organization, has sharply

---

6 As Urry and Abercrombie note, the concept of "services" is unhelpfully nebulous and confusing: who is being serviced? And in what way? For Marx, productive workers are those who produce surplus value. "Unproductive" "service" workers does not mean that people are lazy, but rather that they capture value produced elsewhere: e.g., a teacher paid by the state, through money received through taxation, which extracts value from the productive (of value) labour of workers and businesses. The concept of "services" is therefore broad. It could mean those who service the bourgeoisie (literal servants; think Stevens in *The Remains of the Day*); those who facilitate the circulation of capital and commodities rather than producing them (advertising); those who specifically service capital (accountants, supervisors, corporate lawyers); those who absorb surplus capital through the consumption of luxury goods; those who provide services to other workers (hairdressers, barmen, personal trainers, and so on).

declined since the crushing losses suffered in the 1980s and now sits at 6.44 million workers in 2021, less than half of what it was in 1979. The "intermediate classes" however, have grown and become extremely diverse. Today, professionals are now *the single biggest occupation group in British society*, consisting of 5.7 million people or 21% of the workforce, while managers constitute nearly 10%, or nearly 3.5 million people across all categories (larger than the skilled working class). "Intermediary professions', which incorporates a dizzying variety of roles, constitute 34.5% of the population. This is a near-total inversion of the world of work of sixty years ago, a picture which would have been unimaginable even during the final years of the welfare state.

As Bob Carter argues, the transition to "services", or the "knowledge economy", "information society", or whatever other fashionable term it is called, masks the fact that what has really happened over the last sixty to seventy years is a *reordering of the class structure*. Specifically, the working class has shrunk as a percentage of the population, while the middle or intermediate classes have grown. A. Sivanandan similarly clearly states that "the method of production has undergone such a qualitative change" that the balance of class forces *has shifted to the middle classes*.

Geoffrey Evans and James Tilley sum up these changes clearly:

> It is quite clear that whereas the main point of division in the past was between a large and fairly homogenous working class and a small middle class, now it is between a larger group of heterogeneous middle classes and a smaller working class. There are now more people in the "new middle class" (essentially professional workers, many in the public sector) than in the working class. The transition from a majority working-class society to a minority working-

class society has multiple implications: some psychological, some political.

Just as the base of the economy has changed, so has the class structure shifted. Changes to the world of work constitute a change in class. The working class has emphatically not disappeared, but it *has* shrunk from the period when it was an absolute majority and in which class consciousness was widespread.

Rather than being neatly polarized into two classes — a large proletariat and a small bourgeoisie — the workforce is now complex, and roughly segmented into something approaching thirds. The working class is around a third to a half; then we have a more heterogeneous ruling class, which includes an expanded class of management that directs capital on behalf of the actual owners; and then, at least a full third of the population that are in between. The task facing the left is to categorize and theorize these changes.

The Left Response: Denial and Proletarianization

However, many on the left have not kept up with these structural changes, and as the left has returned to the politics of class, rather than engaging with the more complicated class structure and the rise of the intermediary classes, it has treated the intermediate classes as an afterthought. As mentioned in the introduction, central to the left's return to class has been a return to a dualist class structure, neatly polarized between the elite, on the one hand, and the 99% (the many — which includes us, the left) on the other. The petty bourgeoisie does not feature at all as a concept. While it is accepted that neoliberalism has changed almost every other aspect of modern life, it is *verboten* — perhaps seen as defeatist — to say that it has also changed the class structure.

A popular left response to the effects of economic changes is simply to say that the working class has now just changed *form*: it is no longer white men working down the mines or in the steelworks, but increasingly women and people of colour working in call centres, as cleaners, care workers and so on, clustered in the areas where industrial and manual work was once dominant. The awareness of the changing face and form of the working class has been one of the strongest elements of the left's return to class. It has dispensed with gender divides and realized that women (and other marginalized groups like immigrants) now constitute an enormous portion of the working class domestically and on a *global* scale, paying attention to the role of what Silvia Federici calls reproductive labour. It has also realized that class is no longer as simple as manual/ non-manual, because so much low-paid service work (such as care work and retail) blurs the boundaries between manual and non-manual. Thus, the working class is less homogenous but ultimately it is the same — the *largest* class. Michael Zwieg, for example, pugnaciously argues the working class remains the absolute majority in America.

Of course, it is undeniable that the working class has been recomposed,and is increasingly fragmented. No one would seriously deny this. The intention of this book is emphatically not to categorize cleaners and care home workers as the new petty bourgeoisie. Nor am I denying the fact that the working class remains dominant globally, and that it remains the motor of history.

But within the UK, and more broadly in the Global North, even if you fully acknowledge the fact that the working class has been recomposed internally and now looks totally different and works in different workplaces than it used to, is no longer dominated by white men working in manual jobs and so on, this still doesn't change the fact that, even when you account for the care workers, cleaners and shelfstackers, those in straightforwardly working-class jobs still only constitute about a third to a half of society. It is probably, in my view, still *on balance* the largest class, and it is certainly the most powerful, but it is also surely still a significant leap to look at the dizzying amount of "unaccounted for" "bullshit jobs" and continue to claim a dualist class structure of working class/bourgeoisie.

Having said that, however, this is emphatically "not a problem of numbers". Triumphantly stating the working class, the petty bourgeoisie or the professional-managerial class is now the "objective" majority is not the point. The point is to pay attention to the fundamental reordering of the social relations of society caused by underlying structural changes to the economy and class structure, including how they manifest themselves.

Proletarianization

One of the reasons the left struggles with the concept of the intermediary classes outside the bourgeoisie and proletariat is because even those sections of the middle who would once have felt relatively well-protected from falling into the working class are now in a much more precarious position, and are increasingly at risk of "proletarianization". While once there was a pay and status divide between even lower echelon white-collar work and manual labour, this has been steadily eroded as many of the middle classes have also been hit hard by decades of austerity. The salary, long the difference between the middle class and working class (the working class got paid wages), is no longer taken for granted — increasingly, jobs like teacher, nurse and academic are paid on an hourly, casual, non-contract basis. Much of the "middle" is now increasingly burdened with rising debt for things like mortgages. As well as increasingly suffering economically, the *autonomy* of these formerly respectable professions has been stripped away and they have been deskilled and alienated, reduced to automatons with no creative control over their work.

In response to these changes, while trade union density has massively declined across the workforce as a whole, it has grown across these degraded professions. In fact, trade unionism is increasingly clustered among professional, white-collar groups rather than in working-class occupations and sectors: professional occupations are by some distance the most unionised occupations in the UK. Trade unionism is now disproportionately common in the public sector, and people with degrees, who may earn more and work flexi-time, are now far more likely to be members of a trade union than those without higher education in temporary, low-paid jobs. In fact, foremen and supervisors are now more likely to be unionised than non-supervisors, and managers themselves have almost the same levels of unionisation as regular employees! Trade unionism and trade unionist militancy is now largely (although, of course, not exclusively) the preserve of the middle classes. This again represents a nearly total inversion of the picture in the first half of the twentieth century, where organizing white-collar workers was a permanent headache for the labour movement.

Because large swathes of the middle class now have shit lives, the popular left response to what has happening — exemplified politically by the 99% narrative — is to assume that the degraded middle will merge with the working class. This is sometimes called the "proletarianization thesis", rooted in the *Communist Manifesto*, which, as part of its argument that society was polarizing into two camps, does indeed state that

the lower strata of the middle class — the small tradespeople, shopkeepers, and retired tradesmen generally, the handicraftsmen and peasants — all these sink gradually into the proletariat, partly because their diminutive capital does not suffice for the scale on which Modern Industry is carried on, and is swamped in the competition with the large capitalists, partly because their specialised skill is rendered worthless by new methods of production. Thus the proletariat is recruited from all classes of the population.

As C. Wright Mills describes the proletarianization thesis in *White Collar*, it is the assumption that the middle "will become homogenous in all important respects with the proletariat", that the middle is "merely a peculiar sort of a new proletariat, having the same basic interests", and "with the intensification of class struggle between the real classes of capitalist society... will be swept into the proletarian ranks". Thus, the working class gets bigger by absorbing the degraded middle classes, which are transitional classes that will disappear.

Hadas Thier and Alex Press put forward two recent examples of this approach in *Jacobin*. Press writes that "for everyone else who is compelled to sell their labour in exchange for the freedom not to starve? Welcome to the working class." In an article entitled "The Working Class Is the Vast Majority of Society", Thier similarly states that the professional middle is smaller than previously imagined, and that

> many of those traditionally deemed "professionals" are being summarily shoved into the working class (or "proletarianized"), as computer programmers become routine code writers punching timecards, social workers with enormous caseloads spend their days filling out forms, and academic professorial jobs increasingly give way to adjunct positions.

The assumption is that the squeezing of the middle inexorably sucks it down into the ranks of the working classes. Despite the aforementioned work that points to the expansion of the intermediate classes under neoliberalism, in most popular left work the intermediate classes tend to be glossed over in this way. Because the existence of the 1% demonstrates that society is increasingly polarized into two fundamental classes — Thier approvingly points to Marx's claim in the *Communist Manifesto* that society is increasingly polarizing into two camps — rather than growing more complicated, the middle is an irrelevance, a transitional class that will disappear; and because it is understood as a transitional class, it is only analysed purely in terms of its relation to these fundamental classes (or as parts of them) rather than considering them as distinct or coherent classes in their own right. While Their and Press both put forward sophisticated analyses of what class is, the petty bourgeoisie as a concept or a term remains entirely absent.

I, of course, understand this perspective. The experience of downward social mobility is all-consuming and confusing, and it is the declassed, downwardly mobile graduates who march, who wave placards, who have adopted the accoutrements and iconography of socialism, the working class and collectivism. Hence, it is very easy to buy into the proletarianization thesis, the idea that we are all part of an expanded working class.

However, the increasing closeness of everyone beneath the "elite" in terms of wages and living standards, and the domination of left movements by the intermediary classes, emphatically does not mean an automatic ideological, political, cultural or social alignment between subordinate classes, even if the objective interest of all classes have aligned, not least because class isn't about money. Overcoming the manual/non-manual and gender divides should not be used as a sleight of hand to stop thinking about other (obvious) existing divides, to keep moving the boundary of the working class upwards (class is no longer based on heavy manual labour, ergo, I, a junior academic, can now be working class). While the middle class is precarious and impoverished, this doesn't make it disappear or sink down — it still needs to be understood on its own terms. It remains, and in fact its precarity is precisely what defines it and which produces its distinct ideology.

Growth of the Intermediary Classes as a Tendency Within Capitalism

While it is admittedly incredibly tiresome when people search for trump cards regarding what Marx said on these matters, in this one instance I believe it is actually useful to note that Marx emphatically did not posit a dualist class structure polarized neatly between a working class and the bourgeoisie. Getting rid of this foundational myth about an increasingly polarized class structure is important in appreciating the modern problem of the middle classes and the petty bourgeoisie.

While Marx undeniably states in the *Communist Manifesto* that society was increasingly splitting into two neatly polarized classes, and hence predicted that the petty bourgeoisie would disappear as larger-scale production would swallow it, Martin Nicolaus points out that there is a clear divide between Marx's earlier political polemics (written when Marx was in his mid-twenties and himself involved in revolutionary activity) and his later economic writings, in which he reflected on the evolution of capitalism. In these later writings, Marx unambiguously speaks of a new "middle strata" of "unproductive" "service" workers (such as servants, soldiers and the like) that had been created by the existence of surplus profit, bitterly noting that they developed "like bees" in a hive as surplus profits increased.

In *Capital Volume 1*, Marx actually noted with disgust that the servant class in England were more numerous than the entire manufacturing workforce. Thus, even in the period of industrial capitalism, the "service class" — even though understood largely in terms of literal personal services to individual capitalists, like maids — were huge in number as an "objective" class; in Marx's own writings, they are seemingly objectively larger in number than the proletariat to which he devoted so much time. Marx also mentions — although he does not include them in his stocktake of the working population — the "ideological" classes, such as government officials, priests, lawyers, soldiers, rentiers and landlords (those who lived off interest) and, lastly, the lumpenproletariat of paupers, vagabonds, and criminals.

Marx later wrote numerous passages that captured the clear break he made with his earlier assumptions about a neatly polarized class society, instead emphasizing the tendency for a class of "unproductive" workers to emerge and grow. Dismissing the economist George Ramsay, he wrote:

If this bourgeois ideal were actually realisable, the only result would be that the whole of the surplus-value would go to the industrial capitalist directly, and society would be reduced (economically) to the simple contradiction between capital and wage labour, a simplification which would indeed accelerate the dissolution of this mode of production.

And similarly:

Here we need only consider the forms which capital passes through in the various stages of its development. The real conditions within which the actual process of production takes place are therefore not analysed. It is assumed throughout, that the commodity is sold at its value. We do not examine the competition of capitals, nor the credit system, nor *the actual composition of society, which by no means consists only of two classes* workers and industrial capitalists, and where therefore consumers and producers are not identical categories.

And finally:

What he [David Ricardo] forgets to emphasize is the constantly growing number of the middle classes, those who stand between the workman on the one hand and the capitalist and the landlord on the other.

This is fairly unambiguous: Marx recognised the inexorable emergence of new, intermediary classes within industrial capitalism economically (i.e., the middle classes exist "objectively" or as a "class on paper").

In other words, what Marx said in his later works is the opposite of what he is commonly believed to have said about the class structure, and which underpins the return to a dualist approach to the class structure and the concomitant lack of engagement with the petty bourgeoisie. Rather than polarizing into two major classes, as he states in the *Communist Manifesto*, as capitalism matures the exact opposite is true: the concentration of capital requires increasing levels of oversight, a proliferation of management tiers, with the shift to global supply chains requiring complex logistics and legal and accounting roles, the necessary expansion of finance for the free circulation of capital globally, increased workers to promote the increased surplus product and so on.

Yet we surely shouldn't need to search through Marx for "gotchas" to "prove" that the class structure is complicated. As Erik Olin Wright argues, one only has to look at the class structure and everyday life, the reality of our workplaces, the expansion of the state bureaucracy, human resources, recruitment, marketing and so on, to realize how complicated things are, and the proliferation of roles that don't fit easily into "worker" or "boss".

Capitalism is no longer the simple system spoken of by Adam Smith. Once, capital was "national" and involved, e.g., a big local businessman who ran a chain of warehouses or factories or mines. These operations would involve the owner, a small amount of supervisors, managers and clerks, and then the workers making commodities. Now, however, capitalism is global, stretching across the globe with huge, complex supply chains, with headquarters and factories and R&D sites dotted all over the world. Rather than having just production sites (i.e., places where you make things), there are whole armies of research and development workers; engineers and technicians; logistical arms; communications officers, corporate outreach workers; accountants and lawyers on retainer; advertising and market research gurus — all these roles work to increase the pace of production (while deskilling workers), keep costs low, avoid litigation, improve circulation and sales and so on. And of course, every firm and public sector body now possesses huge human resources arms — including formal supervisory roles — in charge of payroll, admin, but also hiring, firing and disciplining the workforce and helping to keep labour costs low. Many of these jobs are what David Graeber calls "bullshit jobs", in that they are not *socially* useful. Yet they are often not bullshit from the point of view of capital and often fulfil a pivotal role. And because corporations are now global, the global class structure has now also changed, creating a transnational capitalist class and a global proletariat.

On top of the growth of oligarchic capitalism in creating this new intermediary class of "market" service workers, there has also been a steady rise in the state bureaucracy, a process which started during the welfare state period. The state needs a layer of people involved in "non-market services" like health, education, social work, etc. This has also led to the rise of the professional class of administrators both high and low. While the relationship between class and the welfare state is often simply reduced to "the welfare state helped the working class", the state bureaucracy also required people to run it and work in it, and as Christopher Pierson points out, thus helped grow the intermediate classes by increasing professional and administrative employment opportunities in the public sector.

While the public sector has dramatically shrunk from its peak of 30% of the workforce in the 1970s, public sector work still accounts for a huge chunk; but because of privatization, countless roles are now outsourced and duplicated, creating Kafkaesque layers and webs of functions, overlapping laws and regulations and so on — a system in which accountability is impossible. While there is a narrative in some quarters that neoliberalism did away with the state and state bureaucracy, anyone who has tried to pay a bill, change internet provider or challenge a fine knows that the opposite is true. As David Graeber has noted, the transition to neoliberalism, rather than cutting bureaucracy as Thatcher claimed it would, has increased it beyond anything that anyone would have thought possible, both in the public sector, through new public management, and in the private sector. Graeber calls this "the iron law of liberalism": "government policies intending to reduce government interference in the economy actually end up producing more regulations, more bureaucrats, and more police".

The last part of Graeber's "iron law" is important. The transition to neoliberalism has also witnessed an increase in the *authoritarian* functions of the state, which is needed to police an increasingly "surplus" and marginalized working-class population. We have to think about how the changing goals of the increasingly authoritarian capitalist state inexorably requires new workers to carry out these functions. Most obviously, this involves an increase in the repressive apparatuses. Until the Tories began to cut police budgets around 2010, the police had grown steadily since the 1970s. IFS data shows that, "between 1961 and 1991, the police workforce (including civilian police staff) doubled in size from 100,000 to 200,000". Indeed, Thatcher specifically ring-fenced police budgets knowing that she needed more police because there were going to be more unemployed.

As the amount of people on benefits and zero-hours contracts increases, the state also needs more people to administer them. Graeber argues that "all rich countries now employ legions of functionaries whose primary function is to make poor people feel bad about themselves". These new roles occur across the private and public sector and are, as aforementioned, often blended because of privatization. There are now more people working for the DWP than members of the British Army; as the poor get poorer, you also need more security guards and cameras to guard shops against desperate people shoplifting; as more of the surplus poor are jailed and private prisons become drivers of economic growth, they also require staffing and administering by the Ministry of Justice and private firms like G4S and so on.

How to Categorise the Middle? Two Different Interpretations of the Intermediate Classes

Rather than society increasingly polarizing into two classes, the tendency is towards complexity: the inexorable and huge growth in supervisory roles, sales, bullshit jobs, the state bureaucracy, repressive roles and so on. The question is, therefore, how do we categorize these millions of new workers — the salesmen, job centre workers, nurses, administrators, academics, policy wonks? Can we just class them now as part of an expanded working class?

Although he did not devote significant time to the social and political character of the new service strata after identifying them "objectively", Marx clearly places this new class of worker outside the proletariat, commenting of servants that *"no class provides a more worthless section of recruits for the petty bourgeoisie"*. Like Mayer's analysis of the petty bourgeoisie, he here states that the petty bourgeoisie not only expands, but expands by taking on a new fraction, which was different in form and existence from the old petty bourgeoisie, but which nonetheless belonged to the same class. The new service class worked, and had to sell their labour, yet Marx clearly states they are *not* proletarian because of their function and because of their social, cultural and hence ideological proximity to capital and management and distance from the workers.

Developing these insights further, in the early Seventies, numerous Marxist and socialist thinkers mounted serious attempts to get to grips with the complex class structure and the new middle or intermediate class that seemed to be emerging with the decline of industrial capitalism in the developed West. These theorists argued that the new intermediate classes were distinct from both the bourgeoisie proper and the working class, had distinct interests and traits of their own, and therefore had to be analysed on their own terms, rather than collapsed into an enlarged working class. It is imperative that we return to these socialist theories of the middle classes, as these are the missing link that can help us make sense of the increasingly complex class structure we see today.

The most prominent analysis was by the Greek-French Marxist sociologist Nicos Poulantzas, chiefly famous for his analysis of the state. Poulantzas began studying and attempting to categorize "the new middle classes" largely in response to the proletarianization thesis put forward by the French Communist Party, who had claimed that the new middle classes created by the transition to a service economy would relatively easily form part of a hegemonic bloc with the working class, because their interests were aligned. Poulantzas objected, saying that things were not that simple, and argued it was a mistake to not understand the distinctiveness of the new class and their relationship with the working class, which could not be taken for granted.

Poulantzas' main argument was that the new strata of workers produced by the transition to a service economy constituted a "new fraction" of the petty bourgeoisie. Thus, whilst the "traditional" petty bourgeoisie of shopkeepers, artisans and small farmers had undoubtedly declined in number under first welfare state, and later monopoly capitalism, the petty bourgeois as a class had been gradually replenished by the emergence of these new "white-collar" service workers, just as it had been at the turn of the century.

There were, however, obvious differences between the two groups, which makes this argument seem problematic. As already mentioned, the new petty bourgeoisie did not own its own means of production. Moreover, the new petty bourgeoisie tended to work in big capital or the state bureaucracy, fields and phenomena that, as we have seen, were anathema to the old petty bourgeoisie. Relatedly, in order to enter these fields, the new petty bourgeoisie embraced formal education, while the old petty bourgeoisie had eschewed it.

Despite these differences, Poulantzas argued that the new petty bourgeoisie was part of the old petty bourgeoisie because of its precarity within the class structure and its concomitant focus on social mobility. While the working class and bourgeoisie were static classes, this class was mobile, and could move up and down in the class structure. It was this liminal, interstitial position and its fear of falling that inculcated in these new workers essentially the same ideology of anti-collectivist rugged individualism — and its attendant political consequences — of the traditional petty bourgeoisie, and hence placed them as a new fraction of the petty bourgeoisie and which simultaneously split it off from the working class. It was this individualism that allowed the new petty bourgeoisie to thrive in school and embrace its logic of competition; to take up its place in the state bureaucracy and to dominate the working class. While the old petty bourgeoisie was socially isolated by its workplace, the new fraction was socially isolated from fellow workers by their embrace of the logic of competition and obsession with climbing the ladder. Like the old petty bourgeoisie, and like the clerks and recruits to the new petty bourgeoisie at the turn of the century, all the above meant that the class divide between the working class and the new petty bourgeoisie was mutually understood.

The Professional-Managerial Classes

Poulantzas' theory was not the only show in town, however. Another left analysis was put forward by Barbara and John Ehrenreich, who coined the term the "professional-managerial classes" to describe the new middle classes.

Writing in the US in the 1970s, the Ehrenreichs noted the elephant in the room within left activism: while activists argued for the revolutionary role of the working class, the overwhelming majority of activists themselves were not actually drawn from the working classes and instead now came from the upper technical classes based in the universities. The Ehrenreichs defined the professional-managerial classes as "salaried mental workers who do not own the means of production and whose function in the social division of labour may be described broadly as the reproduction of capitalist culture and capitalist class relations", thus making them roughly analogous to Marx's "ideological workers" or Gramsci's "intellectuals".

For the Ehrenreichs, this class is not a "middle class", nor a fraction of the petty bourgeoisie or bourgeoisie, but a distinct class in itself, produced by late-stage capitalism. Like Poulantzas, the Ehrenreichs argued that the professional-managerial class developed "objectively" as the modern state moved away from outright coercion of the subaltern classes and towards more sophisticated methods of social control and rule through consent. Thus the capitalist state "in the West" required not just the police, courts and so on, but a whole complex of "fortifications" in civil society — advertising, education, etc. — to protect capitalism and the status quo.

The notion of hegemony (or rule through consent) is widely accepted, but what the Ehrenreichs argued was that achieving this also required a whole new class of people to undertake this work of pacifying the working class.

The Ehrenreichs detail the various ways in which the pacification of the working class has been achieved and how the professional-managerial class emerged to fulfil this purpose. This process had three pillars. Firstly, the reorganization of the production process within capitalism. This involved primarily the mass deskilling of workers and the end of any meaningful autonomy within the production process, i.e., "undercutting the collective experience of socialized production", which had previously been the backbone of working-class consciousness. This was achieved through: a) the pioneering of sophisticated management techniques, away from outright "factory despotism", for which a new class of managers and supervisors trained in "mental labour" and bureaucracy was necessary; and b) the emergence of new forms of machinery and technology, which automated the labour process and in turn deskilled and atomized workers, for which a new class of technicians, engineers and experts was again necessary. Second, the emergence of a mass state bureaucracy that controlled the populace birthed a mass of teachers, social workers, doctors, as well as a mass culture and entertainment industry stocked with journalists and others. Third and finally, the emergence of a mass consumption society and the creation of false needs for the disposal of capitalist goods amongst the working class brought about new industries of advertising, marketing, but also services to service capital — corporate banks selling loans, finance and so on.

Thus, for the Ehrenreichs, the professional-managerial class was birthed to dominate the working class and perpetuate capitalism, and hence its very existence and function in society — even before one moved on to the subjective social relationship with the class beneath and above it, and the ways in which the class reproduced itself — was antagonistic to the working class. The class interests of the proletariat and professional-managerial class were therefore mutually exclusive: for the Ehrenreichs, people engaged in the apparatuses and professions designed to pacify and subordinate the working class could not, by definition, be part of the working class.

On top of this, the professional-managerial class possessed a distinct culture, aesthetic and habitus — distinct from the petty bourgeoisie *and* the bourgeoisie proper — which continually reproduced itself through intermarriage. Moreover, because of its relationship of domination over the working class, the professional-managerial class also developed a distinct ideology *vis à vis* the working class that it controlled and pacified, defined by a sense of paternalism on the one hand, and disgust and terror on the other. This distinct ideology is indispensable for understanding modern progressive politics.

Finally, the most controversial aspect of the Ehrenreich's work was the assertion that, while the professional-managerial classes once understood their function and accepted it (pacifying the working class and being the right-hand man to the bourgeoisie, running things on its behalf), progressively, its relation to the ruling class and capital changed. While Gramsci and others argue that intellectuals (even if they didn't know it) always did the job of the ruling class, and functioned on its behalf, Ehrenreich argued that gradually, the professional-managerial classes gained more autonomy and distinctiveness from the bourgeoisie, and so this class of experts came to believe that it could run society better than, and in a different way to, capitalists and the elite. The professional-managerial classes' humanist ideology was rooted in its belief in technical expertise and education, and its views on how to run society efficiently frequently began to clash with a bourgeoisie that was narrowly focused on profit. Thus, for the Ehrenreichs, they progressively came to have "anti-capitalist" views and gradually became self-aware, gaining class consciousness (becoming a class "for itself") with distinct interests and ideology to the bourgeoisie proper.

The Fractured Middle

How then to best conceptualize the middle strata? All the professions and occupations that don't easily fit into either the working class or the ruling class? As C. Wright Mills notes, when we think of this deeply confusing "occupational salad", it is often based on our own vision of a particular person or experience, and based on what we think is happening in society. Thus, proponents of the proletarianization thesis will invariably hold up particularly wretched sections of the middle — e.g., nurses using foodbanks, call centre workers, junior academics on short term contracts — and ignore the sections that are doing well for themselves — doctors, salespeople and so on.

The people who inspired this book and who I wanted to focus on were based on those I had grown up around: both the traditional petty bourgeoisie — tradesmen, cops, squaddies, publicans and café owners — and then, through my later experiences at the bottom end of the new petty bourgeoisie — teachers, nurses, call centre workers, salesmen, hospitality workers and academics on precarious contracts. The focus of the book was — and is — on illustrating the boundaries between this lower group and the proletariat beneath them, but as I delved deeper I struck a thorny, second problem: what are the *upper* boundaries of the new petty bourgeoisie? When conceiving the book, I had not thought as much about how far "up" the petty bourgeoisie should be expanded (mainly because I did not and still do not really come into contact with doctors, lawyers, accountants and so on). I was thinking about junior academics rather than senior ones.

The reason the professional-managerial class is important to understand, and why it continually comes back into focus, is because at the upper boundaries of the new petty bourgeoisie — in the degraded professions of social work, teaching, academia and so on — the boundaries between the petty bourgeoisie and the professional-managerial classes get blurred. As the introduction to this book makes clear, there are obvious cultural overlaps between the two, particularly as they both tend to occupy the same political space. But of course, there are also key cultural similarities between the traditional petty bourgeoisie and the working class, and this doesn't put them in the same class, so it's important to try and think through the difference between them. In doing so, this reaffirms what it is that places the new petty bourgeoisie in the petty bourgeoisie in the first place.

Certainly, there are similarities between the groups. Like the new petty bourgeoisie, the professional-managerial classes do not own their own means of production, although crucially they may occasionally direct the production process. The problem with the theory of the professional-managerial classes is that it lumps managers who may direct business on behalf of owners with professionals (like doctors and lawyers) who may not. The most obvious similarity, however, is the shared experience of higher education and the cultural and ideological effects this produces. This is discussed in more detail in the following chapter, but unlike the working class and the bourgeoisie, both these classes require higher education for their career path — the new petty bourgeoisie for social mobility and the professional-managerial class to reproduce itself — and the experience of higher education inculcates in both a particular culture and habitus, a feel for the rules of the game and an awareness of the educational field, as well as an awareness that they are not the same as the working class and a subtle dislike of the class beneath them.

Yet there are key differences between the groups, which split them off and place the new petty bourgeoisie in the petty bourgeoisie. It has lately become clear that the concept of the "squeezed middle" often obscures more than it clarifies, and the impact on "the intermediary classes" and professions has not been uniform at all. Within the complex border areas of the new petty bourgeoisie and the professional-managerial classes, certain professions have been degraded, but some have been protected and enjoy a far stronger market position. The wages of many professional occupations — particularly those that directly service capital — have skyrocketed, splitting them off even further from other middling groups, such as teachers, academics and nurses. Those who went into the public sector need only to speak to their university friends who got on a graduate scheme in the private sector to see how paths can diverge financially. The split is also about autonomy. As Magali Larson has illustrated, much like the old guilds of the petty bourgeoisie, the rise of professionalism was about self-aware professions monopolizing and sheltering the markets and fields in which they work, creating professional bodies that could be used to create and maintain internal standards and laws. Clearly in the modern era, some fields have been successful in defending their autonomy, and have reaped the benefit, while some have not.

But while money is important, class is not based on wages or how much you earn. It is mobility — the ability to move up and down the class structure, and the risk of downward mobility that this carries — which places the new petty bourgeoisie in the petty bourgeoisie. This precarity is why the new petty bourgeoisie is fixated on upward social mobility, which makes it necessarily individualistic as they try to avoid the drop. The professional-managerial classes, however, are not, as a rule, precarious or mobile. They are not, generally, at risk of falling down. This is about assets, to a degree — that is, whether you have a safety net — but precarity/stability also leads to differences in the culture, ideology and habitus of the two classes. Because they are defined by social mobility, the new petty bourgeoisie are often a new class — made up of first-generation members, often recruited from the working class and the traditional petty bourgeoisie. Because the professional-managerial classes are stable and established, unlike the new petty bourgeoisie, it reproduces itself and its culture and habitus from generation to generation; it does not welcome many new recruits. Although they do occasionally recruit from the lower orders, many top professions — such as lawyers, doctors, the military — remain dominated by an elite in terms of their social background. Thus, top professionals intermarry, socialise with one another, go to particular schools, live in particular areas. The children of professionals will generally become professionals. Just as there is a glass ceiling for many in the working class and petty bourgeoisie, there is a glass floor for the professional-managerial classes, beneath which they won't fall. For the new petty bourgeoisie, however, because social mobility often brings it into being from other classes, it will often absorb the culture of other classes, and because of its precarity, their children will similarly often be at risk of falling down within a generation.

Poulantzas' concept of the new petty bourgeoisie was incredibly expansive, covering everyone from the lower end of the middle (e.g., call centre workers) to the higher end (e.g., lawyers, managers, teachers and so on). He essentially makes the new petty bourgeoisie the largest class in society, while his understanding of the proletariat is paradoxically incredibly restrictive, reducing it solely to those who are "productive" — those who produce commodities. The Ehrenreichs' concept is fairly restrictive too — they do not extend the professional-managerial classes all the way down to the "lower middle classes" but instead focuses on the "established" or "upper" section of middle class of professions and managers that has grown enormously in such a short space of time.

Rather than stretching concepts too far, it is better to understand the mass that is often referred to as "the middle class" as being, in reality, split into distinct classes and class fractions, with different interests, values and culture; and having different politics and being potential allies or foes to a working-class movement. It seems reasonable to me to make a distinction between white-collar clerks, foremen, call centre workers, emergency workers, etc., on the one hand, and high-paid, prestigious professions like doctors, lawyers and senior management on the other. The now bloated "middle class" therefore consists of *both* the petty bourgeoisie (both old and new) *and* the professional-managerial classes. There is clearly a difference between these two classes.

The professional-managerial class is a fascinating concept that necessarily recurs, as it is an important character in modern society, and because it occupies a position immediately above the new petty bourgeoisie. However, it is not the main character of this book. I am more interested in the new petty bourgeoisie who, in the current conjuncture, are in particularly precarious positions. Ultimately, Poulantzas' analysis is more helpful than Ehrenreich's in analysing the people and communities who inspired this book — the lower middle classes, not the higher. The second part of this chapter explores the ways in which the new petty bourgeoisie is split off from the working class.

Part Two: Class Boundaries, Class Antagonisms and Ideological Divides

Poulantzas' work not only identifies and describes the petty bourgeoisie — he moves from "grand theory" or a "top down" analysis of the class to theorising class boundaries and class conflict in everyday life.

Poulantzas' relational conception of class, which informs and expands his analysis of the petty bourgeoisie, is elucidated by a series of increasingly complex examples of particularly problematic agents within the social structure — managers, foremen, police and soldiers, the state bureaucracy and so on. These are the problems that usually arise when talking about class in everyday life ("what class would x be then?").

He splits the new petty bourgeoisie off from the working class using three main vectors: function, domination, and culture or habitus ("mental labour"). I discuss "mental labour" and the cultural divide in the next chapter.

Management

From constituting a tiny percentage of the workforce in the early part of the twentieth century, managers now constitute a significant chunk of it. Managers, of course, pose a problem to those who posit the dualist class structure — in which the working class are "anyone who works" and the "bourgeoisie" are an increasingly tiny group of elites who actually own the businesses we all work for. If class is reduced to "ownership" of the means of production, what are the managers who, technically, don't own the company? They are employees. Ergo, they can be included in the 99%.

This might perhaps sound like a bit of a straw man — i.e., who on earth would realistically think like this? — if not for the fact that managers are now prominent and normalized within left groupings, with the Labour Party and trade unionism being extremely popular among managers. Within mainstream British trade unionism, there is no problem with managers and workers being in the same union, and as previously noted, managers are now increasingly likely to be in trade unions. When working as a shop steward for Unison, I was regularly handed cases and disputes where managers and workers were both union members, and indeed, in any big public sector organization, such as local authority workers, it is common for very senior staff and junior staff to all be unionised, or even for trade union representatives to be drawn from the management structure. While landlords are vilified on the left, managers are not.

Poulantzas solves this very simply by pointing to Marx's work, which states that the function of capital is not always fulfilled by the owners of capital themselves:

> the capitalist mode of production has brought matters to a point where the work of supervision, entirely divorced from the ownership of capital, is always readily obtainable. It has, therefore, come to be useless for the capitalist to perform it himself. An orchestra conductor need not own the instruments of his orchestra. To say that this labour is necessary as capitalistic labour, or as a function of the capitalist, only means that the vulgus is unable to conceive the forms developed in the lap of capitalist production, separate and free from their antithetical capitalist character.

Thus, the direction of the labour process is as important as ownership — the direction of capital is all part of the relationship of economic dominance and the "place of capital" in society. The "directing agents" of capital therefore belong to the bourgeois class even if they do not own the means of production: "in all cases the managers are an integral section of the bourgeois class".

While managers are not the main problem we need to discuss, and obviously not part of the new petty bourgeoisie, the example is nonetheless useful because it demonstrates why class is not narrowly about "ownership of the means of production", nor is it just about who works (managers don't own the company, and they do work). Rather, one's class is based on one's function in society *vis à vis* the role of capital and the worker's role in the social division of labour as a whole, which produces distinct ideological and political effects that define them as a class.

Petty Domination as a Class Divide

We have already seen that supervisory labour has grown enormously with the development of capitalism. C. Wright Mills argued that while professional white-collar jobs had been degraded and deskilled, the management and control system had simultaneously been deliberately elaborated into complex hierarchies, which gave more and more people — regardless of their own pay or autonomy — forms of control over others. In the debate on class, the deskilling and degradation of professions and the middle is focused on, but not the proliferation of new forms of social control between workers.

According to the 2011 census, there are 3.3 million people in lower technical or supervisory roles, and more specifically, LFS statistics show that supervisory (i.e., non-management) roles in the UK constitute well over half a million people. In modern, low-paid, white-collar and service workplaces in particular, supervisory roles are widespread, and this is deliberate. Proponents of the proletarianization thesis would note that, in many cases in modern workplaces, these supervisors or line managers are paid just above the minimum wage, maybe a pound more an hour than those they supervise. Again, under the narrow conception of class, which ignores the presence of classes outside the proletariat and bourgeoisie, foremen and team leaders of all grades are often straightforwardly part of the working class: like the workers, they have to sell their labour; they are exploited; they make commodities; they do not own the factory or get to keep their product. They may very well be culturally working class.

Yet the foreman or team leader, like the store manager and managing director, is involved in directing the labour process and dominating the worker, making them work faster and more efficiently for capital. Thus, Poulantzas argues these "workers", through their domination of the working class, and by working to speed up the production process for capital, inexorably come to ideologically side with capital and management and to distance themselves socially, politically and ideologically from the workers that they may share much in common with culturally.

On the topic of supervisors, Erik Olin Wright disagreed with Poulantzas, arguing that supervisors, in practice, have little real authority or power over the workers. Certainly, this is true in many places. But here Wright misses the point, which is that the supervisor will likely *think* and *act* as if their power is real, and this dominance over another worker, whether real or largely illusory, produces social and ideological effects that peel the supervisor off from the working class as they come to identify with management. They internalize their power and relationship of dominance over their subordinates. This is also a two-way street — the workers do not see the supervisors as "one of them" either.

Historically, within Marxist thought, jobs that are often "culturally" working class but which involve domination — soldiers, police, prison guards, and so on — have generally been considered part of the petty bourgeoisie. Poulantzas claims that supervisory labour is also, therefore, generally a part of the new petty bourgeoisie for the same reason. The example of supervisory labour helps further clarify why it is not possible to claim that "all wage labourers" are proletarian.

Indirect Domination via the Bureaucracy

The concept of domination is central to the boundaries between the working class and the new petty bourgeoisie, and Poulantzas argues that domination is on a spectrum from active (supervisors, the police, prison guards, soldiers, etc.) to passive or indirect (social workers, teachers, doctors, nurses, DWP workers, etc.).

Poulantzas' work on the new petty bourgeoisie and class boundaries pays a lot of attention to the state bureaucracy. Channelling Weber, Poulantzas argues that bureaucracy is not a phenomenon that naturally "happens", but is instead a deliberate institutionalization of rules and power relations within everyday life and work. Bureaucracy is one of the tangible ways in which the power of the state and capital permeates people's lives: through bills, council tax, parking wardens and so on. I have already described how bureaucracy has expanded under neoliberalism, so the relationship between the bureaucracy and class position is particularly important given both the left's historic focus on the welfare state and bureaucracy as the ideal form of socialism, but also the related concentration of trade unions and the left in the public sector and education.

Poulantzas argues that the new petty bourgeoisie is clustered in the state bureaucracy, and that people who work in the state bureaucracy may generally be classified as belonging to the new petty bourgeoisie. The new petty bourgeoisie do not always directly dominate the working class like the police or foremen, but nonetheless, for Poulantzas, they often exercise authority ("the induced reproduction of power") over the working class *indirectly* in various ways through the bureaucracy. To take an obvious example, the person working as a job coach for the DWP may be paid very little, be a trade unionist, be from a working-class background and have everything in common culturally with the working class person that sits across from them. They may indeed be empathetic and so on. Yet they are nonetheless the gatekeeper of the government's knowledge — they understand the benefits system better than the working class; they know stuff that the claimant doesn't and ultimately wield the power of the state over the worker.

As Graeber puts it, state bureaucracy

> is felt most cruelly by the poor, who are constantly monitored by an intrusive army of moralistic box-tickers assessing their child-rearing skills, inspecting their food cabinets to see if they are really cohabiting with their partners, determining whether they have been trying hard enough to find a job, or whether their medical conditions are really sufficiently severe to disqualify them from physical labour.

While Graeber's work focuses on the poor who experience it, we also need to think about those who administer it: those who teach, police and even help the working class in paternalistic ways. It is undeniable that the state and other bureaucracies are a hard dividing line for the working class in everyday class interactions, and that the professions and the state bureaucracy have a class character. There is, in all these relationships, a mutual understanding of "us and them", and Poulantzas argues that these boundaries constitute class divides.

What is central to Poulantzas' argument about class positions is that enforcing hierarchy and the state's authority produces ideological effects on the agents who undertake it. He writes that "bureaucratization is a tendency that materializes certain ideological-political effects on unproductive labour [i.e., the new petty bourgeoisie]... this bureaucratization has considerable, if contradictory effects on the agents subject to it". Participating in and enforcing the bureaucracy has ideological impacts on the new petty bourgeoisie, which ultimately splits them off from the working class. The working-class view the bureaucratic agent as Other, and the agent themselves — as we will see in the next chapter — simultaneously believes the working class are *Other* as well. They know that they are also not the working class because they occupy one side of a large, unspoken dividing line (mental labour), and the worker occupies the other.

Bureaucratization impacts whole swathes of society — not just (famously) the public sector, but banking, insurance, advertising, higher education, healthcare and so on. Once we understand how power relations are exercised and the social and ideological role they have in splitting the subordinate classes, we can think about the impact of bureaucratization on the class structure.

Function as a Class Divide and Theorizing State Workers

However, while supervisory roles have proliferated, surely most people do not have direct supervisory or bureaucratic power over the workers? Poulantzas then engages with the more ambiguous agents — i.e., those new skilled, university-educated workers who do not directly dominate or supervise the worker directly. Poulantzas engages with a number of examples here, from engineers and technicians involved in the production process itself to those working outside production, in occupations like teaching, social work, the health service and so on. For Poulantzas, regardless of how progressive these workers are as people, despite their class origins or whether they are being deskilled themselves, they are "objectively" engaged in the subordination of the working class for the benefit of capitalism, and indeed many of their roles essentially only exist to perpetuate the class divide within society and to discipline or pacify the worker and to stabilize capitalism. This ranges from the technician and engineer in the factory, whose skills are used to speed up the labour process and deskill the worker, to teachers and social workers. They cannot be working class, and are placed in the new petty bourgeoisie.

Class here is not defined by ownership of the means of production, but is about one's social function in the division of labour and, hence, society as a whole. This definition is very similar to the Ehrenreichs' account of the professionals, which can be applied to a large part of the professional or, indeed, associate professional class. While Poulantzas places these workers in the new petty bourgeoisie, and the Ehrenreichs place them in the professional-managerial classes, the broader point is to think about one's function in society as a class boundary.

For Poulantzas, function always trumps class origin. It is a popular conceit of both the left and the right in the UK that the class background of agents ultimately determines their class, regardless of the work they do. This extends to all levels of society, which is why it is possible in the UK to have working-class millionaires or working-class MPs. Moreover, it is often implied that, somehow, the class character of the workers can determine the function or nature of the entire organization. Hence, it is not uncommon to hear people saying that the army or police are "working class" because the soldiers and police officers are culturally working class; or even that other state apparatuses like the media are dominated by personnel drawn from particular classes and hence have the "essence" of a particular class and so on.

In contrast, Poulantzas' concept of "social categories" deals specifically with state functionaries like soldiers, the police, civil servants, teachers, prison guards, local authority workers, housing officers and so on. He argues that the class of these individuals, even if they are of different class origins, is defined by the relationship they have to the state apparatus and the fact that they function on behalf of the state (just as managers and foremen function on behalf of capital). The key point is that the functioning of this category or field cannot be reduced to the class origin of its members. He points out that, if this was the case, the bureaucracy as a phenomenon would not be a sociological problem or a problem for socialists — a worker in a bureaucratic role would simply be proletarian and act in the interests of the proletariat. Yet we know from history and daily experience that this is not the case: soldiers break strikes; cops with working-class accents crack skulls; job centre workers sanction people.

So, despite the heterodox class background of the agents involved in these apparatuses, the "social categories" (again, policeman, soldier, civil servant, etc.) exhibit a strong internal unity. The bureaucracy or branches of the repressive and ideological state apparatuses, even if they were hypothetically staffed entirely by the proletariat, still serve class interests other than its own. Ultimately, the ideology of the agents is mediated and formed by the functions it carries out — i.e., the dominance of the state, which is a bourgeois ideology of authoritarianism and capital. Therefore, the workers involved in the state bureaucracy, or indeed anything which has a function of domination, and whether this is direct or indirect, are split off from the working class and placed in the new petty bourgeoisie.

Poulantzas' focus on the relational aspect of class and the ideological and social effects of domination and function allow him to analyse and think about divisions right down to the individual workplace — something which is invaluable for organizing. For example, within traditional industrial capitalism, white-collar clerks would very often earn less than the skilled workers on the shop floor in the factory. Yet their place of work was often *physically* next to the manager (conjoining offices or in the same office, etc.). Moreover, they were generally perceived as associated with management by the workers, and would in turn identify with management and as fundamentally different from the working class both socially and culturally. This is very common in many modern workplaces: HR, payroll, comms, etc. are often (correctly) considered part of the managerial "core", despite the low pay of many of the workers involved in these types of work. As Poulantzas puts it, "*these agents often find themselves involved in legitimizing the power that management exercise over the workers*". He cites David Lockwood's famous assertion that "management ends... with the lowest grade of routine clerk" because the work and messages of management effectively go through this strata of worker. Thus, through their domination and relationship to management, they are removed from the proletariat and belong to the new petty bourgeoisie.

Social Mobility Versus Class Instinct: Petty-Bourgeoisie Ideology Versus Working-Class Ideology

For Poulantzas, the need to get on in life — and perhaps, more importantly, the need to not fall down into the working class — locks people into accepting, enforcing and internalizing a system of domination and hierarchy.

Vitally, when we discuss the increasing proletarianization of the "white-collar" strata, the experience of deskilling and falling wages and working in a job you are overqualified for, these by no means lead the new petty bourgeoisie to give up on the ideology of social mobility and individualism as the left assumes. In fact, the opposite is true. It is precisely this terrifying experience of sinking downwards that drives the desperation for social mobility, and which ultimately places the new petty bourgeoisie in the same camp as the traditional petty bourgeoisie, because it places them in *competition* with one another, and this creates a total mental isolation that precludes thinking collectively. For Poulantzas, the new petty bourgeoisie experience "competitive isolation" from one another in the labour market, an isolation that contrasts with the class solidarity visible within the working class.

For the new petty bourgeoisie, and this is also alluded to repeatedly by C. Wright Mills, precarity inexorably leads them to live a life of isolated, atomized individualism *vis à vis* other workers, who are viewed purely as competition or a threat. Our own survival and career becomes the most important thing in the world — the new petty bourgeoisie become individual islands. So, while the old petty bourgeoisie was driven to individualism by their *physical* isolation (their shop or farm), Poulantzas argues that the new petty bourgeoisie could work in a great office with hundreds of other workers but be similarly split off and isolated from their fellow worker by their own *individualist mindset*.

Poulantzas' analysis of the ideology and values of the petty bourgeoisie is always implicitly contrasted to the working class. This is a key point. To understand the boundaries between the new petty bourgeoisie and the working class, we need to understand the working class. What is it that makes the working class different from the petty bourgeoisie, new and old? What marks the working class out as different?

In *Farewell to the Working Class*, Andre Gorz explores Marx's focus on the proletariat as the only revolutionary class and explains the contrast between the economic position of the petty bourgeoisie and the proletariat and how these inevitably led to different political horizons. The traditional artisan enjoyed independence and autonomy at work and retained their individual identity as skilled tradesmen. They experienced alienation only when their product was sold as a commodity, in that they could not control the exchange value of the product, which was subject to forces beyond their control. Politically, their goals were inherently limited: they wished to keep prices for their products high and preserve the status of their trade and their conditions of work by restricting the amount of people who could enter it through the guilds. Yet as Gorz argues, it was likely that this would be the extent of their political ambitions: "artisans had an interest in defending or improving their respective social positions rather than in calling society as a whole into question or remodel it on a new basis". In this sense they were "prisoners" of their skill and the limited set of interests and ambitions this allegedly created. This was about self-interest and self-preservation within the social structure. The proletarians, in contrast, had nothing: they were not chained to any particular trade or skill, they were uninterested in defending small private property. They had no stake in the system, and it was precisely this which made them truly revolutionary, just as the skill and small property of the petty bourgeoisie made their political goals partial and individualistic. And so "[the working class] are not bound to any particular work or specific production, they are in a place to appropriate them all, to take over the industrial production of the whole world; since they have nothing they are able to want everything and be satisfied with nothing less than the complete appropriation of all riches". In other words, their political interests *had* to be collective, not individual, and had to include total revolution, rather than limited individual goals. As Gorz puts it "the supreme poverty of indeterminate power would be the seed of virtual omnipotence".

While Gorz focuses on the "objective" differences between the political interests and horizons of the petty bourgeoisie and the proletariat, Poulantzas attempts to explain how these differences are lived and manifest in everyday life. Again, this is not about class as an objective "thing", but as a "subjective" and felt experience. It is clear to Poulantzas that the working class are fundamentally different to the new petty bourgeoisie in terms of how they think, feel, and act. They are distinct because of a different form of socialization which produces a fundamentally different worldview and set of values, which in turn helps define the working class in everyday life socially and culturally.

Poulantzas returns to Lenin's concept of "class instinct" as the defining feature of the working class. Class instinct is implicit but rarely articulated within much classic Marxism and sociology of the working class, for example the affluent worker study. Class instinct is not class consciousness (class for itself), which is the ideal of a fully formed, rational, politicized worker. Class consciousness takes time to develop. Class instinct is instead an innate but intangible "class psychology" (much like Bourdieu's concept of habitus) which is already immanent in the proletariat, and which as Anna Krylova argues is created and "nurtured by the social reality of a worker's life". Poulantzas argues that the worker's collective existence under a rigid division of labour creates this class instinct, which inculcates in the worker an innately anti-hierarchical and anti-authoritarian mindset that clearly locates the worker on a particular side of the class divide, whether this manifests itself in coherent political mobilization or "correct" ideology or not. Within the "despotism of the factory" central to industrial capitalism, the worker is oppressed by the foreman and the owner, but as a rule, the working class does not internalize or reproduce within itself these relations of domination/

subordination — because it works collectively and possesses this class instinct, unlike the new petty bourgeoisie in the bureaucracy it realizes what they are and does not come to believe in the legitimacy of hierarchy.

So for Poulantzas, while the new petty bourgeoisie are defined by isolation and individualism — and again, it is this that makes them part of the petty bourgeoisie — the working class are defined by their collectivism and hostility to individualism.

Collectivism does not have to be expressed politically, and is not even confined to the workplace — collectivism was historically also sustained culturally and intellectually by the working class's associational life and institutions — clubs, sports, communities. Collectivism is immanent in the habitus, values, morality, culture and whole way of being of this class.

Central to this collectivism, however, is the fact that the working class (like the bourgeoisie) are a static class. They share many things with the new petty bourgeoisie: they are often impoverished, they don't own their own means of production, they have no autonomy at work. But because they are static, they don't experience the fear of falling that the petty bourgeoisie does, because there's nowhere to go. For Poulantzas, this immobility means that the working class are essentially inoculated against the ideology of social mobility and its attendant individualism. In *White Collar*, C. Wright Mills similarly noted that, unlike the new petty bourgeoisie, the working-class man is *not* on a "career ladder". His horizons and social circle are fixed by the time he is in his early twenties. Rather than making his way up the social and career ladder in order to gain more prestige, his concern is gradually making more money in his job and having a decent work environment and friends. Money trumps status, in other words. Mills argues that this is incomprehensible to the middle classes, and indeed, to many teachers who have to try and socialize the working class into petty bourgeoisie norms of "aspiration". To those outside the working class, this way of viewing the world is apparently unambitious (e.g., to not want to be a foreman because it moves you away from your friends, to *not* want to "get on"). But as Mills notes, the working class are not unhappy here; their horizons and expectations are simply different. The working-class man is not wracked by prestige or status anxiety, or the dislocation that comes with social mobility, and does not fret about continually changing jobs for his career, like the new white-collar worker.

Unlike the new petty bourgeoisie, the working class don't *want* to move up, and because of this, don't internalize or accept the belief in hierarchies and individualism that the new petty bourgeoisie do. They don't have careers or career paths, they have *jobs*. They are not on LinkedIn. This is born out in the limited empirical work that exists: the British Social Attitudes survey of 2016 showed that working-class identifiers generally didn't believe they will be upwardly mobile, while the middle classes still hold a strong belief in the possibility of social mobility, even as it is slowing to a complete halt. The new petty bourgeoisie still believe in the ladder, even though it is covered in grease.

Conclusion

Neoliberalism has inverted many things. The class structure has changed from one that was relatively simple, with a large working class, small middle and small ruling class; to one that is far more complex, with a bloated intermediate class and a more heterogeneous ruling class. The best way to understand the middle is as split into two. The "upper" professionals may be classed as the professional-managerial classes, while the "lower" — which is frequently degraded and proletarianized — may be classed as the new petty bourgeoisie. The lower section is far larger than the upper.

The modern left of downwardly mobile graduates — particularly the young people who campaigned for Corbyn — are rooted overwhelmingly in the new petty bourgeoisie. Yet even though they may likely become a shorthand for the class in the same way that the shopkeeper used to stand in for the whole of the petty bourgeoisie, it is very important not to think that this small group is the totality of the class (or even representative of it, due to the fact this section tends to occupy the upper boundary towards the professional-managerial classes). The new petty bourgeoisie is a sprawling class, which incorporates myriad professions and experiences.

The leap between levels, from "objective" class to a conscious "class in itself", is by no means straightforward and has dogged theorists for years. E.P. Thompson famously stated that class is not a static "category", for instance, but "something which happens (and can be shown to have happened) in human relationships". Class is relational: we become conscious of what class we are through interaction with other classes, as well as with capital, the state and so on. What is so helpful in Poulatzas' work on class boundaries — and how he splits off the new petty bourgeoisie from the working class — is precisely the focus on the relational aspects of class as an active phenomena that exists within society, defined by our relationships to other people from other classes and the same class within everyday life, particularly within the workplace. For Poulantzas (much like Bourdieu), everyday life — and work in particular — involves class *antagonisms* and power relations that determine our consciousness, i.e., make us aware of our class position and create ideological divides, which, in turn, act as class divides. His work helps us understand the divides between "us" (the left), and "them" (the "normal people" that we are attempting to win round to socialism).

Yet Poulantzas' approach to class was highly controversial and was attacked by some of his contemporaries because he appeared to privilege nebulous "ideological" divides over everything else. This appeared to be too radical a departure from orthodox Marxism for people to accept, and he was accused of spearheading "a retreat from class".

For me, the fundamental divide between the petty bourgeoisie and the working class, and which places the new petty bourgeoisie within the petty bourgeoisie, is its mobility and hence precarity. From this liminal position flows its individualist ideology that unites both fractions and influences their political behaviour. This, I hope, is fairly straightforward. However, Poulantzas then adds the aforementioned criteria such as domination, function, culture and ideology, which may understandably seem like he is continually moving the goalposts because he effectively makes so many criteria for membership of the new petty bourgeoisie. This is then why he ends up claiming it is by far the biggest class in society — because almost everyone ticks one of the criteria he provides and because he simultaneously restricts the working class only to those who make commodities.

It is certainly often unclear which level of analysis or criteria he is using or privileging, whether they all have to be in place to form class boundaries, or whether ideological divides trump one's economic position, whether if you tick one of the criteria then you can no longer be working class, and so on. It is natural to feel uncomfortable when his work places so many jobs and experiences which would normally be seen as straightforwardly working class in the new petty bourgeoisie.

His work is not perfect; it is often extremely dense and impenetrable. But class analysis is not a hard science.

Rather than using Poulantzas' theory of the new petty bourgeoisie as a checklist, it should instead be treated as a tool that can help us theorize and make sense of the melange of roles and experiences in the intermediate strata, the bureaucracy, bullshit jobs and the class divides which occur in everyday life.

Despite some of the problems inherent to Poulantzas' approach, his attempts to get to grips with the intermediary classes, and his focus on the world of work, is certainly more useful than saying we are all the same because we have to work for a living, or because we don't own the means of production, ignoring the complex power relations and divides that have proliferated between workers. As Guglielmo Carchedi argues, even while the middle classes or service classes are "objectively" proletarianized "economically", it is equally true that capitalism simultaneously creates new methods of social control and new power relations in the workplace and throughout society, such as increasing the amount of supervisory labour, creating bureaucratic roles to police the surplus classes (the homeless, refugees, etc.) under neoliberalism. So, one can only blithely say that "everyone is working class", or adhere to a framework of a dualist class structure or the "proletarianization thesis", only if you pay no attention to the explosion of management and supervisory roles, the social role people play in the workplace, society and *vis à vis* other workers, or the ideological impact that performing (and experiencing) these roles can have on one's class consciousness.

While Poulantzas' work sketched the outline of a new class, which has since grown objectively, this was never taken further and in many ways seemed to die with him. It is not a mainstream concept; it is totally absent from most contemporary sociological approaches to class. The new petty bourgeoisie, unlike the old petty bourgeoisie, has not been the subject of ethnographies. Unlike the old petty bourgeoisie, the working class or the professional-managerial classes, it is unclear whether the new petty bourgeoisie has its own institutions, culture or habitus. Poulantzas' work is mainly about its "negative" difference from the working class, i.e., the boundaries between it and the working class. In short, though we can say how it is *not* part of the proletariat, we know little about the internal content or lifeworld of new petty bourgeoisie, other than its individualism and status anxiety. Poulantzas is clear that this is a class that is unusually heterogeneous, lacking the internal unity and culture of other classes.

The next chapter focuses on education and how it functions as a class divide, and in doing so, hopefully helps flesh out the internal content of the new petty bourgeoisie.

CHAPTER FOUR
THE EDUCATIONAL ELEVATOR: EDUCATION IN THE MODERN CLASS STRUCTURE AND THE CREATION OF THE NEW PETTY BOURGEOISIE

"...the job of [state] education is to divide and separate the popular classes."

Nicos Poulantzas, *Classes in Contemporary Capitalism*

When I was in primary school, my best mates were two lads called Tom and Justin. Everyone called Justin "Eggy" because his father was called Eggy (his brother was also called Eggy). Both Tom and Eggy came from working-class, single-parent families who had moved to Porthcawl from the "proper" Welsh, working-class parts of Wales: the valleys to the north. We were best mates because we lived on the same street, although they both lived in flats whilst my parents owned our house. We were inseparable. We remained best friends when we all moved up to the comp, and played rugby and walked to school together.

When we were aged thirteen-fourteen, we got placed in different sets. Then we picked different GCSE options. We would still walk to and home from school together and see each other in break, but never during class. Soon, my time spent playing with my mates after school would also be limited — I'd be inside doing homework while they stayed out kicking a football or rugby ball around. Their parents didn't help them with their homework like mine did, but

Tom and Eggy didn't seem to care about homework that much anyway.

We were still best friends, but I gradually also started hanging round with the non-sporty boys in the set I was in too, and stopped seeing as much of Tom and Eggy: like many of my childhood friends, they both left school at sixteen whilst I stayed on for sixth form. I was going to go to university and leave my town and friends.

We began to drift apart, to be separated by forces beyond our control, like shipwrecked sailors in the sea being sucked apart by some invisible current, helplessly watching each other disappear over the horizon.

I don't even remember consciously wanting or choosing this path, it was just how it was. Gradually, we learned that we were different. By the time we were fourteen — still children — and despite growing up on the same street, going to the same school and being from the same community, our horizons and expectations (and of course, reality) had been formed differently. We had been split apart by class in a way that was unspoken but mutually understood.

The central sorting mechanism that separated us into two piles, and made us aware of what pile we were in, was school.

The Function of School

Education is a widely understood proxy for class divides in most societies. Earnings in the UK have historically been higher for those with more qualifications. Educational qualifications are therefore widely understood to be a form of cultural capital that can be converted into economic capital. Discussions of Brexit and "populism" among the commentariat also frequently focus on educational qualifications as a predictor of voting and ideology, becoming an acceptable way of disguising class hatred. Brexiteers and

Trump voters in particular were portrayed as thick and uneducated, their lack of educational qualifications a neat explanation as to why they voted as they did. Relatedly, class dealignment is also increasingly understood through education: the main predictor of support for the Democrats, the Labour Party and "progressive politics" more generally is increasingly higher education rather than income.

When the relationship of the education system itself to the class structure is discussed, it perpetuates the unhelpful assumptions about a simplistic dual class structure: we have the working class, on the one hand, and the elites on the other. Thus, in the UK, we talk about the inequity of the private school system and how it perpetuates inequality, and how many top politicians, lawyers, judges and civil servants went to the same small handful of absurdly expensive schools. Or, at the other extreme, we wring our hands about the educational experiences of the most deprived pupils: poor kids are disadvantaged by the poverty of their parents, they lack the right equipment at home to do homework, they can't afford school uniform and so on. This was particularly evident during the COVID pandemic.

These observations are obviously important, but they are also very partial accounts of the role of education in the class structure. While the focus in the discourse on education is, perhaps understandably, on the dramatic plight, suffering and non-engagement of children eligible for free school meals,[7] what is never really discussed is the experience and function of school for the children just above that group. In most schools, of course, children eligible for free school meals remain a minority. So what about the majority of children in the UK who are not receiving

---

7 In the UK, the most deprived students are eligible for free school meals, and hence free school meal eligibility is the standard measure of the deprivation of a school.

free school meals and who also aren't from comfortable backgrounds? Society isn't made up of chimney sweeps and toffs, so the left's traditional focus on private schools has always seemed a bit of a red herring, which glosses over class divides between the subordinate classes in the state sector. It tells us nothing about the new petty bourgeoisie — i.e., the children just above those who are eligible for free school meals, who are their friends, who don't go to private school but *may* go to university — and how they experience education and how this forms their ideology and class consciousness *vis à vis* both the bourgeoisie and the working class.

School and formal education play a particularly important role in the formation and socialization of the middle classes, and the new petty bourgeoisie in particular. Education is where the character of this class is developed and the social, cultural and ideological boundaries between it and the working class are formed and hardened.

Education in the Capitalist System

Education plays a central role in capitalist society. It must reproduce and inculcate in students not just capitalist "ideology", but the entire set of capitalist social relations of production, from the division of labour to the class system itself.

Education has evolved to meet the changing needs of the capitalist system. This is a general rule that applies to all countries, but of course different countries have different education systems, which reflect their different economies, class structures, political cultures and political priorities. "Politics" does not simply reflect class divisions passively but plays an active role in shaping class and class divides as different parties and movements seek to mobilize or co-opt particular classes or groups, or seek to reward or expand their social bases in different classes. This is often done through education policy.

During the early years of the Industrial Revolution, the poor lived in horrendous conditions and child labour was common. The little education the poor did receive was ad hoc, and largely through religious organizations and Sunday schools. Even in these contexts, the focus was often on moral and spiritual education. As late as the 1850s in the UK, half of all children did not attend school, normally because they were working.

During the early industrial period, education was reserved for the rich, despite the fact that the children of the rich, much like the children of the poor, at this stage of capitalism actually had little need for an extensive formal education. Capital had not yet been collectivised: there was not yet any "professional class" of managers and overseers, but rather a stark division of labour and simple class structure between a relatively small amount of owners, landowners and workers. In other words, education did not "create" the bourgeoisie, for it was already in place anyway, and hence the education the rich received was in the humanities, subjects that helped them rule, rather than subjects like science, which would help them produce.

The bourgeoisie had much to fear from the education of the working class and hence initially prevented it. Yet mass public education nonetheless rapidly developed — and, indeed, was encouraged by capitalists — for two interrelated reasons. First, the maturation of capitalism itself; and second, the rationalisation of the modern capitalist nation-state. According to Hobsbawm, the first Industrial Revolution (taking place from the mid-eighteenth century until the early nineteenth century) was largely led by countries without an educated populace. The industries and technology that stood behind the early Industrial Revolution (iron and textiles) were relatively primitive and required not so much technical skill as brawn and a mass of cheap, desperate labour. Skilled craft labour, as we have seen, was mainly concentrated in the petty bourgeoisie. Yet technological advances, specifically the increasing role of chemicals and electricity in production techniques, drove "the increasing penetration of industry by science", which underpinned the second Industrial Revolution (which took place in the mid-nineteenth century); and hence drove the need for a more educated workforce in a way that had simply not been necessary from the point of view of the bourgeoisie in the first industrial period. As technology developed and became increasingly important to the production process, it became impossible for countries lacking effective mass education systems to become or remain industrial powerhouses. It was therefore the self-interest of capital, rather than moral appeals from liberals for the virtue of education, which drove the creation of mass public education.

Alongside this was a need to rationalize the modern nation-state, which often involved binding troublesome regions and potentially revolutionary subaltern classes into the state. Male suffrage was to be granted, and mass education was therefore required to inculcate nationalism (and, in many multinational states, a standardized national language) and to promote uniformity and ideology throughout, ensuring loyalty to the status quo. During this period, national bureaucracies emerged (e.g., the civil service, education, militaries), and compulsory education, including national universities, was central to this.

Thus mass elementary (i.e., early) education emerged in the UK and across much of Western Europe in the latter parts of the nineteenth century. As a result of these combined drivers, illiteracy was largely eradicated. At the start of the nineteenth century, around 50% of the British public were illiterate. By the start of the twentieth century, this was around 3%. Hobsbawm argues that it was literacy that represented the major split between the advanced industrial economies and the underdeveloped.

The introduction of mass education had a complex impact on the class structure. While the elites remained where they were, mass literacy among the working class impacted on the new petty-bourgeois fraction of clerks in particular. Previously, literacy had been a key dividing line between the new petty bourgeoisie and the working class, both in terms of market position and general prestige, and so, with mass literacy, they now risked losing the slender status and benefits they had had over the working class. Significantly, as John Foster argues, much of the opposition to mass working-class education during this time came from elements of the petty bourgeoisie who viewed it as a threat to "tradesman exclusiveness" and hence their status.

As the democratic capitalist state became formalized and rationalized, with suffrage being increasingly extended to the ever-expanding and dangerous proletariat, and as the economy evolved and unproductive roles grew, the newly created middle classes beneath the owners sought a route into the latter, and a way of distinguishing themselves from the now somewhat educated proletariat, who seemed to be biting their ankles from below. The method for obtaining this social mobility, demonstrating one's class position and status in society, was formal education, and hence the middle-class focus on education as a vehicle for social mobility began. As Hobsbawm put it:

Schooling provided above all a ticket of admission to the recognized middle and upper zones of society and a means of socializing the entrants into the ways which would distinguish them from the lower orders.

Secondary education had previously been rare, but with the new need for distinction between the middle and lower orders, secondary education to the age of eighteen expanded in terms of numbers attending far beyond the size of the bourgeoisie proper, which was still relatively small, and for whom education still remained divorced from the industries they owned, and served primarily to win connections and roles within government and empire. Education was therefore of disproportionate importance for those with new money but not status, for whom social mobility was of the utmost necessity to avoid falling down the social ladder: the new professional and managerial classes and the children of the increasing amounts of self-made men who were becoming owners.[8] Formal education thus became the chief vehicle of social mobility, the primary indicator of which class you belonged to and was therefore prized by the middle classes because of their desire to set themselves apart from the lower classes.

Hobsbawm argues that the expansion of education was a conscious hegemonic strategy on the part of the ruling classes. Within a society riven by glaring divisions, the elites came to recognize the value of education in creating social stability, creating a loyal buffer class between them and the proletariat. The expansion of education was therefore specifically designed to co-opt the aspirational middle classes and keep them onside by providing an attractive hierarchy and "social stairway" to the upper orders. Of course, the ladder could rarely be climbed, and certain positions then rarely held, but what mattered was

8 For this reason, these schools in fact did not impart "technical" education for future members of the nascent professional-managerial classes, but instead subjects like Latin — schools were explicitly about inculcating "cultural capital" and training wannabes in the habitus of the bourgeoisie.

that the middle classes *had to think that it could be*. This would keep them onside and ensure that they identified with the hierarchy, rather than throwing their lot in with the lower classes and fermenting revolution. After all, people are not inclined to smash a system they think they can get to the top of, and the educational divides ensured that they had a class beneath them to look down on and define themselves against. From the very beginning, social mobility via education was an ideological strategy designed to shore up the status quo.

The expansion of education continued unabated following the turn of the century. The 1902 Education Act formally enshrined public secondary education into law and brought schools under the control of local authorities, leading to increasing standardization in teaching and curricula. The 1918 Education Act then raised the school leaving age to fourteen, although these rapid improvements and changes were then paused until after the Second World War, whereupon the implementation of the 1944 Education Act (also known as the Butler Act) promised secondary education for all and formally enshrined mass secondary education up to age fifteen — previously all schools were elementary (for ages five-fourteen) — and ended fees for secondary local authority-maintained schools.

Free education for all was a cornerstone of the Beveridge Report that underpinned the welfare state and a central ideological pillar of the Keynesian consensus. And yet, as Derek Gillard repeatedly demonstrates in his history of education in England, the executors of this ostensibly egalitarian policy — the Labour Party — retained a deeply confused attitude towards education and class from the very start, which greatly hampered any efforts to equalize society through education. On the one hand, the party was motivated by a sense of egalitarianism and levelling the playing field for the working classes, but on the other, they still essentially accepted as normal the idea of "natural" class divides in the education system, and hence society as a whole. This was reflected in the fact that the 1944 Education Act also provided for a tripartite school system of "grammar schools" for the most academically able (entry decided by the eleven-plus exam taken at aged eleven), "technical schools" for skilled trades and "secondary modern" schools for everyone else. From the get go, although the mass public education system was based on "ability", inevitably this school system reinforced a *de facto* class divide based around which type of school one attended.

Contrary to popular belief, the majority of grammar school pupils came from working-class backgrounds. Yet within the grammar school system, the home background and the social origins of the pupils continued to have the main bearing on pupil performance and life chances, and the children of the burgeoning professional-managerial classes (a category used in the Gurney-Dixon report into the class composition of grammar school pupils) dominated academic performance, with the children of semi-skilled and unskilled workers tending to struggle. So, even grammar schools, the most effective tools for social mobility the UK has ever seen, still could not overcome the effects of class and deprivation, and pre-existing class divides were reproduced even in a form of school that, on paper, was meant to abolish unfair advantage. Moreover, while the grammar schools were undoubtedly *seen* as a vehicle for social mobility, the *actual* social mobility of working-class children was limited, with the children of the professionals tending to go onto further education.[9]

---

9 While further education was still rare and specialized, under 8% of the children of unskilled workers went onto further education following grammar school (with under 2% of boys), while 33% of the children of the professional-managerial classes did.

Secondary modern schools, on the other hand, which were attended by three-quarters of all children, became seen as a "dumping ground", particularly for the children of unskilled workers, and therefore as somewhere to be avoided at all costs by those with aspirations of social mobility. Despite the largely illusory nature of social mobility, educational divides between grammars and secondary moderns nonetheless became a common tool for class distinction within society and between the lower classes in particular. Respectable and aspirational working-class and petty-bourgeois families cherished the idea of the grammar and looked down on the secondary modern children.

Increasing concerns about the unfairness of grammar schools eventually led to them being scrapped (by Labour MPs who had, of course, attended them). The 1953 Labour Party manifesto promised to abolish selective schooling and, in 1954, the first "comprehensive school" opened. The election of a Labour government in 1964 saw the gradual introduction of the comprehensive system, which was designed — on paper at least — to again try and level the playing field. The move to comprehensivization in the UK was strongly opposed by right-wing educationalists and Tories, who published a series of influential critiques of the "progressive" changes — some deeming it "the egalitarian threat" — known as "the Black Papers".

During the "winter of discontent" (1978-79), the collapsing Labour government, like many a developing nation, was pressured into accepting an IMF loan. As Gillard details, in return it agreed to make cuts to public spending, which in turn impacted on education. As the crisis bit, throughout the late 1970s teacher unions became noticeably militant, striking on numerous occasions alongside members of manual unions. Not coincidentally, moral panics about the "low standards" of comprehensive education then began to emerge in the right-wing media: comprehensives were slums, the children illiterate, unruly, violent, with the teachers' "progressive methods" failing to raise standards and so on. Typically, rather than withstanding these moral panics, Labour capitulated, with Prime Minister Jim Callaghan joining in the criticisms of the comprehensive system, seemingly endorsing the views of the notorious "Black Papers" written against comprehensives in the process.

Faced with the narrative of failing comprehensives, early neoliberal views about "teacher accountability" and "parental choice" began to inexorably seep into Labour's own approach to education. Clyde Chitty argues persuasively that the end of the post-war social-democratic consensus took root firmly in the education system as early as 1976, which meant that, when Thatcher was elected in 1979, her campaign against the state system was made a lot easier.

As a previous education secretary, education was central to Thatcher's hegemonic strategy, and would become a laboratory in which the previously niche ideas of the new right (i.e., neoliberalism) could be incubated and spread throughout society. Keith Joseph, Thatcher's closest ally and arguably the chief domestic intellectual force behind Thatcherism, was made education secretary precisely because education was seen as central to changing the common sense of society.

Thatcher was passionately opposed to the collapse of the grammar school system and the rise of comprehensives, but by the time she took power, comprehensivization was too far gone — by the mid-Eighties, the majority of schools were comprehensives — and could not be undone, so all she could do was protect the remaining grammars. Unable to undo comprehensivization, neoliberal policies had to saturate the existing comprehensive system as it was. Thus "traditional values" were pushed within the curriculum, exemplified by the Section 28 clause that attacked the discussion of homosexuality in sex education, dishonestly presenting it as "promoting" homosexuality. In addition, brutal cuts were made to the education budget. Teachers' pay was cut and unions were attacked. An ideology of parental choice and competition between schools was championed, and social mobility was championed through the "assisted places" scheme, which aimed to allow tiny numbers of "brighter" children to leave their "sink schools" to attend private schools.

As Thatcher gradually shored up her position within the Conservative Party — and society was dragged to the right behind her — Tory policies and interventions in education became increasingly radical. The transformation of education culminated in the 1988 Education Reform Act, which Ken Jones describes as "the major achievement of educational Conservatism":

> Not only did it change the institutional pattern of schooling, but it also substantially modified its social relations and reshaped its values, meanings and objectives. To put things more strongly, it destroyed the educational culture which had developed between 1944 and 1979, and began the work of creating a different one, in which old "social actors" were marginalised and new ones rendered powerful. What it created was successful: it established enduring ground rules for schooling in the 1990s and beyond.

Clyde Chitty argues that this was the final ideological break with the post-war consensus and marked the total capture of education as a sector — and as a concept — by neoliberalism. Nowhere (other than perhaps housing) was the societal and institutional cultural shift to the right more reflected as in education: the very concepts of knowledge and education swiftly shifted from a public good to a commodity for the individual to hoard. Schools and universities became sites of competition against one another. The working class, who Thatcher despised, were left to rot, and anyone who had any sense would be trying their best to escape them.

New Labour's Legacy

John Major's tenure as Prime Minister represented something of an interregnum, and in education (as in all fields) the role of his government was primarily to reinforce the changes put in place by his predecessor. While in broad societal terms New Labour represented a continuation of Thatcherism, they also made a number of distinctive interventions in the education system that reshaped the British class structure and the relationships between classes within it.

Like Thatcher, Tony Blair also saw himself as a revolutionary, and similarly saw education as a pillar of his hegemonic project. Even before he was in government, Blair's focus for societal reform was, in his words, based on the slogan "education, education, education". Before he got into power, he had played to the Labour left and had promised to abandon selection for all secondary schools, a long-term source of class divisions. Of course, when in power, Blair's educational policies retained much of Thatcher's neoliberal logic (even if it was rhetorically now implemented for egalitarian ends instead of openly embracing inequality).

Despite all evidence to the contrary, Blair — and all subsequent Labour leaders — became obsessed with the idea that schools could compensate for and solve all the ills of society. Under the banner of solving poverty and facilitating social mobility, competition between schools and pupils was deepened with the introduction of school "league tables" and the reintroduction of testing. Parental choice was now the name of the game, and hence school league tables were necessary so middle-class parents, as consumers, would know which school would be best for their children, and know which schools to avoid.

Education policy was enforced by fanatical Blairites like David Blunkett and later Andrew Adonis. Blunkett lambasted "non-traditional" teaching methods and regurgitated Black Paper rhetoric about the dangers of it. In a damning indictment of New Labour, his obsessive focus on a return to "traditional" prescriptive teaching methods was seen as too authoritarian, even by the original authors of the Black Papers. But while teaching methods had to remain "traditional", the subjects had to be "modernized". As part of the transition to the "knowledge economy", under New Labour things like enterprise, business and entrepreneurship became embedded in schools. The curriculum narrowed to focus on STEM (science, technology, engineering and maths), literacy and numeracy, while subjects that could not support the knowledge economy were marginalised and defunded. Labour's zealous belief in social mobility led to huge pressures being placed on teachers and schools to achieve increasingly impossible demands, particularly as the wider economy and society left thousands of families struggling to cope.

School policy ultimately reflected New Labour's version of progressive neoliberalism, in which socially liberal politics were combined with brutal authoritarianism and the paternalism of the professional-managerial classes that motivated the entire project. Thus, on the one hand, the homophobic Section 28, which was introduced by Thatcher, was repealed; and yet, on the other hand, education was increasingly sucked into Blair's shameless crusade on the "feckless" working class. Government-backed drugs-testing was brought into schools, mass campaigns against truancy were launched and he introduced the Islamophobic Prevent policy, which attempted to make schools part of the repressive state apparatus.

Of particular significance for the deepening of class divisions within the state education system was the promotion of academic selection within comprehensives. In 1995, David Blunkett had promised the Labour Party conference: "Read my lips. No selection, either by examination or interview, under a Labour government", signalling to Labour's supporters a clean break with the grammar system and hence class divisions in education. Yet after being elected, Labour not only supported grammar schools, it accepted and promoted selection of pupils on academic aptitude by state schools. As Blair himself put it, comprehensive schools should "cease meaning the same for all", and so New Labour then pursued a policy of transforming "failing" schools by making them "specialist colleges" that would allow academic selection.

The narrative that comps were "failing" led to the eventual introduction of "academies" — autonomous, state-funded schools that were no longer run by local authorities, placing them instead in the hands of charities and businesses who, in return for financial sponsorship, could control the board of governors, influence the curriculum and so on. This was a classic case study of privatisation, justified by Blunkett as the market stepping in reluctantly to save "failing" schools (i.e., we had no choice). Chitty argues that the new academies were, effectively, "private schools paid for by the state", although unlike the classic liberal values of the private school system that historically developed the individual without the constraints of employability, these new privately run but publicly funded schools would be driven by a neoliberal, KPI, jobs-market orientation. Their introduction marked Labour's final, total break with the ideal type of universalist state education that underpinned the welfare state and formalized the privatisation of state education.

As ever during the Blair years, academization was brought back to the need to speed up social mobility, stopping a cycle of "low expectations" among the working class. Gillard recounts how Adonis explicitly stated that he wanted academies to be "the new grammar schools", offering a path out of poverty for (a few) bright but disadvantaged children.

Glaring class divides — which had previously largely been between the secondary modern and grammar system, and between the state system and the private system — were now formally built within the state system itself with the abandoning of comprehensivization. This was not an accident, however, and was the result of political calculations. Blair understood his electoral base very well, and enshrining class segregation within the ostensibly unified education system, while devastating for the working class, had the specific aim of helping the professional-managerial classes and upwardly mobile new petty bourgeoisie. For Chitty, the education initiatives of the Blair years "seemed to involve the creation of many new types of secondary school, which would attract the support of the middle and aspirant classes, and thereby help to secure the government's new electoral base."

The formal stratification of comprehensives by either selection or academization allowed progressive professional or aspirational lower middle-class parents — people who were outwardly in favour of state schools and who probably openly abhorred the concept of private education at dinner parties — to circumnavigate "failing" schools, which were overwhelmingly in areas of high poverty, and send their kids to what were effectively private schools (with hardly any free school meals-eligible children). (This is, of course, what the Blairs themselves did with their son, Euan.)

Like Thatcher, these policies endorsed and accepted the idea that certain comprehensives were sink schools for the growing underclass. While Thatcher perhaps more honestly encouraged "smart children" to leave the state system and escape to the private school system, New Labour instead went about creating opt-outs within the state system for the professional-managerial classes, while the lower orders were left to rot in their failing schools. On the ground, of course, this "rigid hierarchy of [state] schools" served chiefly to undermine the Blairite rhetoric of "equality of opportunity", and to sharpen class divisions and insecurities as class divides between schools and places became more visible. The grammar school system was no longer in place, but education and what school you went to or sent your kids to became supremely important for the aspirational classes and to everyday class divides.

Finally, central to New Labour's focus on social mobility, as well as its zealous belief in the UK's transition to a post-industrial "knowledge economy" — populated by "knowledge workers" — was a huge expansion of higher education. Thatcher's regime had tampered with higher education — introducing fees for international students and tightening research criteria, for example — but had certainly not been interested in expanding higher education to the lower orders. Indeed, she *cut* funding to universities. The expansion of higher education under New Labour was therefore an enormous structural change that has had profound implications for the class structure of British society. Predictably, for all the egalitarian rhetoric about expanding opportunity, the mass expansion of higher education inevitably led to a crisis in how to fund it. This led to the abolition of maintenance grants (free university) and the eventual introduction of tuition fees in 1998, a move Labour had — of course — strenuously opposed before taking office, and which had previously been proposed, unsuccessfully, by Keith Joseph.

Thus, just as the state sector was privatized, by introducing tuition fees the higher education sector was also privatized. This had enormous effects on the character of higher education, which will be discussed later on.

By the time the Tory-led coalition entered government in 2010, the state education sector had been turned into a bewildering mosaic of different types of school. The most significant change within education since the 2010 Tory-Lib Dem coalition — later continued by the Tories on their own — has been the introduction of austerity measures, which have predictably devastated education as they have every other part of life in Britain. The Tories cut the school building programme, cut school meals budgets and cut the Education Maintenance Allowance (EMA). Despite adopting the language of social mobility, the Tories have returned to their original position of helping their traditional base and leaving everyone else to rot. Under Theresa May, the Tories expanded the grammar school system, thereby returning to the formal class divides within education promoted by Thatcher. State school funding was slashed while funding for private schools has risen enormously. The A* grade was introduced at A-Level, representing a further barrier in access to university for children from poorer areas, and university fees jumped from £3000 to £9000 in a single year.

Class Inequalities Within Education: The Marginalisation of the Working Class

Today, the class inequalities that were already latent within the education system have magnified. Schools have been expected to do more work with less money, leaving the teaching profession on its knees. The class divides that formerly occurred between grammars and secondary moderns are now occurring within the state system. Class divides are glaring between schools, typically mediated by geography. Schools in nice areas have no or very low numbers of children on free school meals or with Special Educational Needs , as well as modern buildings and facilities, while schools in working-class areas have obscenely high levels of children receiving free schools and with Special Educational Needs, with buildings that are falling down and staff shortages. Schools in deprived areas often now resemble huge anti-poverty centres, hosting wrap-around child-care provision, breakfast clubs, providing free school meals, free school uniforms, psychiatrists, doctors and nurses, social workers and so on.

Despite the never-ending surfeit of policies designed to end poverty and aid social mobility, things have gotten worse. This is consistent with all the evidence that you cannot teach your way out of poverty. By every measure, the working class are being increasingly marginalized within education. Poorer children remain far less likely to get good GCSEs compared to those with more affluent parents. More acutely, the most deprived children — those receiving free school meals, a crude but fairly accurate proxy for "working-class children" — achieve terribly at GCSEs. A 2019 Sutton Trust report showed that, in 2018, nearly 50% of the most disadvantaged children did not get an A-C grade (a "standard pass") in maths or English — a huge barrier to accessing many occupations later in life.

Many working-class students do not even take GCSEs in the first place but instead opt for other vocational qualifications. If you *do* take GCSEs, what subject you take at GCSE is also overwhelmingly determined by your class and your horizons and expectations in life, which will be already be set by the time children pick their choices at age fourteen. Poorer kids take subjects like Health and Social Care and avoid STEM subjects and the arts. Unsurprisingly, working-class kids leave school as soon as possible, and a 2019 Children's Commissioner report showed that, in the UK in 2018, 37% of children receiving free school meals left school without basic qualifications.

Working-class non-engagement with education has occupied sociologists for over a century. Discussions of educational performance in the modern press often replicate the attitudes of Victorian reformers in their view of the working class.

There are a lot of reasons why working-class children struggle in school. As children had to work from home during COVID, it came as a shock to many people to learn that many did not have a dedicated space in the house where they could do homework, did not have iPads or laptops, and had parents who were too busy working to help them with their schoolwork. Class produces "hidden injuries" — ultimately, you will struggle to engage with school if you're stressed and upset that your parents are fighting or your dad has gone to jail, or your relatives are unwell or you have unpaid carer duties, or any number of the traumatic incidents that the working class (of all races and ethnicities) disproportionately experience. Poverty is traumatic and dealing with it is difficult for children, let alone then having to face the relentless testing regime in school. Poorer children face stigma because of their poor uniform, the shoes and the coats they wear, the fact they receive free school meals and so on. All these factors can simply make school an extremely miserable experience.

For decades, the working class — unlike other classes — have had no political patron. Working-class communities have been hollowed out; the steady jobs that people used to rely are no more. Children have eyes and they are not stupid: if someone tells you can work hard, bust your ass at exams (with little or no help at home) and then go to university, when everyone you know has not gone to university or even done A-Levels, and you can see there are either no jobs in your town, or certainly none which require degrees, it is unlikely you'll care or listen or respond to the promises about delayed gratification and learning how to pass exams. You may also have seen or worked with recent graduates laden in debt and angry at false promises.

What is also frequently missed in the handwringing over the working class's "lack of aspiration" is that even when working-class children *do* want to go to university, or to become doctors or architects, these aspirations are rapidly managed. As Jessie Abrahams' research has shown, in school they are frequently told that that path is not for them. "Why don't you try something a little bit more realistic?"

Yet again, as C. Wright Mills repeatedly argues, this handwringing assumes that working-class people and communities *want* the same life and career — have the same "aspirations" — as the middle classes, when this simply isn't the case. School simply isn't seen as relevant for many of the roles that working-class kids will eventually take up in society. If you want to be a builder or a plumber, you will get most of your training on the job. Children realise this. Many pupils also realise the current market situation of jobs like construction to be very strong, so not being interested in overly academic subjects is entirely rational as it's eminently possible to build a very good life for yourself, living in your own community with your mates without worrying too much about school and having to go to university. This perspective is, of course, entirely alien to other classes (and social mobility "tsars") who wish to "get on" and get out, and who can only see success and the good life in their own terms. Who on earth would want to stay in their small town and be next to their families? How parochial and narrow minded. Hence, these entirely rational life plans are often seen by other classes as lacking "aspiration".

It is also certainly true that the institutional habitus of the school generally clashes with the habitus and culture (i.e., behaviours, worldview and norms) of the working class and the roles they do in society in countless ways. Generally speaking, the jobs and roles that the working class often take up in society do not require (or even value or respect) the social practices, behaviours and values that school and the white-collar workplace teaches you — deference, seriousness, work as a place where laughter and humour is parked and a new face and personality is put on (regardless of how many pool tables or beanbags are placed in the breakroom). The famous book *Learning to Labour*, which explores why working-class pupils get the same working-class jobs as their parents, argues that working-class children are primarily socialized *outside* school — in their community and family — and the personal qualities that are treasured in this milieu (e.g., wit, strength, camaraderie) are rooted in the workplaces of their parents. Hence, it is natural for working-class children to reject the norms, values and expectations that are imposed upon them in school. Precisely because of this glaring culture and values clash — whether it be how teachers or other kids talk to them — working-class children become aware of their own class via school, and soon realize that school and what it represents is not for them. They reject school as a place that is to be endured and finished as soon as possible.

School and the Creation of the New Petty Bourgeoisie

While school is not seen as relevant to working-class children, it *is* relevant for the intermediate classes, and for the new petty bourgeoisie in particular. Education is the primary site where the new petty bourgeoisie and the working class are split off from one another and whereby the social, cultural and ideological class boundaries between the two groups — outlined in the previous chapter — are first created.

To understand the function of school and its special role in forging the new petty bourgeoisie as a class, it is important to emphasize that, for other classes, education is primarily about reproducing and maintaining their position in society. The "fundamental" classes of the bourgeoisie and proletariat in particular are static and do not change class. They are not mobile — they don't move up or down. Therefore it doesn't matter that the children of the bourgeoisie get bad grades — for example, a Royal getting Ds with class sizes of eight and the best tuition money can buy — because these kids aren't ever falling out of their class position; it just doesn't happen. School is where they go to confirm their place in the elite, just as it always has been, and accordingly, the actual subjects and qualifications you get taught are secondary. What matters is learning and developing contacts that you will use for life, and the *bearing* of the ruling class: their unshakeable self-belief and confidence and the ability to bluff and charm people, even if you don't have a clue what you're talking about. The experience of the professional-managerial class is slightly different. One of the ways in which they are split off from the bourgeois proper is the fact they have to actually care about education. The ruling class can take over their daddy's business (or country) with no qualifications, but you can't simply inherit being a lawyer or doctor: you have to actually gain qualifications, go to university, pass exams and so on. You will have a massive advantage over the working class and the petty bourgeoisie in obtaining these, but you do still have to pass things.

Equally, for the working class, it doesn't really matter what grades you get if you are going to work in Amazon, or on-site, or with your dad or cousin or uncle, or join the army. The imposition of alien values onto the working class, and their subsequent rejection of the logic of school and the "chance" of social mobility, of course ultimately serves to reproduce the class structure and the working class's lowly place within it. It ensures the class remains static. School therefore reproduces the position of the working class, albeit less consciously than private school (i.e., it is reproduced "negatively" for the working class).

The petty bourgeoisie's relationship with education has historically been complex. Historically, the traditional petty bourgeoisie rejected the logic of formal education, preferring common sense and learning on the job (often the family business) — something they shared with the proletariat. Thus, education — and its attendant culture and habitus — has traditionally been one of the ways in which the different fractions of the petty bourgeoisie were separated. On the other hand, the traditional petty bourgeoisie, because of their emphasis on social mobility and class distinction, regularly encouraged their own children to engage with the education system that they themselves rejected, creating an intergenerational trend whereby the new petty bourgeoisie were often the offspring of the self-employed. Today, the old fraction of the petty bourgeoisie increasingly do attend university (mainly business schools), but educational divides are still most important for the new fraction, and it is this new fraction that is focused on in this chapter.

As the previous chapter demonstrated, just like the old petty bourgeoisie, the new petty bourgeoisie's main obsession and overriding concern in life is how to get on; and equally, they are continuously and desperately trying to avoid slipping down into the class they are closest to and from where many of them originated.

Education, as C. Wright Mills put it, is an "elevator" that can take the new petty bourgeoisie where they want to go in life, and education therefore assumes a disproportionate role in the life of the new petty bourgeoisie as one of the central mechanisms of "getting on". Mills argues that education is more important to the new petty bourgeoisie than property was to the old petty bourgeoisie. So, while education for other classes is about reproduction, for the new petty bourgeoisie it is disproportionately important and actually creates the class by splitting it off from other classes.

"Mental Labour"

In the previous chapter, I briefly introduced some of the ways in which Poulantzas argued the new petty bourgeoisie was split off from the working class. One of his key theories is the recurring (and somewhat nebulous) concept of "mental labour". Poulantzas repeatedly argues that it is "mental labour" that primarily distinguishes this new class from the working class within society.

My interpretation of mental labour is one that can be read narrowly or expansively. The narrow reading is basically that the new petty bourgeoisie and the working class simply have different habituses. In his discussion of technicians and engineers, for example, Poulantzas writes that

the dominant ideology does not just exist in "ideas"...

but is embodied and realized in a whole series of material practices, rituals, know-how, etc., which also exist in the production process. The technological applications of science are here directly present as a materialization of the dominant ideology.

In effect, what Poulantzas is saying here is that the new petty bourgeoisie, regardless of their earnings, even if they are not in a position of direct authority or domination *vis à vis* the working class, possesses a different habitus to the working class. The problem, however, is that it is unclear what the habitus of the new petty bourgeoisie *is*, other than "not being like the working class".

A more expansive reading of the concept is of both symbolizing and constituting a deeper, social, cultural and ideological divide, which is strong enough to split the new petty bourgeoisie (and, indeed, all other subordinate classes) off from the working class. Mental labour for Poulantzas is not simply about "blue-collar versus white-collar", or "clean work versus dirty work", or "skilled versus unskilled labour", or even the possession of educational qualifications versus not having them, but instead involves something much deeper again. Mental labour represents an unspoken, social and ideological dividing line in society, based on the legitimacy and superiority of certain types of knowledge. This dividing line is the "concrete manifestation of the political and ideological elements in the structural determination of class". This is a widely understood but unspoken and intangible line in society between the working class ("them") and everyone else ("us"), which plays a key role in a class-divided society. Poulantzas makes it clear that mental labour *is what workers do not have*. It is being on the side of "mental labour" that fundamentally splits off the new petty bourgeoisie from the working class. The new petty bourgeoisie, regardless of how little they earn or however much they become proletarianized, are always on the other side of the mental labour dividing line "with respect to the working class". To the new petty bourgeoisie, the working class are "them", and this is mutually understood.

For Poulantzas, it is education that, more than any other field, splits the new petty bourgeoisie off from the proletariat, and school is one of the places in society where his concept of the mental/manual divide becomes most tangible.

Learning How to Obey

Historically, schools have reproduced capitalism and the class structure in two ways. The first is *formal*, through the curriculum. So, at the most basic level, if we viewed school crudely as a place where our current hegemonic ideology was simply passed on to children through the curriculum, then it is clear that the ideology of competition, business, entrepreneurship (and the individualism that these promote) are certainly formalized in the British school curriculum and have been since the 1970s. The idea that social mobility is good, and that the primary focus and aim of schools is to get kids to pass exams, that the best thing that can happen to a working-class child would be to go on to university, is by now hegemonic within the education system. That education should be a vehicle for social mobility is explicitly stated in government documents and enshrined in curricula across the UK, and many state schools in poor areas are explicitly oriented to this end, with a massive focus every year on increasing the amount of children who go to university, with the dream of getting some into Oxbridge.

In order to prove you can do the tasks that the "knowledge economy" requires and get a good job, you need standardized exams. The "intermediate" classes who form the new petty bourgeoisie — school teachers, nurses, social workers — see education and the accumulation of qualifications as central to the (stressful) process of social mobility. The new petty bourgeoisie require certain skills and qualifications to be able to take up their place in the class structure and to hopefully move up it. You need GCSEs and A-Levels — and an enormous amount of emphasis and stress is placed on getting the right ones.

The second way that capitalism is reproduced is *informal* — through the social relations, norms and values of school and education that exist beyond the formal curriculum. Success in school of course involves technical qualifications — doing the right GCSEs, staying on for A-Level and going to university — but on the whole, children are taught that their success and their social mobility is not simply predicted on technical expertise and formal qualifications, but instead on the possession of things inculcated in the "hidden curriculum" — the nebulous "competencies", qualities and values that they must cultivate for the roles that they wish to take up.

Thus, more important than GCSEs or A-Levels is learning the rules of how to succeed in the white-collar world: not just how to pass exams but the importance of exams themselves, the value of hard work and delayed gratification, working to deadlines, completing tasks on your own in isolation. Formal credentials and qualifications — whether it is your degree or A-Levels — of course often have no bearing at all on whether you can do the job. Instead, achieving these targets are more important for what they say about your loyalty and adherence to a set of values, which dovetail with the capitalist system. Children thus learn how to behave appropriately and, above all, how to defer to authority. Althusser states:

But besides these techniques and knowledges, and in learning them, children at school also learn the "rules" of good behaviour, i.e. the attitude that should be observed by every agent in the division of labour, according to the job he is "destined" for: rules of morality, civic and professional conscience, which actually means rules of respect for the socio-technical division of labour and ultimately the rules of the order established by class domination. They also learn to "speak proper French", to "handle" the workers correctly, i.e. actually (for the future capitalists and their servants) to "order them about" properly, i.e. (ideally) to "speak to them" in the right way, etc.

To put this more scientifically, I shall say that the reproduction of labour power requires not only a reproduction of its skills, but also, at the same time, a reproduction of its submission to the rules of the established order, i.e., a reproduction of submission to the ruling ideology for the workers, and a reproduction of the ability to manipulate the ruling ideology correctly for the agents of exploitation and repression, so that they, too, will provide for the domination of the ruling class "in words".

Children who deviate from or question these deferential qualities — primarily working-class children — are punished, and "the others" learn that you must not be like that under any circumstances.

The anecdote at the start of this chapter is somewhat misleading, and omits my own role in the dissolution of my friendship. The fact is, as secondary school progressed, I remember gradually becoming terrified of sitting with my friends from primary school in class. They'd sit at the back, mess around, talk while the teacher was talking, answer the teacher back, make wisecracks. I, on the other hand, had been taught to sit obediently and to learn and was increasingly terrified of getting in trouble, because I knew that school was the key to my future. I couldn't get my head round the lack of respect they had for authority and how little they cared about school — *didn't they realise how important this was?* Thus, when we did get separated into sets, I was somewhat relieved that I would no longer get "dragged down" with them. I could now focus and be a good boy and impress the teachers with no distractions.

In the early 1950s, C. Wright Mills identified the distinct qualities that white-collar workers had to cultivate and learn from an early age. He claimed that, while the self-employed were entrepreneurial and focused on making short-term profits for their business, the new petty bourgeoisie were also entrepreneurial, but in a different way. He argued that every white-collar worker developed the personality of a salesman, but rather than selling a product or trying to make profit, over their lifecourse they learn to *sell themselves* and their personal qualities in the "personality market". In this market, of course, we are in competition with others. The school thus inculcates in the new petty bourgeoisie the ideology mentioned in the previous chapter, which was contrasted with the working class: a need to rise to the top as *individuals*, a view of the world in which others are a threat, competition. In school we are taught that we are the most important person in the world, that we are special and that getting ahead and selling ourselves (ahead of others) is crucial. In school, children learn the competitive individualism that leaves them isolated from others, sat on their own desks, hiding their answers from their friends, putting their hand up in class, trying to be first.

The Ideological Split

So, in school, the new petty bourgeoisie learn the qualities of deference, individualism and all the things they need to succeed and climb the ladder. But Poulantzas — through the concept of mental labour — argues school is about more again than just learning new modes of behaviour, than someone being quiet and persistent and listening to the teacher and another not listening and not bothering with homework. It is the manifestation of a deeper ideological divide.

Educationalists, particularly anarchists like Francisco Ferrer, have long argued that there is an informal but deep-rooted split within the school system between "mental" and "manual" education. At an early age, children are divided into different streams based on whether they are academic or "non-academic". Some kids are encouraged to subjects like Design & Technology, some are encouraged to do arts, humanities and sciences, and so on, and these traditionally corresponded to wider societal class divides. The new petty bourgeoisie — those just above the proletariat — who go on to work in white-collar roles, are overwhelmingly shuffled into the "mental" (academic) path in school and rapidly begin climbing to the top of the pile. While educational theorists have historically focused on how this split and the societal prioritization of particular forms of "intelligence" deprives children of a holistic education — that is, it deprives working-class children of a chance to engage with high culture and turns "academic" children into helpless adult-children with no practical skills — Althusser and Poulantzas focus on the ideological consequences of this split and the impact it has on the subordinate classes' relationship to one another.

Being sorted into the "academic" stream in school is central to the early socialization of the new petty bourgeoisie. This is not just narrowly about who passes what subject, who is in set one or set four, who passes their exams and who doesn't, who leaves school at sixteen and who stays on to go to university; it is also about accepting the deeper notion that particular types of knowledge and the forms of behaviour that are valued in school — the forms that *we* have, but the working-class kids lack — are not just important for getting ahead in school, but also that these qualities and forms of knowledge — deference, hard work, etc. — are valuable and correct within society more generally.

This has a vital *relational* aspect — accepting these rules and norms (that allow you to succeed in school), while others reject them, tells you that you are different to the other children, that you know more, that you are better than them both in terms of the things you know and the way you behave. In other words, being put in the top set for everything has social, cultural and ideological effects: we are in set one because we are brighter; we have certain qualities that they don't. They don't know what we do; they can't behave like us. Success in school, climbing to the top of this small ladder, inexorably leads the new petty bourgeoisie to believe in the justness of hierarchy, competition and social mobility more generally. And after all, why wouldn't they? School is ostensibly a "meritocracy" and they tend to do well in school because they possess these qualities. They hence accept and internalize the rules of the game.

Absorbing and accepting that this form of knowledge and intelligence — this way of being is superior and fundamentally different from the proletariat — is a prerequisite of learning your place in society (we know who we are by knowing who we are not) and forming new aspirations and expectations based on this. This includes learning that certain jobs (i.e., manual, low-paid work) are "not for us", alongside the related, implicit assumption that they *are* for "others" — i.e., those who don't have the qualities we do. The widespread belief, even among "progressives", that certain forms of knowledge are superior is a component of capitalist ideology because the taken-for-granted acceptance of the superiority of "mental labour" ultimately justifies hierarchy and class divides throughout society. We accept that some people are where they are because they know more, or they know better, and others are where they are because they lack the relevant qualities or forms of knowledge.

Accepting and internalizing these rules and norms in order to succeed, but also learning that the working classes are different to and inferior to us, is why the petty bourgeoisie, later in life, accept and enforce the laws of the bureaucracy or the white-collar world. Preparation for their role and function in society — their willingness to climb the bureaucratic ladder, and their career of enforcement and domination over the working class, as well as their fundamental difference to them — begins in school.

University: The Top of the Educational Elevator

When universities were for a small minority of the population, the economy was based on manufacturing rather than services, and when the class structure was a lot simpler, the sorting function of universities within society was more obvious. The expansion of participation in universities since the late-Nineties has been a hugely significant development that has had profound but complex effects on the class structure.

In the 1950s and 1960s, when the British economy was based on industrial capitalism, university was a minority pursuit. In the second half of the twentieth century, as capital reached a particular level of development and increasingly required particular managerial skills to operate successfully, universities became essential for growing, training and socializing the newly formed — but at that stage relatively small — professional-managerial classes. It was necessary for those who had to manage industry or learn how to improve production (engineers, scientists, bankers, accountants) and for those who had to ensure the ideological and social reproduction of society (teachers, doctors, social workers), but no one else.

There was a limited amount of upward social mobility for children who went to grammar schools, but this was still a minority experience. In the 1950s, only 3% of the population went to university. University participation grew, although participation in higher education in general remained relatively low — at around 15% — right up until the 1990s, when it began to dramatically rise and then skyrocket under New Labour, as Blair set a target of getting 50% of all pupils into higher education.

Today, there are over 2.5 million students in higher education. The university sector is now a bloated behemoth and a huge driver of the UK economy. Universities bring £95 billion a year to the economy and employ 815,000 people. In major cities, they are huge employers as well as landlords, owning large tracts of land and housing. The sector is beset with all the usual hazards of privatization: an increase in bureaucracy, hollowing out of job security, rising mental health problems among staff and students under ever more pressure to succeed, and more besides. Universities are neoliberal hell-holes for everyone involved in them.

Despite the "progressive case for fees" being written by those with a vested interest in the university-industrial complex (the more fees you charge, the more money the university has to expand access programmes, the more working-class kids can come), the original hopes of "widening access" did not last, and nor could they. In response to the introduction of fees, UCAS reported an immediate fall in the number of working-class university applications. In effect, the door for working-class social mobility slammed shut almost as soon as it had been opened. Today, very few working-class children actually go to university, and they certainly do not go to elite universities. Most working-class children continue to leave school at sixteen. Only approximately 10% of the most disadvantaged children go to university; according to UCAS's own latest reports, advantaged applicants are currently nearly fourteen times as likely to enter university as the most disadvantaged.

The reality is that university is still overwhelmingly for the better-off sections of society and only a very small percentage of the student population come from poorer backgrounds. Russell Group universities are dominated by the professional-managerial classes, while the deprived students who *do* manage to somehow access higher education, against all the odds, overwhelmingly tend to go to less prestigious universities (children who are not eligible for free school means are three times more likely to go to more prestigious universities than those who do), instead going to universities they are geographically close to, often not leaving home while they study for financial reasons. Theirs is a very different "student experience" to everyone else's.

However, not every one of the 2.5 million students are from the elite. The expansion of higher education has been significant primarily because it has seen the new petty bourgeoisie (as opposed to the working class) enter university in large numbers. It is new petty-bourgeois families, concerned with upward mobility, who will shell out for student fees, believing in social mobility (the other demographic that has benefited from the expansion of higher education are less academic rich kids, who will now always be able to find a place somewhere as long as they can pay).

For many new petty-bourgeois entrants to university, getting there is the culmination of the path you were placed on in school. As one of the "smart kids", this is where you belong, or have at least been encouraged to think you belong. Many probably couldn't wait to get away from their small town and their parochial friends and family, who they were taught to think they were so different to. Many of the skills that were developed in school — working hard to pass exams, for instance — now come into their own. While as a child their main way of marking themselves out from their peers was educational prowess, as they reach early adulthood in university, they can now add to this a plethora of aesthetic and cultural markers, as well as more subtle forms of distinction: changes to their personality — a new accent maybe; new tastes, new fashion; progressive politics. Moreover, *geographic* mobility — for years a corollary of social mobility for the professional-managerial classes — is a significant experience that marks this class out from the working class and old petty bourgeoisie, who are traditionally geographically fixed in place (the latter being tied to an area because of a business). The majority of graduates now move from towns to large or medium cities. This has myriad effects, but the fact you've "been away" to university and have experienced the wider world is important for everyday class distinction, allowing the new petty bourgeoisie to become more cosmopolitan and progressive — or at least *believe* that they are — than the people who stayed behind.

Moreover, it is also significant that universities are (and always have been) what Walter Benn Michaels calls the "research and development" arm of neoliberalism. Universities are the "top floor" where capitalist ideology is created and refined before being disseminated into the wider populace. The new cohort of new petty-bourgeois students, including many of those who end up on the left, spend at least three years being immersed in the new, strange culture, language and norms of the professional-managerial classes, which, as Catherine Liu notes, are hegemonic within the field of higher education. The aspirant new petty bourgeoisie may well absorb the culture of the professional-managerial classes and learn new ways to distance themselves from the working class, particularly on social attitudes. University thus finalizes the social and cultural split with the working class for the upwardly mobile new petty bourgeoisie.

But this is more than the moulding of habitus, more than looking and sounding a bit different and not being able to talk to your old school mates when you see them in the pub over Christmas. Like school, university inculcates ideological effects, which split off the new petty bourgeoisie from the working class: it deepens the "mental labour" divide. As with your GCSEs and A-Levels, getting a degree is not the point. The point is that entering university is designed to firmly place the upwardly mobile individual on one side of a dividing line and to inculcate certain ideological effects in them. Whilst at university, far more even than school, you learn to compete against others. You learn to become *even more* individualistic, how to sell yourself on the job/personality market. You accept the hierarchy; indeed, getting to university in the first place, getting your foot on the first rung on the ladder of success, proves to you that society *is* fair, that the ladder of social mobility *can* be climbed. You are now, in effect, "officially" better than the people and community you left behind. There are few students in higher education who do not internalize this logic of competition and the new role of education and their new place within society.

Yet the effects of university on the new petty bourgeoisie are not uniform. Just like our experiences of state school, the experience of university varies massively depending on what class you are from. For the rich, much like private school, university is either a finishing school or a place to while away three or four years; a place where you can have a laugh, have some banter, play rugby, shag, drink (now called "the student experience"). But don't work too hard, because after all, it's not important what degree you get — more than likely you will get a "Desmond"[10], because you are going to be fine anyway: you possess the right connections, you possess the right cultural capital, you don't feel out of place managing people, and even if you do bum around for a while, you're never going to be poor and you're never going to be homeless. You don't care about social mobility, you care about maintaining your position, and for the rich that's what education is all about. For the professional-managerial classes, it involves more studying and training, although they are very well-supported and prepared for their journey — everything is in their favour. You are not likely to mess things up from here.

For the new petty bourgeoisie, however, the experience is more complex. The *established* middle classes (the professional-managerial classes) are defined by *ease* — they are at home in these milieus and don't need to impress anyone. They know they are going to be OK whatever happens and don't have to worry about downward mobility. This is not the case for the new petty bourgeoisie: they can't afford to mess around in university, because the chances are that their parents are paying a lot for their degree; it feels like an enormous sacrifice, and they will be put under far more pressure than their peers. It has been well-researched by now that, despite being one of the "academic" kids in school who from a young age are encouraged to split themselves off from their peers and focus on getting to university, many students from the petty bourgeoisie or working class who do attend universities feel very rapidly like a fish out of water in the rarefied environments of the

10 A 2:2, i.e., a second-class degree.

university. For the first time in higher education, they feel the sting of being the lower class after a lifetime of being the higher class, at least relative to the working class. After a lifetime of realising they are not the working class and are fundamentally different to them, the new petty bourgeoisie at university frequently finds that they are also not part of the professional-managerial classes, and that they may in fact have more in common culturally and socially with the friends, family and communities that they were so desperate to leave all along.

While state schools are frantically focused on teaching to the test, passing exams and getting kids to university, so that they can move up the league tables, it means that many of the new petty bourgeoisie who go to university do not actually possess the same amounts of cultural capital as their new peers. The cruel irony is that, in school, they are *not* generally taught the soft skills that the bourgeoisie and the professional-managerial classes are cultivating at the same time — confidence, leadership, all the qualities that you need to move beyond a certain point on the ladder. The qualities they have been taught — deference, diligence, not making a big deal of yourself — can actually only get you so far.

One of the underexplored manifestations of the cumulative experience of social mobility, even when that is blocked, is on the habitus of the new petty bourgeoisie. In *The Uses of Literacy*, Richard Hoggart outlines how those working-class children who *did* manage to successfully negotiate the grammar school system and experience genuine social mobility then experienced significant dislocation and discomfort. In the name of social mobility, they were encouraged to leave their home and community, shed their old personality and accent and to don a new one, cultivate qualities and values alien to their background and family, only to end up in an alien middle-class milieu in which they resented everyone.

The notion of habitus is limited when it is constrained by the dominant notions of "working-class habitus" versus "middle-class habitus", and when it ignores the issues of social and geographical mobility and the complexity of class fractions. It is hard to explain the habitus of the new petty bourgeoisie if we are constrained by thinking in these black-and-white terms. As a result of their social mobility and interstitial position, they may develop — and this is certainly my own experience — a habitus that Bourdieu calls "cleft" or split. The school may socialize the new petty bourgeoisie enough to feel comfortable in university in some ways (e.g., the academic expectations, the rituals of exams and so on), while uncomfortable in others (e.g., other aspects of the university experience and the forms of cultural capital that are drilled into the bourgeois in *their* schools but not in state schools). Simultaneously, they may feel comfortable around the working class who they have grown up around (especially those with working-class family connections), but uncomfortable in others, as the experience of social mobility and the rejection of local, family norms and the immersion in new norms in school and university makes the habitus clash with their background even more acute. Hoggart argues that these poor, socially mobile individuals ended up fitting in nowhere: feeling not entirely at home in their professional milieu, nor in their home communities after a lifetime of consciously distancing oneself from the working class. The cleft habitus leads to a "hysteresis effect" — a persistent anxiety and unease about their social position and place in the world.

Thus, while university completes the socialization of the new petty bourgeoisie and its place on the side of mental labour, continuing the splitting-off from the working class that was begun in school, it may simultaneously reinforce its liminal position in society and its distance from the elite — in school, they learn they are not working class; at university, many (not all) may learn they are also not the bourgeoisie or the professional-managerial classes.

Conclusion

Education streams children towards different roles in the social division of production, guiding some students towards BTECs, vocational courses and apprenticeships, whilst guiding others to A-Levels and university. As capitalist society has evolved, so school now functions to socialise the unproductive, white-collar workers of the service economy. Thus, as well as being where the working class inadvertently "learn to labour", school is also now needed to teach the majority of children (i.e., those above the working class and below the minority that enter the professional-managerial classes) to sell, answer emails, do administrative work, use computers, to learn all the things you need to take up either a bureaucratic or bullshit job within society.

Formal education is disproportionately important for the new petty bourgeoisie compared to the bourgeoisie and the working class, precisely because they are focused on getting ahead in life so as not to fall back into the working class, and education is the elevator that can facilitate this social mobility. Education is where the new petty bourgeoisie is created and where it is split off from the working class ideologically, socially and culturally, and is very helpful for explaining the leap between objective classes or "class on paper" and class consciousness, i.e., how we come to understand our position in society. Therefore, Poulantzas argues, "differences within the education system and different attitudes towards the function of education are decisive class barriers".

School inculcates the petty-bourgeois attitudes of getting on and differentiating yourself as an individual. Moreover, over many years in the UK, education policy has grown the middle classes and, indeed, this has always been a conscious strategy of the ruling class, who throughout history have used the education system to "seal the "[ideological] alliance" between the middle classes and the bourgeoisie and to stabilize the capitalist system through the ideology of social mobility. This is how successive education policies, including the expansion of higher education, should best be understood. By splitting the subordinate classes, by splitting the new petty bourgeoisie off from the working class in school, by permitting them limited amounts of penetration into institutions designed for the upper classes (universities, the professions), inculcating in them an individualist desire for social mobility — which, of course, obscures any class consciousness as we are encouraged to think like individuals — these classes are prevented from identifying with the working class.

While the new petty bourgeoisie have far better odds of "reaching" the bourgeoisie or professional-managerial classes than the working class, their chances of actually doing this are still largely illusory. Social mobility — the ideology that keeps the middle classes onside — is undoubtedly, and by now quantifiably, a lie — indeed, the great lie of our time. While social mobility saw an absolute increase within the UK for people born between the Fifties and late Seventies (ironically probably helped by the grammar school system), it has objectively declined since then and downward mobility has increased. You are now more likely than ever to stay in the same class you were born in. There are not enough "knowledge economy" jobs for everyone, the white-collar world has been massively deskilled and the massification of higher education has seen a huge devaluation of degrees, as predicted by C. Wright Mills back in the 1950s.

There is now a huge oversupply of graduates, and graduates are increasingly experiencing unemployment (although nowhere near as high as non-graduates); across the UK, over a third of all graduates are now working in non-graduate roles. This is over four million people with blocked social mobility. Moreover, the movement into graduate roles from this cohort is small, meaning that more and more people are actually getting stuck in non-graduate roles for longer and longer, and for many people this will be forever.

The "graduate premium"[11] remains there for some, but it is also increasingly not for others. On the whole, the graduate premium is stalling: those who enter university rich will leave rich. Outside some professional roles, university — like grammar school — thus cements pre-existing class positions rather than actually improving social mobility.

It is increasingly likely that, of all the classes who go to university, it is the new petty bourgeoisie — those who start off closer to the proletariat, and who may have proletarian families and parents, maybe the first in the family to attend university — who are in fact less likely to prosper and will be proletarianized. Of course, this does not apply to the entire class, but for some members of the newest generations of the class, this will be their experience, and this is likely to increase as the economy tanks. With graduates now loaded up with debt and useless educational qualifications, they are shut out of the housing and job market.

---

11 The assumption that over a lifetime, graduates will earn more and have a more comfortable life than non-graduates.

Thus, educational capital can no longer generally provide social mobility; it can no longer be converted into riches or status. Instead, it increasingly remains solely a form of distinction for the new petty bourgeoisie. Like the old petty bourgeoisie, class distinction is of disproportionate importance to the new petty bourgeoisie, as they seek to define themselves against the working class. While the old petty bourgeoisie have traditionally relied on vulgar displays of wealth, of piety and morality or on conservative politics to accomplish this, the new petty bourgeoisie utilises educational qualifications, high-brow cultural capital and many of the behavioural norms and socially progressive views they will have absorbed from their time in the lair of the professional-managerial classes. Yes, you may work in a bar, but you have a degree; you like French films and niche hip-hop; you're an anti-racist and so on.

Ironically, because of their blocked and/or downward social mobility, the new petty bourgeoisie in the modern era experiences the same "status anxiety" that previously defined the traditional petty bourgeoisie. As Mills noted, by basing their prestige and status solely on educational qualifications and skills that are rapidly devalued and largely irrelevant in the world of work beyond school, they "open themselves to a precarious psychological life" that is redolent of old petty bourgeoisie's permanent state of anxiety. For the declassed graduate, "among those who are not allowed to use the educated skills they have acquired, boredom increases, hope for success collapses into disappointment, and the sacrifices that don't pay off lead to disillusionment".

Yet while status anxiety and the threat of downward social mobility — and the need to do anything to prevent this happening — drove the traditional petty bourgeoise to bitter, reactionary politics, the experience of blocked social mobility has radicalized large swathes of the new petty bourgeoisie to the left, or at least progressive politics generally speaking. It is unsurprising that Corbynism can trace its lineage back to the student protests of 2010, because that is perhaps when the reality of proletarianization and blocked social mobility began to dawn on many new members of this class. It may also be possible to conceptualize their turn to the "left" — which is, in reality, often simply support for socially liberal politics rather than redistributive ones — as part of the process of distinction, rather than as a genuine socialism or fundamental polarization towards the working class.

CHAPTER FIVE
HOUSING AND THE CLASS STRUCTURE:
A NATION OF LANDLORDS?

When I was sixteen, I was very briefly a labourer for my best mate's dad, a very successful local plasterer. Rob was about as culturally working class as it was possible to get. He was from the Valleys, left school at a young age and had been a plasterer ever since. He loved rugby, his family and singing along to Celine Dion in the work van. He also loved Margaret Thatcher. He worked his arse off and, like most people who have spent a lifetime on the tools, had utterly broken his body in the process. He proudly owned a couple of rental properties that he called his life insurance as, being self-employed, he had no pension.

The football club I am currently coaching and playing for is in one of the most deprived parts of Wales. One of our sponsors is a small property development company set up by one of the players: a steelworker who has taken to doing up and flipping houses with his friends from work. It's relatively easy for them as they are skilled workers. His property company's Instagram regularly flashes up with news of another house sold. If any of the other lads think about this at all, it is seen as a positive — well done son, making money, good on you.

Over the last decade, I have either rented or lived back with my parents, who have a big, "middle-class" house that they bought for £20k in 1980. I have rented off two landlords in particular who considered themselves to be very progressive. One was a staunch Plaid Cymru supporter, the other was a socialist and trade unionist. Both were "incidental" landlords who had "fallen into it" by obtaining a surplus house following a divorce or through inheritance. Neither saw any contradiction between their landlordism and their "radical" politics, and both went to great lengths to say how different and caring they were, to try and minimize the enormous power inequality that existed between us. However, this always resurfaced rapidly if I was a day late with rent, if I complained about having no hot water or if I wanted my deposit back.

I am now renting in Splott, a deeply working-class part of Cardiff, where nearly 40% of people live in poverty. My street is comprised mainly of elderly people who own their small terraced houses; many of them are ex-steelworkers who used to work in the local works which dominate the skyline. The area is also home to some of the most marginalized people in society: the formerly homeless now moved into the private rented sector; Romanian families; refugees crammed into houses of multiple occupancy (HMOs) by slum landlords, who are now valued partners of the Welsh government.

Although people used to joke that Splott is impervious to gentrification, it is slowly but surely changing. More and more young, hip people with posh accents are renting in the area — after all, there is nowhere else anyone can afford in the city. In 2002, a two-bed terrace in Splott cost under £100k. In 2022, the same house costs over £250k. Our street regularly gets flyered by landlords and letting agents, who have been driven into a feeding frenzy by Cardiff's skyrocketing prices. "Are you looking to sell or rent your house? Get in touch! Big money to be made!" I would regularly chat to my neighbours about the house price situation. They'd say how awful it was for young people these days, a palpable sympathy for us having to rent our shithole house.

When old people in our street die, their houses are often sold at auction or to "cash buyers only" — a codeword for property developers, as no normal person has the full price of a house lying round. Once the house is sold, teams of builders flood in, working morning till night, gutting the old houses and fitting them out in an aesthetic that would appeal to city-dwelling young professionals — wood flooring in the bedrooms, keep the original tiled floors, maybe some exposed brickwork, lots of plants — and then immediately placed back on the market at enormously inflated prices, to be bought by young, often Welsh-speaking professionals working in the bloated state bureaucracy, who then love to joke about living in Splott and how fab it is really!

I was briefly active in my local branch of ACORN, the tenant's union. They are very passionate about improving housing standards, taking on bad landlords using direct action, and are arguably one of the most effective "indie" unions in the UK. Their activism and passion has helped make housing a central pillar of modern left discourse. ACORN is full of very well-spoken and highly educated young people, many still in university and many others renting late into their twenties and early thirties, the overwhelming majority of whom were central to Corbyn's Labour movement.

In ACORN, people were very keen to branch out from their base in the student population and engage with real people "in our community". I thought how hard it was going to be to connect with communities and talk to them about the harms of gentrification when none of your members are actually from the community (or even south Wales, in many cases), and when you are yourself the unwitting faces of gentrification, even if you're not actually responsible for it.

Once, ACORN did an outreach session in Splott. Scores of doorknockers — this group were from Bristol — scoured the area, asking people what their main bugbears were. For most people, it was not rogue landlords, simply because they owned their house and had done so for years. The main problems were litter, drug-dealing and kids flying up and down the road on scramblers. Anti-social behaviour. Socially and culturally, there was a gulf between ACORN and the people of Splott, but also in terms of policy — the things that were important to us. It was an experience many Momentum members would have faced over and over again while campaigning for Labour in 2017 and 2019, and the problem of Corbynism in a nutshell.

This is not to pour scorn on ACORN — indeed, rarely have I encountered such passionate and well-meaning activists — but merely to show that nowhere is class more complicated than in housing.

***

Understanding the role of housing within the class structure is vital for understanding modern politics and society. It plays a particularly large role in demarcating the class boundaries of both fractions of the petty bourgeoisie.

Housing is not just shelter or a nice place to live. It governs where we live, how often we see our neighbours, what neighbours we have, i.e., the type of community we live in and how we relate to other people. Through rent or paying a mortgage or other bills, it mediates the nature of our relationship to capital (whether these be financial institutions or individual owners of capital, whether individual firms or people), the environment and the state (council tax; if we pay rent to the council or housing associations).

Housing's impact on social relations means that the structure of housing in society, by its very nature, has "ideological" effects, if we understand ideology in the

Althusserian sense as the representation of the individual's imaginary relationship to the world. Changes to the housing system change the way we live our lives and, hence, change our relationship to society and the way we think about the world.

Housing has become central to the politics of the left wing of the Labour Party (and indeed, the wider left more generally) because housing is now the main concern of its main social base, the element of the new petty bourgeoisie (socially mobile graduates renting in cities) who have been locked out of the housing market. The battle between the two main social bases of the Labour Party — the new petty bourgeoisie and the professional-managerial classes — is often mediated by housing and housing policy. While Corbyn's policies were driven by the new petty bourgeoisie, the party's recapture by the professional-managerial classes has been reflected in a housing policy that is again pro-landlord, pro-development and happy to throw renters under the bus, simply because these are not the people that Starmer's Labour Party is pitching to.

Perhaps more than any other issue, housing is forcing the left into structural explanations for political behaviour, and there have recently been a glut of thoughtful articles on the relationship between housing and Tory hegemony. The link between housing and politics has also been picked up by some of the more sociologically inclined British journalists. Among the small cohort who are at last attempting to move beyond the "red wall", "redneck" cultural discourse as a way of explaining Tory dominance, a few are beginning to explore the link between housing — particularly home ownership — and political behaviour.

In the *New Statesman*, George Eaton argued that home ownership correlates with Tory dominance:

In 2019, 57 per cent of owner-occupiers and 43 per cent

of mortgage-holders voted Tory (against just 22 per cent and 33 per cent for Labour). Of the 365 seats won by the Conservatives, 315 have home ownership levels above the UK average of 64 per cent, compared with just 53 of the 202 won by Labour.

In the United States too, Trump's support was also increasingly linked to home ownership. Political scientists, in their own inimitable way, are also beginning to study the correlation between home ownership and political behaviour. The logic is fairly sound on the face of things: more home owners vote Conservative, ergo home ownership makes you conservative (and therefore not owning a house is likely to mean that you vote Labour).

It is a welcome change that people on the left have begun to explore political shifts in a more thoughtful way — as structural, and about class and assets and how material conditions have ideological effects — rather than the relentless hopelessness of "rainy fascist island" or calling everyone racist or reactionary. However, in housing in particular, the issue of class is increasingly confused. For one, housing is where the inane "socialism of fools" of intergenerational conflict is most often invoked. The discourse of "generation rent" divides the UK neatly into young (left-leaning) people, who have to rent, and older, (implicitly conservative) people, who were lucky enough to live under Keynesian conditions during the post-war boom (and, because of its after-effects, were able to buy their house). Increasingly on "left twitter" — inasmuch as this can be taken as a gauge of debate on the left — one frequently witnesses intergenerational resentment, which effaces proper class analysis. Thus, "Boomers" are privileged; older people own their houses and love rising house prices; they hate us; my parents had it so easy because they could buy their house for peanuts whereas I'm stuck renting; my life is awful, etc.

To many on the left, housing tenure is now seen as a straightforward class divide *in itself*. In the *Guardian*, for example, Owen Hatherley, perhaps the best writer on housing in the UK, writes that "housing is England's greatest divide". Here, home ownership is a class divide, or a proxy for class, that is more important than the work you do, the education you have and so on. Home ownership trumps all other divides.

This assumption is now widespread and has even been used to gloss over the glaring regional disparities in the UK — actually, London cannot have it better than northern areas, because working-class areas in the north have higher home ownership per capital than in London; ergo, these people have better lives, and so regional disparities in infrastructure can't be bad because if you own your own house, your life is sorted. The horror of renting and the jarring experience of downward social mobility is all-consuming and has given the left tunnel vision, a blinkered view of society in which it feels uniquely hard done by, and in which anyone who owns their own home must be doing great.

Housing and the Class Structure Throughout History

Housing has always been central to class struggle and to a class-divided society. The history of housing is complex, but to simplify a complex story, during the early part of the Industrial Revolution the working class lived in squalid conditions. The new workers flooded into the cities where housing was scarce, leading to slum conditions with families crammed into damp, overcrowded tenements with inadequate sanitation, which led to high levels of disease and death.

In certain places workers lived in accommodation provided by paternalistic owners of whatever industry they worked in ("company towns" like Bourneville in the UK or Pullman in the US), and small-scale charitable organizations provided small-scale accommodation. However, the primary mode of housing for the new proletariat was overwhelmingly privately rented; it was extremely rare for a worker — even a skilled worker — to own their own home.

During this period, housing separated the subordinate classes in a number of key ways. Firstly, as Foster has outlined, many of the petty bourgeoisie not only tended to own their own houses, but also consciously aimed to live away from the working classes, in the nicer parts of towns and cities, if at all possible. Physically distancing oneself from the working classes was central to the early boundaries between the petty bourgeoisie and the proletariat, and to the ambitions of social mobility that define the petty-bourgeois condition.

But separation between the proletariat and the petty bourgeoisie was not just a case of physical distance and a difference in tenure. Although this was the first era of large-scale industrial capitalism, worker accommodation was in fact *not* owned by the large capitalist, but largely (if not overwhelmingly) owned and operated by the petty bourgeoisie — the shopkeeper and small tradesman only one step above the worker. Geoffrey Crossick notes that this was particularly the case in slum housing, "in which large capital had little interest"; thus, "the typical owner of working-class housing in European cities throughout the nineteenth century was a small businessman". In town after town across Europe, it was the small tradesman and shopkeeper that owned (and often built) working-class housing and who managed slums. A report to the Royal Commission in Salisbury stated that landlords of worker properties were "generally persons of small capital, hard-hearted, and destitute of feeling towards the tenants".

Then as now, small businessmen saw housing as a precious investment, central to social mobility and separating themselves from the class immediately beneath them. However, their lack of significant, genuine wealth also meant petty-bourgeois landlords were unwilling or unable to shell out in order to maintain the properties that they managed, leading to terrible conditions for their working-class tenants and huge tensions between the classes; petty landlordism brought the petty bourgeoisie into direct antagonism with the class immediately below them.

However, much like the expansion of education, capitalists soon began to take an interest in worker housing, largely because overcrowded slum conditions were driving public health crises, such as cholera epidemics, and leading to a sick workforce. Improvements in housing stock were seen as essential to improving public health — a link that has largely disappeared today — and hence healthy workers and reproducing capitalism. Moreover, the emerging managerial classes needed somewhere to live and wanted to become homeowners. Thus, big capital began to muscle in on housebuilding, and in time housing began to better respond to need and became rationalized/industrialized. The increase in supply was politically opposed by many of the petty-bourgeois small tradesmen who were also landlords. As homeowners, they wanted to preserve their status, and as small housebuilders and landlords, they also bitterly opposed the introduction of new bureaucracy regarding building standards. However, they lost out, and the 1878 Building Act introduced minimum standards for housing construction, leading to significant improvements in sewerage systems, which greatly improved public health.

The interwar period again saw a huge increase in building and a huge increase in owner-occupation. Land and building costs had fallen, and building houses had always been vital to economic stabilization. Demand was driven by the growth of the new white-collar groups of clerks, the first generation of the new petty bourgeoisie, as well as the popular demand for "homes for heroes" following the First World War. Although now it seems like an impossible dream, during the First World War, when housing demand still outstripped supply, rent controls were introduced in order to stop landlord profiteering. This dramatically disincentivised petty landlordism and, as a consequence, private renting went into rapid decline. As Mike Savage illustrates, the interwar period saw private renting being supplanted as the dominant tenure by social renting and owner occupation: on top of a huge increase in privately built homes, the state built millions of council houses via local authorities creating the new tenure of social renting. Between 1920 to 1940, over 4.6 million houses were built, of which 1.2 million were council-owned.

Before 1914, only around 10% of the British population owned their house. By the late 1930s, however, it had risen to 33%. Tenure was split along class lines, with the majority of professionals, such as teachers, doctors and civil servants becoming homeowners during this period. They were soon joined by many of the new petty bourgeoisie of technicians, foremen and clerks, because their income at this stage was still generally more than skilled manual workers. Building societies, largely manned by the petty bourgeoisie, were crucial in enabling the lower middle classes to obtain sufficient credit to buy their own houses. Home ownership was likely to have still been a significant financial burden for the new petty bourgeoisie, yet it was a core aspiration and status symbol and therefore central to the formation and boundaries of this class, who saw owner occupation as a reinforcement of their class position. The Thirties witnessed the creation of the suburbs, as housebuilding began to expand into areas outside the centre of cities and towns, further aided by slum clearances undertaken after the 1930 Housing Act. This, in turn, increased the spatial segregation of communities along class lines, with the new petty bourgeoisie favouring smaller houses for their smaller families in the suburbs.

Following the Second World War, there was famously a huge expansion in council house building, with over one million council houses being built between 1945 and 1955. Jim Kemeny argued that housing was the "shaky pillar" that supported the welfare state and its underlying ideological values. Social renting expanded significantly during this period, and by 1979, 32% of all homes (6.5 million) were social rents. The new council tenants benefited from security of tenure and below-market rents. Private renting, which was as high as 76% immediately after the war, declined dramatically. Housing construction and quality also improved rapidly, with the majority of new houses having insulation, indoor baths, toilets and showers. Slum conditions were virtually eliminated. Moreover, the UK's lack of supply was eradicated. Although it is hard to believe now, the scale of the house-building programme meant that the UK achieved a housing *surplus* by the 1970s, with the bulk being built before 1971, with council housing — built by Tory governments as well as Labour — comprising a sizeable chunk of this supply.

While left hagiographies of housing and the welfare state are understandably fixated on the achievement of the mass expansion of council housing and the positive experiences of social renting, it is less well-known that working-class owner-occupation also steadily increased during the post-war period. The then Minister for Health, Nye Bevan, had essentially eliminated the construction of new houses for owner-occupation, because he believed that speculative building for private ownership "was not a plannable instrument", and hence contradicted the socialist view of housing, which was to fulfil a need. But this did not end owner-occupation, as people now simply bought existing houses second-hand. Harold Carter notes that, as landlordism was disincentivised by rent control and land nationalization, former privately rented housing stock was sold by landlords on a huge scale to working-class owner-occupiers. Indeed, the sales of these former rented homes — three million of them — were double the eventual sales of council houses under right-to-buy.

Although Bevan himself was opposed to the privatization of housing, as the welfare state wore on, the Labour Party and Labour governments increasingly committed to increasing owner-occupation as they came to accept Tory arguments on the necessity of a "mixed" housing market. At a local level, many Labour councils increasingly wanted to appeal to the increasingly affluent sections of the skilled working class and the petty bourgeoisie proper, and to this end often offered loans to people to let them purchase these older former private rented sector houses when building societies would not. In 1964, the Labour government introduced the option mortgage scheme as a way of growing working-class owner-occupation.

By 1960, 42% of housing was already owner-occupied, and this was largely driven by private sales of existing stock rather than from new building. However, private housebuilding for owner-occupation continued to increase after the Sixties, and between 1960-1975, 2.6 million private new-builds were completed. As the welfare state wore on and boomed, the working class continued to prosper and working-class owner-occupation continued to expand.

By the 1960s, council houses were already increasingly oversubscribed and now had a waiting list, and so local authorities decided that they would be reserved primarily for those on low incomes. The private rented sector was not an option; thus, for skilled manual workers and the petty bourgeoisie alike, owning one's home was "the only game in town". By the early 1970s, owner-occupation stood at 50% (it had been 29% in 1950). Over half of the new white-collar intermediate classes owned their home, and nearly half of all skilled workers.

Significant changes began to occur in the 1970s. The world economic crisis meant that fewer council houses were being built. The existing stock was therefore increasingly reserved solely for the most marginal, in-need groups in society. In terms of tenure and the class structure, for decades after the Second World War, council housing and social renting was in fact widely regarded as the preserve of the skilled or "respectable" working class, with the petty bourgeoisie being consolidated in the suburbs as homeowners. However, in the 1960s, the Tories mounted a concerted campaign against those "undeserving" and "affluent" working-class people who still rented council houses, claiming that these workers were too rich to live in social housing and were, in effect, receiving subsidized housing and "bed-blocking" the council stock. Much like the attacks on comprehensive schools, Labour began to accept this narrative rather than challenge it, and council rents were subsequently raised to attempt to remove these "limpets" by forcing them to give up their council properties and move into owner-occupation, thereby freeing up council housing stock.

Because of the deliberate restriction of council stock and the subsequent prioritization of those in absolute priority need, council housing, formerly the preserve of the "respectable" working class, was increasingly demonized as the lair of the *lumpenproletariat*. Discursively, the same right-wing media that had earlier demonised "limpets" now spun a new narrative of an "underclass", which seeped into the mainstream imagination. In turn, council housing — which was now increasingly of the high-rise variety — stopped being as sought after by the skilled and respectable working class, its previous tenants. Aled Davies notes that, "culturally, the idea of an archetypal council house and tenant shifted from high-quality and 'respectable', to low-quality and poor". After a period of relative equality in housing, it now started to re-emerge as the mediator of class as the working class began to get poorer. Class divides opened up *spatially*, with certain areas being demonized as crime-ridden ghettoes. Housing became central to the everyday process of class distinction between the working class and middle class, but also mediated divides between the "rough" (i.e., unskilled) working class and the respectable working class.

Right-to-Buy

During the 1960s, the concept of right-to-buy was confined to a pet project of a small number of ultra-right-wing neoliberals within the Tory Party.[12] The Tories as a whole had little interest or appetite in the idea. Enoch Powell, for example, rejected the concept of right-to-buy, and before it was implemented, Thatcher herself privately worried that it might backfire if council house sales to aspirational working-class people affected property values of traditional Tory voters (i.e., it could potentially have split the new

---

12 The Monday Club, a right-wing group borne out of distaste for the moderation of the Macmillan government, published a paper in 1966 arguing that, by compelling councils to sell their housing stock, the Conservatives could destroy socialism in the UK.

and old Tory base). Yet, in the 1960s, Tory councils began to implement pilot schemes that sold council houses to their tenants, which proved popular. Gradually, and with ceaseless lobbying, like so many other formerly marginal ideas within the Tory Party, the issue became mainstream and politicised. The "freedom" of being an owner-occupier and the "aspiration" to become one gradually replaced the concept of housing as a basic human need, and as ever, social mobility was key to sowing interest in the concept of right-to-buy.

While right-to-buy is often talked about as a radical, society-altering policy that just suddenly appeared overnight, the reality is that the steady rise in owner-occupation under successive Labour governments meant that by the time the debate about right-to-buy had entered the mainstream, it was pushing against an open door. In other words, the structural foundations of public support for right-to-buy predated Thatcher by some way. Owner-occupation was already extremely popular (if not totally dominant) as a tenure amongst the working class by the time it was introduced. Due to rent raises in the council sector, initiated by Labour in order to free up council housing, owner-occupation was in fact cheaper in many cases than council rents (which, as Davies notes, had risen by 90% — and outstripped wage increases — in order to subsidise new council builds); and more council housing was not being built so the majority of the working class could not access it anyway. The working class and petty bourgeoisie still wanted to own their own home, but there was no supply and social renting had been squeezed. So, when right-to-buy was finally implemented on a mass scale by the Tories in 1981, it was inevitably extremely popular and accounted for a huge increase in owner-occupation during this era, creating a new generation of homeowners from across the working class and the petty bourgeoisie.

Today, a popular interpretation of right-to-buy among the left is that those who aspired to be owner-occupiers were innately conservative Thatcherite social climbers. An alternative, better interpretation is put forward by Harold Carter, who argues that right-to-buy instinctively appealed to the type of groups who had become owner-occupiers between 1945 and the 1970s through buying private rented sector stock: "the skilled, better paid, upper working-class families that had for so long been the life and soul of local Labour Parties", overwhelmingly drawn from the first wave of social renters rather than the "rough" (i.e., unskilled) working class who had recently been moved into council housing following slum clearances. So rather than being down to grasping individuals, structural forces like the limited supply of socially rented housing and the demonization of council housing simply made owner-occupation the most attractive and secure option to many people who would have hitherto been perfectly happy living in a council house, but for whom this option was no longer a viable option.

So popular was right-to-buy that it became impossible for Labour to oppose it, and by 1985 the Labour Party formally dropped its opposition to the policy. Yet although right-to-buy is understandably focused on, there were other hugely significant policy developments during Thatcher's period that have also greatly influenced the contemporary housing system and how we live in the UK today. The 1988 Housing Act, just like the Education Act of the same year, further introduced the logic of neoliberalism into the housing market in a number of ways. First, it restricted the ability of local authorities to build new council housing, instead transferring responsibility for social housing to newly created "housing associations", which were handed new abilities to seek private finance for homebuilding, giving them a huge advantage over local authorities. In turn, local authorities began to transfer their council house stock *en masse* to these new housing associations as a cost-saving measure. Before the Act, housing associations had been minor players in housing, but now almost overnight became responsible for huge swathes of social housing (or more accurately, owning all the houses but with none of the attendant responsibilities). Rents were raised and lifetime tenancies were ended. The Act essentially privatized the provision of council housing and ended it as a feasible option for the majority of people.

Next, Thatcher aimed to grow the private rented sector — people who couldn't get the vanishing council houses had to go somewhere — and the Act immediately shifted the balance of power in this sector away from tenants and towards landlords. Prior to the Act, tenancy in the private rented sector had been relatively secure, with tenancies able to be passed between generations. The Act changed all this and allowed landlords to repossess their houses. It also introduced short-hold (six-month) tenancies, which destroyed any form of long-term stability that tenants previously enjoyed. Finally, rent controls that had stabilized prices in the sector for so long were removed, meaning that landlords could now price gouge.

On top of right-to-buy, these policies entirely changed the face of housing tenure in the UK. In one fell swoop, it decimated social renting (i.e., council housing rented from local authorities) through privatisation. The private rented sector, which had fallen dramatically since the end of the First World War until it was a tiny percentage of provision up until the early Eighties, began to level off and then gradually start to grow. Alongside increasing owner-occupation through right-to-buy, housebuilding for owner-occupation by private developers soared. Unsurprisingly, owner-occupation itself skyrocketed.

Major and Blairism's Impact on Housing and the Class Structure

Just like the education system, the Major government's housing policies did not depart in any real way from those of his predecessor: home ownership was entrenched across society as a positive thing (and one which seemed to benefit the Conservatives by catering to their petty-bourgeois base). Right-to-buy trundled along, albeit not at the same pace as under Thatcher. Local authority spending on housing was halved and the transfer of council housing stock to housing associations was expanded. Inner cities, formerly associated with crime and decay, began to be lined up as arenas for "regeneration" (i.e., gentrification). However, the biggest single policy intervention of Major's tenure was the introduction of new "buy-to-let" mortgages in 1996. This new scheme turbo-charged the private rented sector and allowed larger capital to get involved. Perhaps more perniciously, though, it further cemented in the popular imagination that housing was a market to be played by more and more people — the policy essentially encouraged small-scale landlordism.

New Labour entered government in 1997 on a crest of huge optimism. However, as in education, Blair's housing policies were a continuation of Thatcher's paradigm shift. In its first term, Labour spent less than the Tories on social housing: less, in fact, than in any of the previous eighteen years of Tory rule. Right-to-buy increased to levels higher than under the Major government, housing stock transfers from local authorities to housing associations were continued — 80% of all stock transfers have occurred since 1997.

As Owen Hatherley argues in *The New Ruins of Great Britain*, certain housing policies of the New Labour era also left a legacy in their own right, particularly in terms of our cityscape and the class divides within it. Of particular significance during the New Labour period was the ramping up of gentrification of inner-city areas under the guise of "urban renaissance", a policy and interest that remains central to many Labour councils across the UK. As Claire Colomb notes, central to this was the introduction of "mixed development", a policy which was marketed as a progressive "attack on social segregation by class via housing, the decades-old tradition of keeping social and private housing apart". This would be done by changing planning laws to allow owner-occupiers in socially rented estates, and by demanding that new-build private estates included some "social housing" (allowing people to buy flats outright in council estates and to have an element of social housing in new-build estates).

Although Blair typically obscured this by effective use of social justice language of "local communities", in reality this was a plan to "civilize" inner-city sink estates by filling them with owner-occupiers, who it was hoped could be good "role models" for the feckless poor. As Neil Smith argued at the time: "the class nature of the process... is assiduously hidden in the verbiage of the British Labour government". In practice, "mixed tenure" was a one-way street that involved middle-class professionals — now priced out of the desirable areas they *actually* wanted to live in — buying flats in poor estates (ideally next to Tube stops), rather than poor people moving into more affluent areas. This created visible class divides within formerly homogenous working-class estates — particularly noticeable in London today — as former "rough" estates are now dominated by young professional homeowners. Empirical research suggested that there was barely any interaction between the newcomers and the old residents, who existed together like oil and water.

Class divides had previously been glaring between different places and neighbourhoods. New Labour's policies intensified the role of housing in social class divides *within* the same formerly working-class neighbourhoods, not just in terms of aesthetics and the process of class distinction between the gentrifiers and working-class residents, but in terms of actual conflict over the use of urban space, such as the changing of communal areas into things that would service the new residents rather than the old community. Just like all forms of privatization, gentrification is sold as a rescue mission and compared positively with the crime and poverty that preceded it (although, as Samuel Stein argues, areas will often be consciously neglected as a deliberate precursor to gentrification as a way of justifying new "investment"). Yet we all know by now that, while it is nice to finally have your bins collected on time and to have a new coffee shop to go to, in reality this is a zero-sum game. The reorientation of an area towards the needs of the newcomers inevitably means that old institutions that facilitated social capital among the old working-class community (pubs, cafes, markets) get displaced by the institutions of the incoming richer folk who have different, more civilised tastes. "Social mixing", in reality, meant the changing of class dynamics in areas, largely achieved through housing policy. It led to the displacement of older, working-class residents and the increasing domination of inner-city areas by the professional-managerial classes, all facilitated by the Labour government.

Of course, the generation of young professionals who benefited from these policies in the cities also just happened to be the electoral base of New Labour. During the Blair era, this class — which had to move to the cities for work in the industries that were concentrated there — took them over.

While the new middle classes benefited, the working class was marginalized and ghettoized as the city was magnified as a site of class struggle.

Over the last decade of austerity since the Tory coalition government, the marketization of housing has deepened. Housing benefit was cut to sub-cost levels, causing homelessness to soar. In 2013, George Osborne announced help-to-buy, a loan scheme designed to help people get on the housing ladder, but which in practice acted as a pyramid scheme that sent profits for big housebuilders skyrocketing.

And yet, home ownership is falling, or at least seems to have levelled off, due to a deliberate suppression of supply but also, unsurprisingly, falling wages. Owner-occupation today is at 62.7%, only 7% more than when Thatcher entered office, having peaked at 70% in 2002 during the Blair years. Home*building* is also at a record low, under half of what it was in the 1960s. The new houses that are being built are by large house builders in new-build estates and are often heavily subsidised by schemes like help-to-buy.

Because of the deliberate suppression of supply, house prices are now through the roof and have risen way beyond wage inflation. Having largely given up on the idea of building council housing, councils now attempt to meet their meagre obligations to build social housing through things like Section 106 Agreements, which ask big builders to ensure that a percentage of new builds are dedicated to social housing (everyone wins!). In reality, developers frequently circumnavigate their obligations to build social housing and simply give councils a small bribe to *not* build social housing (social tenants on the estate would cause house prices to fall). Thus, these new-build estates remain dominated by owner-occupiers. Barely any social housing is being built now, and that which is, is almost always done by housing associations rather than by local authorities. Housing associations have since raised social rents to pay for new social housing. Private renting now is over 20% of the market and growing, more than social renting, and is being actively encouraged by governments across the UK. In 2014, almost two hundred thousand buy-to-let mortgages were approved, and as home ownership has stalled, this will likely only get higher. Far from the "mixed" situation of "complementarity" between social renting and owner-occupation that was envisioned when Labour embraced owner-occupation in the 1950s and 1960s, the situation now is one of owner-occupation for the majority, and then the rest split between social renting from housing associations and the private rented sector.

Housing and the Class Structure: "Coming to Terms with Owner Occupation"

The way we live now is extremely different to how it was fifty years ago. The rapid transformation in housing tenure is extremely significant for the class structure and ideology of society and how we understand class itself. Yet, as the vignette at the start of this chapter makes clear, the relationship between housing and class is far from straightforward, and has in many ways played a very complex role *vis à vis* social class in a way socialists have struggled to get to grips with.

The hard right of the Tory Party certainly firmly believed that right-to-buy and home ownership (creating "a property-owning democracy") was key to killing off socialism by inculcating individualism. They had made no secret that they believed that increasing home ownership would not just ideologically prove to be anathema to collectivism, but also that it would essentially create a new base of working-class Tory voters that were motivated not by the deference that had previously characterized working-class Tories, but by ruthless aspiration and social mobility — i.e., it was a policy that would spread the historic values and ideology of the petty bourgeoisie into the wider population beyond the class itself. It was widely interpreted that buying your council house magically turned people Tory, and Thatcher herself apparently believed that it was this policy specifically that won her marginal constituencies.

The situation of mass working-class owner-occupation that confronted the left in the Eighties would have been utterly unthinkable to previous generations. It was a historical anomaly that was simply unprecedented, and which turned many leftist assumptions about the working class on their head. The left were simply unable to come to terms with its popularity. Presumably working backwards from the problem in front of their eyes — i.e., we now have mass owner-occupation and also Tory hegemony, therefore these must be linked — they by and large came to the same conclusions as the Tories: home ownership made working-class people Tory.

This was in effect a return to the underlying assumptions of the thesis of "embourgeoisement" that had emerged among panicked left intellectuals during the welfare state period — the idea that as workers became increasingly affluent, they would inexorably adopt and internalize "bourgeois" values and ideology, and would hence abandon Labour as more of them bought their own home and moved to the suburbs. Yet John Goldthorpe et al's famous "affluent worker study" in the late Sixties — conducted to test the embourgeoisement thesis — concluded that, despite now owning and living in nice new houses amongst the middle classes and petty bourgeoisie, the affluent workers remained avowedly proletarian in politics and culture. They still worked in difficult, monotonous manufacturing jobs which, while comparatively well paid, nonetheless left them under no illusions as to their class status. They socialised together rather than with their affluent neighbours, remained in trade unions and still voted Labour. In other words, affluence — which led to owner-occupation — had no bearing on the class structure or the subjective class of the workers. The workers knew what side they were on because of what job they did, and owning a house and earning more money didn't change this, just as earning less money does not mean that the struggling elements of the professional-managerial classes and new petty bourgeoisie become proletarian.

The return to the assumptions regarding embourgeoisement therefore raised many uncomfortable questions. What was it about owning your own house that made you more likely to be Tory? If owner-occupation was "Tory", why had it only become conservative *now*, given that, as we have seen, owner-occupation was dominant among the skilled working class since the Second World War; that increasing owner-occupation was also a Labour policy and working-class owner-occupiers had historically been a pillar of labourism in the UK?

These ambiguities are discernible in the recent forays into the relationship between housing, class and politics on the British left. In *Tribune*, housing activist Nick Bano bemoaned Labour's new emphasis on displacing the Tories as the party of homeowners. Echoing the sociologists of the Eighties, Bano was "uncomfortable" with the new focus on owner-occupation, arguing that home ownership was an innately conservatizing force in society and a tool used to encourage individualism and, hence, undermine socialism. But while Bano's piece implies that owner-occupation is innately conservative, he is then at pains to say that homeowners are not natural Tories. George Eaton's aforementioned piece in the *New Statesman* says home ownership produces conservative ideology, but then notes confusingly that Liverpool and South Wales, which have very high rates of working-class home ownership, are solidly Labour.

One of the ways of squaring the circle and avoiding the uncomfortable splits within the working class caused by working-class owner-occupation was simply to argue that home ownership made the working class petty bourgeois. Owner-occupation, therefore, did not just destroy revolutionary consciousness, it also, in effect, functioned to *change the class* of the working-class owner-occupier, shading them into the petty bourgeoisie.

In another *Guardian* article — one of the few mainstream articles to ever mention the petty bourgeoisie in the wild — Owen Hatherley returns to this approach, and argues that owner-occupation is mainly concentrated amongst the petty bourgeoisie, and it is *they*, not the working class, who, through the ideology of home ownership come to prop up the status quo politically:

> It's... not difficult to work out exactly whose interests the housing crisis serves. The capitalist class does very well out of it, which is why names like McAlpine, Wimpey and Barratt turn up so often among Conservative donors; but more interestingly, it also buys consent from a large proportion of the "petit bourgeoisie" who have an interest in the value of their only asset, their only piece of property — their house — getting higher and higher, however much that might be against their interest in other respects.
>
> The housing crisis has the benefit of dispossessing a propertyless proletariat, by forcing them to move from potentially lucrative housing, of giving the property-owning petit bourgeoisie just enough to buy their allegiance, and of funnelling enormous quantities of money into the pockets of capitalists.

The historical reality of working-class owner-occupation in the UK, and the split within the working class created by owner-occupation, is here skirted over. As in previous eras, the implication is that home owners cannot be working class, because owner-occupation is incompatible with being working class, as the working class are, by nature, those who own no property. Home ownership must therefore concentrated in the petty bourgeoisie, and owner-occupation *makes you* petty bourgeois.

Home Ownership Is Not the Biggest Divide in Society

Of particular interest in the 1980s were those theories that claimed that the structural changes to housing were so significant that housing tenure now constituted *a class divide in itself*, and that "*housing classes*" were a better way of describing society than classes formed in work. Sociologists like Peter Saunders argued that class was no longer constituted by the bourgeoisie, the petty bourgeoisie and the proletariat, but instead by different housing classes of landlords, renters, social renters, owner-occupiers and so on.

This is implicit in many of the new left claims that housing is now the primary divide in society — that society is divided between helpless renters (which includes the left) and owner-occupiers. It is easy to see the appeal and logic of these arguments. Housing clearly does bring different tenures and groups into competition — for example, those who make money off house prices rising are in direct antagonism with first-time buyers, who now have to save even more for a first home, and with those forced to rent; homeowners associations frequently oppose the expansion of social housing, fearing that it may cause their property values to fall. Gentrification also clearly demonstrates the competition between different classes mediated by housing. Representatives of the petty bourgeoisie have and continue to defend small property interests on town councils everywhere.

Saunders' hypothesis — that housing ownership constituted "a real material change in the basis of class relations" — has been returned to by Martijn Konings et al.'s recent work on the "asset economy", which argues that, given the constant increase in the price of housing over and above inflation and wages, the ownership of assets is now the major determinant of class position. Yet while Saunders' work on the changing class structure involved the mass *expansion* or "democratization" of home ownership, Konings' work focuses on the subsequent "*locking*" of the housing market with the ostensible end of the expansion of owner-occupation. As Konings puts it:

> we have moved then from a brief period of relative wealth democratization (with some sectors of the former working class making real class shifts), to a period of lock in, where social mobility is freezing and the bridge between home owners and renters is closing.

As this gap has closed, and home ownership has become impossible in the way it once was for the majority of people, Konings et al. argue that what matters now in the modern class structure is family asset ownership. Those who previously managed to somehow get a house and their offspring now constitute one group, whilst other families who own no assets are on the other side of the divide. Ownership of housing trumps everything else, including other previous determinants or class signifiers, because it begets access to other "assets" such as education: if you own a house, it becomes easier to afford things like higher education, as parents with houses can act as guarantors for students who want to rent a house, allow children to stay at home if needs be and so on. Thus, for Konings, two people doing the same job would be of a different class if one owned a house, or even if one's family owned a house and one didn't. He writes:

> the escalation of house prices in major cities around the world has carved deep chasms of inequality between classes of people who earn the same wages but are differentiated by their status as homeowners or renters. Where once we might have placed these people in the same class based on the kind of work they did, today it is obvious that these people belong to different echelons of the social scale. In such an environment, class can no longer realistically be identified as a simple function of wages from labour (working, middle and upper class) or professional status (blue collar or white collar) and must instead be rethought in terms of asset ownership.

These arguments are, on the surface, very compelling. Yet the idea that assets and home ownership are a *determinant* of class, which are now more important than everything else, is an unhelpful simplification of the relationship between housing and class, which obscures more than it illuminates.

In response to Saunders, sociologists like Mike Savage, Simon Clarke and Norman Ginsberg put forward a series of counter-arguments against the idea of housing tenure as a class divide, which remain highly relevant today. Primarily, these critiques centre on the problems of eliding the glaring class divides within the categories of owner-occupiers and renters, and hence, in grouping very different groups of people together purely on the basis of home ownership.

For Savage — whilst in theory, of course, there is potential for wealth to be made by anyone who owns their own house — it is unclear if, in practice, all homeowners accrue wealth from their homes, or even want to. In practice, there are huge divides within the category of "owner-occupiers" in terms of house quality, type of mortgage, rate of interest, wages and also — to take Saunders' and Konings' main criteria — on the potential for wealth to be extracted from housing when income from wages is either stagnant or in decline. Evidently, it is generally better to own a house than to not, but surely it is not controversial to say not all experiences of owner-occupation are the same — the most obvious example in recent memory being the cohort of largely working-class people who were sold dud mortgages way beyond anything they could afford, who got destroyed by the 2008 crash, all of whom were, of course, "home owners".

This is not to say that working-class owner-occupiers do not or cannot extract wealth from their houses: anyone can click on the listing history of a small flat on Rightmove or Zoopla and see that the price of some flats have sometimes gone up by £100k in a small amount of time. Lucky bastards, I often think. Then, once you look at the photos more closely, very often the photos in the listings are of a dead old person's house, still adorned with photographs of their children and grandchildren, with handrails and other modifications in the bathrooms. This leads to another key point — the majority of the people ("boomers") who have been "privileged" enough to have a house that has gone up in value are not, in fact, property speculators who have realized profit in their lifetime, but simply working-class people who bought a house when they could afford it over fifty years ago, when worker power was at an all-time high, and then have done nothing more than live in it for their whole life. The majority of working-class people are not mobile; they tend to live in one family home for life and do not seek to flip their houses in the housing market as Konings implies. "Assets" may devalue, or become worthless, as people who bought flats with shoddy cladding have found out; and similarly, for many people houses are money holes that take up most of their money and time.

In contrast, the professional-managerial classes, who are geographically mobile in order to be upwardly socially mobile, *do* tend to make significant profit from housing, simply because they tend to move around a lot more as part of their professional careers and therefore have the opportunity to flip their houses more frequently. Savage's empirical research in Bristol demonstrated that only the professional-managerial classes regularly moved house and saw housing as a way to make extra money. Thus, property ownership may undoubtedly be a significant source of wealth above and beyond wages, but not for all classes or owners equally. Next, as Savage points out, profits realized through real estate assets are spatially contingent. Houses in desirable areas are the ones that increase in price the most. While almost all house prices increase in value, those in metropolitan areas will have seen the biggest rises, whereas places like the East Midlands and the North East will not have, although, of course, these are places where the new petty bourgeoisie and professional-managerial classes do not want to move to, so they don't seem to count. Moreover, even within the cities outside London, some areas are simply not that profitable for flipping houses. Location is everything.

Home ownership clearly *does* complicate class position and political leanings. In some circumstances, home ownership may give fractions of the working class interests that are contradictory, and which cause them to align with capital, putting them at odds politically with the increasingly marginalized strata of the working class that lives in socially rented housing and the private rented sector, for example — in a way that may be analogous to gender divides, race, the role of the aristocracy of labour, etc. In this sense, owner-occupation is no different to the historic divisions that have beset the working class and which have to be overcome. Yet we can say that housing has become a very important and complicating factor in class divides and class struggle without then saying that housing tenure determines class or constitutes a class divide above and beyond your job, or that it is the biggest dividing line in society

It is surely not hard to see that, if we extend class determination to housing tenure and asset ownership, we will descend into chaos and lose any analytical grip on class. Under the framework put forward by Konings, for example, the ACORN canvassers in Splott were now the working class because they were renting their homes, and the old homeowners were now the middle class. Indeed, perhaps one of the appeals of this theory is precisely that it allows progressive young graduates to believe that, because they do not currently own a home and are *temporarily* renting, they are the working class

It is worth continually reminding ourselves that "class is a social relationship". Basing our analysis of class solely on the ownership of fixed assets that are more or less valuable precludes any dynamic and relational understanding of class, which is to say a conception of class as a social relationship of production. In one fell swoop, this reduction removes an understanding of the processes of socialization, the role of ownership of the means of production, the social relationships of domination between classes in the workplace and beyond, which is represented in complex and nuanced ways by ideology (and values) and which split classes off from one another.

Housing, Toryism and Ideology: A Nation of Landlords?

Konings and Saunders imply that, because housing *complicates* traditional models and understandings of class (and it undoubtedly does), we should do away with the old model of class (or societal divides) altogether, adopting a new one based on housing above everything else, rather than simply acknowledging that home ownership complicates things and then working through the increased complexity. It is ultimately an entirely unnecessary step; a cop out that attempts to simplify something that cannot be simplified. Instead, we should continue to think through the ways in which housing complicates and works around or on top of class position.

As I have argued in the previous chapters, contemporary capitalism wants to spread petty-bourgeois ideology beyond its base in the class itself, so that all classes become aspirational, while their possibility of actually advancing in practice is undermined by making everyone's conditions precarious and individualised (i.e., the historically precarious position of the petty bourgeoisie writ large).

Housing is where the success of these attempts, and the concomitant destruction of collectivism and the dominance of individualism, is most tangible. Within the wider context of financialization and the collapse of secure work (including the destruction of wage labour as a source of wealth), the increase in precarity and the risk of downward social mobility, securing a house — the one asset that retains its value in society — is the *only* guarantor against downward social mobility. As Poulantzas frequently argued, political behaviour is as much influenced by what classes stand *to lose* as what they stand to gain. So long as rising house prices stave off downward social mobility (as much as facilitating *upward* social mobility), it is obvious why subordinate classes who own their own home become easily co-opted into a ruling bloc and begin to oppose any egalitarian policies — such as mass housebuilding — which could be felt to destroy the value of this asset. This helps explain why housing can split classes, and people vote for parties that may work against their class interest in other ways.

Rather than saying housing *changes* your class, or speaking of distinct "housing classes" that exist independently of or parallel to the "regular" class structure, it is sufficient to simply say that housing has complicated class and has blurred the boundaries between classes. One of the most egregious examples of this is the proliferation of small-scale landlordism. Following the extension of owner-occupation, the introduction of buy-to-let mortgages and the encouragement of the private rented sector following the deliberate suppression of social housing, small-scale or petty landlordism has become a significant force in modern society. There are now 1.5 million landlords in the UK. Nearly half of this cohort are smaller "accidental" landlords who own only one rental property. As the vignette at the start of the chapter shows, many self-employed people invest in housing as a guarantor against their lack of employment rights and pensions. Landlordism, property improvement and speculation are also obviously far easier to get into for tradesmen, and the self-employed accounted for 16% of all landlords in England in 2018. This is a continuation of a historical feature of the traditional petty bourgeoisie, and the increase in insecure self-employment amongst the petty bourgeoisie accordingly increases the likelihood of those moving into this sector investing in property as a guarantor against future crises — i.e., as the amount of people moving into self-employment grows, it is likely that we will also see an increase in small-scale landlordism.

But what is also significant are the 450,000 "workers" (i.e., employees) who now own a rental property. In electoral terms, this is a small amount, but it is not insignificant in terms of its wider impact on the amount of people enmeshed in landlordism as a norm and aspiration (and this is a lot of people). Moreover, the political economy of landlordism is in itself a new cottage industry, with letting agents and estate agents constituting a new strata of people who have a vested interest in landlordism and house price inflation.

This is also a global phenomenon. In *Planet of Slums*, Mike Davis demonstrates that slum areas across the world have witnessed an explosion of petty landlordism:

> petty landlordship and subletting are *major wealth strategies of the poor*... homeowners quickly become exploiters of even more impoverished people. Despite the persistent heroic image of the squatter as self-builder and owner-occupier, the reality in Korogocho and other Nairobi slums is the irresistible increase in tenancy and petty exploitation. [My emphasis.]

The modern housing market — both the expansion of owner-occupation and the deliberate suppression of social housing — has undermined collectivism and promoted individualism through the increased potential for the exploitation of others, even making it a *rational* act (via small landlordism), and in doing so, changing the relationship those "workers" previously had with the rest of the working class.

Owner-occupation did not *create* new classes, but has certainly split the working class socially, culturally and politically. The marketization of the housing market has blurred the boundaries between the petty bourgeoisie and elements of the working class (best exemplified by the proliferation of small landlordism). This has inculcated petty-bourgeois values in large swathes of the working class, bringing them far closer to the petty bourgeoisie.

Generation Rent? The New Petty Bourgeoisie and the Housing Market

While housing and its role in social mobility has blurred the lines between some elements of the working class and the petty bourgeoisie, it has sharpened the boundaries of the *new petty bourgeois* fraction within the intermediary classes. Many graduates now enter the labour market much later in life. As well as being in debt, many have a very weak market position because of the devaluation of degrees and the proletarianization of white-collar industries and the public sector. Moreover, they tend to live in cities where houses are even more unaffordable and are hence shut out of the housing market. To some of the elements of the new petty bourgeoisie that form the modern left, it is in housing where the lie of social mobility and one's precarious position is most viscerally revealed; above all other issues, it is housing that has politicized and radicalized this group, splitting them from the professional-managerial classes (which it is often culturally and politically close to in other ways) and polarizing them towards the most marginalized elements of the working class, at least on this issue.

However, just as there are class differences within owner-occupiers, there are class divides within the bloc that is currently mobilizing around being locked out of the housing market that are often overlooked. Where Konings' work *is* very valuable is that family asset ownership often offers a more accurate predictor of class and life chances among the sections of the left that are temporarily renting than the *current* precarious living situation that many of these young people find themselves in. While some of the young housing activists drawn from the new petty bourgeoisie will genuinely be locked out of the housing market for life, many others — particularly the children of the professional-managerial classes — who are currently renting in larger cities have parents who own their own house back in their regional town. As Danny Dorling points out, what is happening is that as elderly relatives live longer, people who will typically come into inheritance — and hence a way into the housing market — are now simply having their path into housing security delayed by a decade or two. There is a fundamental difference between those who are *temporarily* renting, and who will inevitably be able to access the market one day, and the more marginalized — including many elderly people — who will be renting for life. I had resented the lads on the other side of the bar because they had gained property, but the reality is that like many of the young people on the left, while I am renting and miserable now, one day I will likely (hopefully) be able to access "help" to "get on the ladder" from my family in a way that they would not.

The Geography of It All: Barratt Britain

Understanding the different relationships that different fractions of the petty bourgeoisie have to housing (including how housing helps distinguish and define the new and old petty bourgeoisie) can be bolstered by thinking about the geography of class and housing. Since rapid urbanization and agglomeration is one of the defining features of capitalism since its industrial phase onwards, the battle over "the right to the city" has become central to modern socialist thought and organizing. Significant swathes of the proletarianized elements of the new petty bourgeoisie live in urban areas, particularly big university cities and London, and are defined by their lack of access to the overheated urban housing market (hence "generation rent"). They are in the cities despite not being from there, because you have to move to the city to be upwardly mobile and get a job.

But as Olly Durose argues in *Suburban Socialism*, the new petty bourgeoisie's concentration in (and subsequent focus on) the city has led to a neglect of towns and suburbs and, indeed, other social experiences beyond the urban. The horror of renting and downward social mobility has driven an assumption on the new petty-bourgeois left that their urban experience of the housing market is universal when it is actually not. As the opening to this chapter demonstrated, one of the reasons housing precarity does not resonate with everyone is because, while it is particularly acute among the left's social base in the cities, beyond the cities their housing market and work (and family) situation is more complex than the familiar refrain of "I'm never going to get a house".

Although the levels of people with mortgages are dramatically falling because of spiralling house prices and the suppression of wages, the majority of most work sectors in the UK — managers, administrators, professionals, intermediate, self-employed, and technical — still have mortgages or own their homes outright. Even those in the semi-routine and routine categories constituted around 50% of homes owned outright or mortgaged. This is not that surprising when you think about it. Consider the young men I was so jealous of in this book's preface, compared to a graduate now living in a large city, laden with debt. A tradesman who has worked since he was sixteen (instead of "going travelling" and going to university) may well, by the time he's in his mid-to-late-twenties, have saved up enough cash for a deposit in an area of low-cost housing relatively comfortably. A nurse and a cop who get married in their late twenties and stay in their small- or medium-sized provincial town will have a combined income of around

£50-60k and will likely be able to buy a £120k new-build before they are thirty. Others still (who have not gone to university) may have gained a house through finance deals and put themselves in even more debt, but they will have a house and a mortgage.

As Danny Dorling's work repeatedly reminds us, one of the main things about class is that it is spatial. Different areas have entirely different class structures based on the type of industries that are clustered there. For example, London is where all the media and creative industries are clustered, hence it will have an over-representation of people living there who work in these sectors. People with degrees tend to live in certain areas and not others; people who are less healthy live in certain areas; ethnic minorities live in different areas; family structure varies between areas; where you live may determine whether you own a car or not; and of course, whether you own your home outright, have a mortgage, or rent, varies between areas as well.

While the element of the new petty bourgeoisie that comprises the left is concentrated in the cities, the traditional petty bourgeoisie are not so concentrated, and are spread out across the UK. As a percentage of the workforce, solo self-employment is highest in London because this is where high-tech industries are clustered (for the richer elements of the petty bourgeoisie), as well as being where the gig economy is clustered, so it is equally where many of the poorer self-employed live. Outside London, there is huge variation. Rural areas have higher incidences of self-employment because of the prevalence of small farming (nearly a quarter of the population in Powys, for example), while in more deprived areas the incidence of self-employment is smaller but of a different type. While London has the highest percentage of the self-employed who are graduates, Wales has the highest percentage of the self-employed who are non-graduates.

To understand the modern petty bourgeoisie and how it is shaped by housing — but also how housing is not a standalone issue, instead related to the new forms of work, family structure and infrastructure — it is important to think about suburbia and regional divides.

One of the most perceptive accounts of the role of housing in mediating the changing face of the British class structure is Duncan Weldon's *Barratt Britain*, a very useful corrective to the solipsistic focus on the city that defines most left analysis. It is one of the first journalistic accounts to approach a materialist analysis of society that moves away from cultural explanations for the rise of Tory hegemony — i.e., people vote Tory because they're selfish and racist — and instead reflects on the fact that social relations of society have changed in a way that makes Tory-voting and individualism a logical outcome.

Weldon notes that the restructuring of former Labour voting areas has occurred through the prevalence of new-build housing estates, generally built next to motorway junctions and designed to service the majority of people who commute to work by car. Thus, former mining areas previously defined by close-knit terraced houses are "now ringed by developments constructed over the past 20 to 30 years by the big-volume housebuilders — the likes of Barratt Homes, Persimmons and Taylor Wimpey".

Like my home constituency of Bridgend, "Barratt Britain" is swing-voter territory — places that have a mixed class structure but which, because they have voted Labour, have been treated as homogenously working-class or as "left behind" in the media. In these areas, homes are relatively affordable if you have a joint income with a partner, and so they have higher levels of owner-occupation compared to cities. Traditional family structures remain dominant in these places because a dual income helps to get a mortgage. The people who live in these estates are close to family support networks (like grandparent childcare) and often commute to work. They are reliant on cars (because of terrible rail infrastructure) and hence don't really care about green initiatives or improving public transport. Weldon argues that, rather than horny-handed men of toil, "red wall" places are increasingly defined by this new demographic. *Barratt Britain* paints a picture of people who are actually doing OK, or at least feel like they are in relative terms: again, a constituency and experience that is absent from leftist discourse.

For Weldon, these estates are home to what Jim Pickard in 2010 branded "motorway man": "an aspirational character, maybe a sales rep or similar, who lives in a new housing estate in a former mining area next to a motorway. He used to vote Labour, or his parents did, but is now a Tory." This picture is very similar to Savage's class of "new affluent worker": mainly male; mainly working in sales; tending to not be graduates or, if they did go to university, it was to post-1992 institutions; homeowners with middlebrow cultural tastes; and those clustered in post-industrial areas where call centres have replaced heavy industry.

"Barratt Britain" and Savage's "new affluent worker" are just new iterations of "Essex Man" and "Mondeo Man" — new ways of trying to capture the petty-bourgeois experience: the aspirational classes, "lower middle class suburbia". Although it is not *entirely* comprised of the petty bourgeoisie, Barratt Britain essentially paints a useful picture of the modern petty bourgeoisie outside the cities: both the old who live in the towns because they're rooted there (cops, the self-employed of all stripes, hairdressers, etc.), as well as those elements of the new petty bourgeoisie that have *not* been proletarianized (and there are a lot of these too — the associate professionals, call centre workers, salesmen,[13] estate agents, junior supervisors and so on). Barratt Britain is also a useful way of not getting caught up in the belief that certain fractions of the new petty bourgeoisie (i.e., young Corbynistas) are representative of the *entire* class. Instead, they are one group within a much larger, sprawling class. To reiterate: not all of the class is proletarianized by any means.

Weldon's picture of the suburban experience is one that, for me, is normal (and desirable), but was evidently a shock to Weldon himself and for the urban-dwelling people who make up the progressive forces in the UK. Of course, the very point of this book is that the petty bourgeoisie's suburban lifeworld (and the ideology it produces), which Weldon described, is a far more common lifecourse and lifestyle than people think, and certainly more common than the life experiences of the commentariat and the political class (both left- and right-leaning). This experience is by no means restricted to the "red wall" (although it is necessarily more prevalent outside cities).

Housing and Distinction: In Defence of Deano

As Savage notes, the house is now the biggest purchase that anyone ever makes. In the face of the significance of housing, all other forms of consumption have become secondary. Accordingly, in every community across the UK, class divides are expressed, understood and lived through housing aesthetics: council estates or detached houses, new-build versus tasteful Victorian terrace, AstroTurf garden with faux olive trees versus bohemian rewilded

---

13 In Weldon's analysis (as in Haywood's), it is significant that the focus was on the salesman, a profession that Poulantzas argues is firmly located in the new petty bourgeoisie because of his commodity fetishism.

garden to help the bees. This operates right down to divides within the street or estate: walk down the road and we can see the everyday process of distinction at work — the type of door you have, whether houses have numbers or names, whether your front garden is tidy or unkempt, whether you put your bins out correctly or not and so on. Consumption practices and aesthetics are very important in reproducing and entrenching class boundaries subjectively in everyday life, in shaping how people understand what they are and what they aren't.

Different classes have different housing aesthetics, and these are widely understood. They are promoted and perpetuated by those who sell lifestyles through various forms of media. Different estate agents, different housebuilders and different department store interior design departments target different classes.

Class distinction via housing has always been particularly intense between the petty bourgeoisie and the proletariat (and, indeed, between the respectable and rough fractions of the working class). Because the petty bourgeoisie is the most insecure class, they are the most invested in an exhausting arms-race of class distinction, constantly attempting to remain above the working class. Living in different, nicer areas was previously what separated the petty bourgeoisie from the working class, but increased working-class home ownership, wage stagnation across the board and rising house prices have forced the classes closer together economically. In terms of housing wealth, for example, the self-employed in the UK are actually highly comparable to the employed. Neither the petty bourgeoisie nor the working class are geographically mobile and, thus, they increasingly live in the same towns and even the same estates, very often in "Barratt Britain" together. These places are now a blend of the aspirational, owner-occupying working class and the petty bourgeoisie. Housing thus no longer separates the classes like it used to.

The closer the petty bourgeoisie come to the working class economically, the more common owner-occupation is, the harder they work to distinguish themselves from the working class socially, culturally and aesthetically. Thus, of all the classes, it places the most emphasis on not just gaining property but also showing it off and distinguishing it, which manifests itself as finding their "forever home" and posing with keys outside their new-build. (The cover for this book was prompted by the absolute domination of my own social media world by housing: Instagrammed shots of new house keys to smart new-build housing, house accounts, home improvements, AstroTurf lawns and so on.)

The process of class distinction via housing has also been reinforced by the dominance of housing as aspirational light entertainment: shows that promote home improvement, interior design, as well as petty landlordism and speculation, are incredibly popular. Within this milieu, petty-bourgeois experiences and aesthetics have become more culturally visible if not more politically understood. One of the biggest stars on social media in recent years is the endearing "Mrs Hinch", perhaps the modern personification, along with her friend Stacey Solomon, of petty-bourgeois aesthetics and lifestyle, complete with the requisite heteronormativity: Mrs Hinch is a stay-at-home mother from Essex whose husband is, yes, a sales manager. Her tips on keeping an immaculate home — a long-standing trait of the petty bourgeoisie and the respectable working class — have made her an inspiration to millions.

However, one of the cruellest ironies of distinction is that the petty bourgeoisie's pretensions only confirm their subordinate status and proximity to the working class in the eyes of the classes above it, particularly the professional-managerial classes, who laugh at the petty bourgeoisie's lack of taste. Whilst Mrs Hinch has been a lifesaver for many, she has predictably also turned into someone people can define themselves against. Her aesthetics (crushed grey velvet) are "tacky" and relentlessly mocked.

Indeed, so prevalent and widely understood is the petty-bourgeois obsession with distinction mediated by housing that it has become its own meme: "Deano", a call centre supervisor who lives in a new-build, has whitened teeth, who likes FIFA and banter. His new wife (you need a dual income to get a new-build) is also a call centre supervisor. His house is decorated with IKEA and Sofology sofas — imagine! The petty bourgeoisie has become a figure of fun to mock — their aspirations seen as somehow aberrant, a scapegoat for the excesses of individualism and consumption in society. Of course, class *disgust* is a central part of distinction and learning who you are not. Elements of the left are justifiably angry about housing, but as the popularity of twitter accounts like "newbuild hate" attest to, it is also often these very same people who love to ridicule and define themselves against the petty bourgeoisie, whose tastes and aspirations they clearly find utterly alien. They are apparently desperate for housing, but ugh, not a new build! This class snobbery reveals the true roots of much of the left in the professional-managerial class.

Conclusion

In *The Housing Question*, Engels argues that a disproportionate focus on housing in political society is symptomatic of the emergence of the petty bourgeoisie as a political force. Housing was always a problem to the working class in capitalist society, but became prominent politically only when the petty bourgeoisie were finally affected by these issues and faced blocked social mobility.

The emergence of housing as a mainstream political topic — by those who defend the current system and those who want to change it — similarly demonstrates the growing size of the petty bourgeoisie and their significance as a political force within contemporary society.

The restructuring of the housing system has simultaneously sharpened and dissolved class divides in society. The individualist ideology that was historically the preserve of the petty bourgeoisie (born of insecurity) is now a widespread condition being felt by the entire population: petty-bourgeois ideology now extends far beyond the class itself, and housing has been one of the key delivery systems for this. Mass owner-occupation and the right-to-buy has blurred the boundaries between aspirational elements of the working class and the petty bourgeoisie, as housing has also split the working class, helping to demarcate the *lumpen* and most marginalized element that is stuck in social housing or the private rented sector. The rise of owner-occupation has also facilitated an increase in small-scale landlordism — formerly the exclusive preserve of the petty bourgeoisie — encouraged by housing policy and the locking-in of assets.

For swathes of the working class, the traditional and non-proletarianized elements of the new petty bourgeoisie, who live in the suburbs and provinces, housing is central to their life and aspirations, and they have a political interest in keeping house prices high in order to stave off downward social mobility. Thus, housing has politically united much of the owner-occupier working class and the petty bourgeoisie, absorbing them into a power bloc.

Housing has also demarcated many members of the new petty bourgeoisie, who are also split from the working class and traditional petty bourgeoisie by their educational experiences. Often clustered in university cities and locked out of the housing market — and hence unable to be co-opted into the power bloc — the housing situation has served as the primary radicalising topic and driven large swathes of it — at least for now — towards the most marginalized sections of the proletariat (a group they have nothing in common with otherwise), which has served to distinguish them from the professional-managerial classes.

Because of its role either facilitating or blocking social mobility, housing has therefore played both a conservatizing and radicalizing role to different fractions of the same class, even if the core ideology of both remains the same — social mobility and aspiration — one achieved and defended jealously; one blocked and resented.

While housing has complicated class and created complex cross-class political alliances, as this chapter has argued, the concept that housing is a class divide *in itself* is unhelpful. Perhaps most perniciously, the idea of housing tenures as proxies for class, or as divides which supersede all other divides in society seems, to me at least, to efface the role of capitalist ideology and the state's hegemonic strategy. Instead, in classic liberal fashion, it individualizes the problem — focusing on the personal qualities of people who own their own homes, who are selfish Thatcherites, etc.

It is vital to not individualize this issue or reduce it to some innate acquisitiveness, or wring our hands about people being corrupted by greed. As Poulantzas repeatedly reminds us, the *aim* of capital is to build hegemonic alliances between classes that can be integrated into the ruling bloc. Therefore a more productive way of understanding housing and housing policy is as part of the ruling classes' hegemonic strategy, which in turn structures people's lives. The transition to a homeowner society is not something that has happened "naturally", but was deliberately fostered by successive right-wing governments in order to buttress the forces of capital and marginalize the left by co-opting sections of the working class and the petty bourgeoisie into the ruling bloc. Thatcher's famous aphorism that economic policy was merely a method for changing people's hearts and souls arguably applies to housing more than any other area of society.

Housing both reflects changes to society and drives changes itself. Thinking about the suburbs that dominate post-industrial areas is so important because it reveals a whole host of societal changes that are bound up and reflected in the modern organization of housing. Previously, certain industries brought the working class together in large factories and communities; similarly, close-knit housing emerged around these industries. But today, these forms of work have disappeared, and so have the communities around them. The new organization of housing reflects the new world of work in post-industrial areas — call centres, care homes, retail parks. While housing was formerly clustered around the steelworks, it is now built around hospitals or next to motorway junctions.

Community has always been key to developing collectivism beyond the workplace. Like the destruction of old collective forms of work, the restructuring of housing has facilitated an individualism and atomism that is not conducive to collectivism as people become private islands. This is evident on the thousands of new-build estates across the UK: workers live there but they are rarely communities, just places to watch Netflix with a takeaway in between commutes.

As with right-to-buy, "aspiration" and the reason people are so excited to show off their new-build, the achievement of gaining an asset finally signals some security, staving off downward social mobility and ensuring that they are not going to be sucked down into the working class from which many of them have come and fear falling back into. When you believe you've prevented this happening forever, this is justifiably cause for celebration. It is unlikely that people (like me), whose parents own large semi-detached houses in leafy suburbs, get as excited about purchasing a new-build because there is already a family safety net, not because they are less grasping. As Brett Christophers notes, removing the social safety net makes acquisitiveness of property rational; it represents finding a life raft in a storm.

In a more practical and banal sense, having a house as an asset means that it is collateral against future risks, and acquiring this asset, which acts as a safety net, directly leads to an unconscious individualism and an opting-out of society. It is far easier to begin to undo other aspects of the collective social safety net once people have this all important, *personal* safety net. For example, the gutting of pension plans encourages people to buy houses, and even second houses. In turn, if more pensioners have their own houses that are collateral for privatized care, the incentive for an effective, public care system is removed.

Jim Kemeny's research demonstrates that, in countries with higher levels of owner-occupation, there is far less of a welfare system, and in those with a strong welfare state, owner-occupation is far lower, because there is less desperation and hence less need to acquire property. Home ownership in the UK will be one of the ways in which the ongoing privatization of the NHS becomes normalized and accepted, as people use housing wealth as collateral for private health plans.

Thus, just as socialized housing was an ideological and social pillar of the Keynesian consensus, the privatization of housing is a central pillar of neoliberalism because it facilitates the gutting of the welfare state — once you privatize housing and shelter, you can privatize anything. However, just as housing was the "shaky pillar" of the welfare state, it is also the shaky pillar of neoliberalism. Owner-occupation is arguably the only lasting material concession made to the lower classes by neoliberalism, and high house prices that prevent downward social mobility are perhaps the only thing binding working class and petty bourgeois homeowners into the ruling bloc and stabilizing the system. The ruling class realize how unstable this coalition is, which is why so much effort is expended in artificially keeping prices high. If this fragile thread ever breaks, then huge swathes of the petty bourgeoisie would become instantly detached and society would be thrown into chaos.

CONCLUSION
THE PETTY BOURGEOISIE AS A MODERN
POLITICAL FORCE

The petty bourgeoisie, far from dying out, as Marx predicted, is instead now a major political force in contemporary politics. It has displaced the working class in the political arena. The working class has largely withdrawn from politics into a seething, resentful, yet nonetheless still hugely powerful mass.

It is vital that we understand the petty bourgeoisie and see it as a distinct, specific and historic class with its own experience, values, ideology and aesthetic, rather than simply cram it down into the working class or see it as a nebulous "middle class". By exploring the nature of the petty bourgeoisie, we can arrive at a better understanding of many of the changes and political developments in modern capitalist society, because many have been driven by this class and its instincts and interests. Moreover, as this book has argued, the petty bourgeois social condition of isolation and the competitive individualism that this produces has spread beyond the confines of the class and is now a widespread condition under neoliberalism.

Engaging with the petty bourgeoisie and the changing class structure will necessarily lead to a better understanding of class today in general (and hence all other classes). Finally, it can help explain the struggles of the contemporary left, because we can now understand the class base of the majority of the modern left (in the new petty bourgeoisie), as well as the allied subordinate classes and the ways in which these classes interact.

The point of all this is not to understand the class for the sake of it. We are in the midst of a crisis where society is rapidly collapsing and in which instability is spreading like wildfire. It is a crisis that the left has to win for the good of humanity, to avoid climate catastrophe, fascism and war between the large imperial powers. The only way to win is by building class alliances between the petty bourgeoisie and the working class.

Unless there is an alliance of subordinate classes — and unless the working class is mobilized — the crisis will be resolved and won by the right, who have repeatedly displayed a better understanding of class, and particularly the petty bourgeoisie, than the left.

Building a hegemonic strategy requires, as Stuart Hall notes, the articulation of different composite elements and values into a whole, just as Thatcher did, and to do that requires an understanding of both fractions of the petty bourgeoisie as well as the working class. This cannot be done if we treat the subordinate classes as a homogenous mass. This obscures the specificity and interests of the different subordinate classes and class fractions, and hence prevents understanding and achieving points of unity.

The Petty Bourgeoisie in Modern Politics

Undoubtedly, the petty bourgeoisie is far more heterogeneous than the "fundamental" classes either side of it, and this book has only scratched the surface of its complexity. The petty bourgeoisie has two fractions or strands, like a DNA double helix. On the one hand, the old, "traditional" petty bourgeoisie, comprised primarily of the solo self-employed; on the other, the new petty bourgeoisie, comprised of a sprawling mass of educated, primarily white-collar workers who are increasingly deskilled and struggling.

Both strands have grown exponentially under neoliberalism. Both new and old are split off from the proletariat and bourgeoisie socially, culturally and ideologically. Although the different fractions have different work, life experiences and culture, they are nonetheless united in a number of key ways, particularly ideologically.

Similarities between the new and old petty bourgeoisie are also evident in their political behaviour. In fact, the behaviours (and failures) of modern left/radical movements reveal their roots in the petty bourgeoisie, because the tactics, ideology and trajectory of the modern left is in fact consistent with the political tendencies of the petty bourgeoisie throughout history.

While socialist movements in previous epochs struggled to graft the old petty bourgeoisie and new petty bourgeoisie/professional-managerial classes onto the workers' movement, what has happened in the twenty-first century is the inverse of this situation. When Poulantzas was writing in the Seventies, the task of the French workers' movement was to bring the smaller (but expanding) petty bourgeoisie along with it. Today, in the absence of an organized labour movement and in the face of the mass disengagement of the working class, Corbyn (and Sanders) actually *started* with those non-working class elements as the pillars of their coalition. Finding their path to social mobility, leadership and material security blocked, realising they were lied to and going from being the smart kids to the ones working in coffee shops, created a potent political ideology of resentment and dissatisfaction. Many of the educated and frustrated fractions of the new petty bourgeoisie found Corbynism attractive and formed the nucleus of his support. This has happened around the world — Sanders in the US, Podemos in Spain, Syriza in Greece, the Arab Spring and more.

Yet, like the student protests of 1968, the Corbyn moment, for all its huge strengths and promise, failed to then engage with or graft the working class onto it in a meaningful way, despite having an obvious common interest in doing this. As Dorling notes, insofar as the Corbyn project engaged the working class, it was a movement based on "helping the poor", but not being "*of* the poor". It looked upon the working class with a mixture of fear and paternalism. As Alex Hochuli, George Hoare & Philip Cunliffe argue, this was "socialism without the masses". Corbynism — and indeed, many other social democratic movements around the world — did not and could not engage with the working class precisely because it was animated by the desires, needs, interests and ideology of the new petty bourgeoisie and the professional-managerial class; those involved simply did not understand or appreciate the scale of the glaring class divide between them and the people they wanted to appeal to.

Chapter 1 illustrated the evolution of the petty bourgeoisie throughout history and how its liminal social and economic circumstances repeatedly translated into chaotic political tendencies, which saw it become both the social base of Jacobinism, Owenite socialism and the social base of fascism. Because of its interstitial, precarious position, the class could be radicalized to the left and right at different periods and circumstances, based on whether its social mobility was upward or downward; whether they were unhappy with their precarious position and were angry with the status quo, or whether they were relatively secure and wanted to lock in and preserve their position (i.e. happy with the status quo). Thus, while the new petty bourgeoisie's downward mobility at present has translated into left politics, as Chapter 3 argued, it is not innately left-wing. In the contemporary epoch, it has been attracted to left movements both because these offer the best prospect of achieving social mobility and as a form of class distinction. At different times, different fractions have been polarized in different directions based on the trajectory of their social mobility.

The new petty bourgeoisie, like the old petty bourgeoisie, has oscillated wildly in its positions, veering towards the working class in one moment and then the bourgeoisie/the state in the other. As Oliver Eagleton notes, the "radicalism" of "generation rent" (i.e., the new petty bourgeoisie) has been massively overstated. When push came to shove in the UK, the majority of the new petty bourgeoisie supporting Corbyn threw their lot in with the professional-managerial classes over the EU, reflecting both a rational calculation regarding the positive role of the EU, and globalization as a whole in their own life plans for social mobility, as well as a latent fear of the "nativist" working class, which repeatedly emerged during Brexit and the subsequent fall out. In a recent article for *New Left Review*, Mike Wayne similarly claims that the pivot towards the "second referendum" position was reflective of the predominance of the new petty bourgeoisie and professional-managerial classes within the Labour Party, which eventually created a wedge that drove Corbynism increasingly away from material issues and towards social liberalism:

> While Corbyn's supporters were open to policy sentiments that offered a route back to social democracy (now anathema to social liberalism), they were also aligned to — that is, under the hegemony of — cultural values much closer to liberalism, of which the EU seemed to be the single most important symbol.

This, in turn, "created a fatal fissure between the membership and the broader electoral base in the northern constituencies".

While Corbyn himself and his manifesto were focused on a (very modest) redistribution of wealth, it seems fairly obvious now that many of his young radical supporters were (and are) not primarily animated by economic factors regarding the redistribution of wealth (at least, not beyond housing), but by socially liberal issues of "social justice" and representation, which have become fused into the fabric of the Labour left and "socialist" movements across the world. On top of this, for all Corbyn's huge strengths and qualities as a human being, the MPs in the party — and its local face — were still drawn overwhelmingly from the leftovers from the Blair era, the professional-managerial classes. It therefore had no chance of appealing to the working class or the traditional fraction of the petty bourgeoisie.

The political instincts of the new petty bourgeoisie are towards *reform*, just as they were for the traditional petty bourgeois-led leftist movements in the late-nineteenth century. Indeed, this has happened time and time again in new petty bourgeois- and professional-managerial class-led leftist movements over the last decade: the Arab spring, Podemos, Syriza, and will likely now happen in Chile, where, while the government was toppled by workers, the "broad front" electoral alliance that has now entered power is led by the new petty bourgeoisie and professional-managerial classes, who are rooted in the student movement rather than the worker movement. This is likely to become a passive revolution, just like Syriza and Podemos' tenure.

Leftist movements with their main base and leadership cadre in the new petty bourgeoisie have flourished, ridden and led "progressive coalitions". Then, just like social democratic movements of the past, they have almost immediately capitulated and embraced reformism upon taking power. As Marx and Engels repeatedly noted, while the petty bourgeoisie often agitated for revolution, it was never in the last instance willing to give up its relatively privileged social position in the class structure *vis à vis* the proletariat; it was never willing to fully dismantle a system in which it had a slim advantage. It was precisely this — having something to lose: a stake in the system — that led to the Marxist belief that, while the petty bourgeoisie could act as a powerful political force, it could never truly lead a radical movement. Just like the traditional petty bourgeoisie throughout history, new petty bourgeois-led movements are animated by vague, yet strongly felt "anti-establishment" sentiment, but this tends towards reformism and issues such as social justice, increasing participation and "democratization" rather than socialism. The latter is important because it is not about smashing the state or state institutions, but rather opening them up so that the "radicals" might climb up them.

Corbynism was ultimately a collection of frustrated individuals — *I* thought I would be *x*, *I* want to be able to buy a house, *I* stand to gain from this; the system needs to change, but primarily to accommodate me and my individual goals. It reflected a deep-seated and genuine anger with the system and at blocked social mobility. But it was a frustration also still ultimately tied to a belief in and acceptance of social mobility and hierarchy — wanting social mobility, being angry that social mobility is blocked — and the attendant individualism and solipsism that this entails, which has historically defined the ideology of the petty bourgeoisie.

The new petty bourgeoisie, just like the traditional petty bourgeoisie, undoubtedly experience genuine anger and, like the proletariat, are exploited. Yet this ideology and anger is refracted through the new petty bourgeoisie's experiences and values — primarily, its individualism, isolated work environment and pre-existing beliefs in social mobility. As Poulantzas puts it, "even when the new petty bourgeois adopt working-class positions, they invest them with their own petty-bourgeois ideological (and cultural and social) practices". Bechhofer and Elliot brand this specifically petty-bourgeois politics as "instrumental collectivism": temporarily relying on the collective to facilitate individual advancement, which is a fundamentally different political motivation from the solidaristic collectivism of the working class. Whenever the petty bourgeoisie has engaged with progressive movements throughout history, this has been its view.

Many may well now be reading this and vehemently disagreeing with me. You may be one of the four million graduates in the UK who are stuck in non-graduate roles. You were ripped away from your community and mates, your parents are very proud of you and so you are desperate to do well; your parents spent a fortune on your education so you don't have to do the same job your old man did. So, unlike the posh kids you met in university who messed around for three years, you worked your bollocks off to get a 2:1 or a first, only to find that you can't get a graduate job or the job you wanted — either you're not confident enough, relaxed enough or you don't know the right people — and you gradually realise that all the skills you cultivated, all the sacrifices you made, all the qualities that you were praised for in school, all the debts you took on actually mean very little in the real world. So you're faced with a choice: either continue to rent in a shithole in the big city and work as a barista, or go back to your small town and do the same thing you were doing before you left school, all while living in your old bedroom, managed by people who you are more qualified than. All the original advantages you had over your friends who didn't go to university were for nothing. You are now in debt and you also don't feel like you fit in properly anywhere. Undoubtedly, many precarious graduates see themselves — as I did — as the vanguard of the working class. And it is now the proletarianized degree-holders — rather than the working class — who are more likely to be in unions, to be leading strikes, picketing, etc., across the service economy. It is perfectly natural in these circumstances to feel defensive or precious about your own class. But it is important to realise that classifying people is not a moral judgement, and being part of the petty bourgeoisie is not a moral failing — a belief that it is culturally specific to the UK.

Downward social mobility — "proletarianization" — does not mean that one is now of "the proletariat". Economic proletarianization does not mean a cultural, social or ideological convergence with the class that they are at risk of falling into. This is not just about the cultural differences between the graduate and non-graduate working the same dead-end job; it is not about the difference in what type of movie or music one likes, or whether one puts #BLM in their Twitter bio and doesn't have Twitter at all. It is a lot deeper than that. The fundamental difference between the graduate call centre worker and the non-graduate call centre worker is that the proletarianized graduate did not expect to be in a low-paid, deskilled job. They had different horizons and fundamentally different views of the world and their own place in it. It is unlikely that the proletarian colleague with no degree has a LinkedIn profile, for example, or is continually applying for other jobs. While they are sharing the same experience now, their experiences and ideology are not the same as the static life experience of the working class. They are being radicalised precisely because they are unhappy about being close to the proletariat, who they are different to and better than. This is implicit in all new petty-bourgeois moaning — *I* should not be working in a dead-end job with the thick kids from school; this job is not for *me*, but it is for *them*. This is a different, limited and individualized form of political radicalization (and one which does not require a total overhaul of the capitalist system) than that which has historically motivated working-class collectivist politics. Moreover, these goals and expectations also profoundly influence how and in what form this element of the new petty bourgeoisie gets involved in politics, the policies they focus on and, when they do get involved, how they behave and what they expect.

While the new petty bourgeois-led left has oscillated and erred into reform, the old or traditional petty bourgeoisie is again emerging as a significant and dangerous political force. Increasingly, the traditional fraction of the petty bourgeoisie are re-emerging as the face of a powerful anti-government and anti-authoritarian movement that is increasingly global. Most notably, this includes the *Gilet Jaunes* movement in France, a country with a long tradition of petty-bourgeois militancy, and over the course of writing this book, there have been trucker protests in Canada, fuel protests in the UK and farmer protests in mainland Europe. As in previous epochs, these are reactions against state bureaucracy — in the case of farmer's protests, it is the EU overstretching and meddling — in which the small self-employed and small businessman has featured prominently. These movements have been rural as well as urban, and as in previous epochs, they have been very willing to deploy violence and to attack the state in a way that the new petty bourgeois-led left simply never would.

The Future: How to Build Class Alliances

For all the above reasons, for all its power and influence, as throughout its history, the petty bourgeoisie is incapable of building a mass movement on its own. Only the proletariat is truly revolutionary, simply because it has nothing to lose and hence has to push for a total, rather than partial, transformation of society. No fundamental social change can be won or sustained in the long term without an alliance with the working class — in which the organized working class leads — and the new petty bourgeoisie and the professional-managerial classes give up their leadership. So, how can this be achieved?

With Corbyn and Sanders gone, Labour and the Democrats are again dominated at the higher echelons by the professional-managerial classes, with only residual elements of the new petty-bourgeois surge remaining in positions of power. The fight for the soul of the left in the West is one which is being fought between the new petty bourgeoisie and professional-managerial classes, with the working class as ever excluded and understandably not interested. In the UK, many are naturally gravitating to the Scottish and Welsh independence movements as surrogates for the same social mobility ideology that drove Corbynism (and again, in these countries, the battle is between the new petty bourgeoisie and professional-managerial classes, with the working class again totally excluded). In England, it remains to be seen where these potent energies will be channelled into. While many more young people are waking up to the true nature of Labourism, remnants of the British left continue to cling onto the Labour Party, incapable of breaking out of their closed circles.

One of the major steps in building coalitions is, as I stated in the introduction, an awareness of class divides and a crucial yet uncomfortable reflection on the corrosive effects of the domination of the left by sections of the new petty bourgeoisie and the professional-managerial classes — and the ways in which the boundaries between these two classes have blurred — and how the norms, values and policies of the classes that dominate the left are felt and interpreted by the working class (and indeed, most people outside the left). This is emphatically not about using the corrosive language of "privilege" and applying it to class within leftist movements, but simply about attempting to develop self-awareness.

The problem with some of the Blue Labour-type critiques of the Labour Party and left more generally is that they contain a large grain of truth that cannot be grasped by those who are too immersed in it, and who, because of their class, feel at home in the left in a way others do not. Overwhelmingly, the Labour Party — and indeed, the labour movement — is represented in parliament and the media (and sometimes on the streets) by the professional-managerial classes — a strata of people who are (justifiably) the most widely detested people in society: people whose sense of their own superiority and self-righteousness is far more unacceptable to working-class people than the traditional economic bourgeoisie or even the aristocracy. As aforementioned, one of the biggest problems is that the section of the new petty bourgeoisie that constitutes the social base of the left is that which shares a boundary with the professional-managerial classes, primarily through its experience of education. The blurring of cultures and attitudes between this group and the professional-managerial class is an enormous problem for the left precisely because of the extent to which the professional-managerial class is despised throughout society and the extent to which the policies and values it espouses are anathema to the working class. As Mike Wayne puts it,

> among the huge barriers to be overcome in repairing the unravelling of solidarities, is the deep class resentment and suspicion now emanating from the working class to the middle-class "left", whose priorities seem more and more remote every day from working-class lifeworlds.

This is not hyperbole. Despite this, and despite claiming to have "learned the lessons" of 2019, it is clear that the new petty bourgeoisie still do not really get the depth of the resentment that exists towards the Labour Party or the left more generally, or the ways in which the left excludes people.

The dominance of these classes over the left takes many forms and alienates people in myriad ways. Leftist activism is best understood as a "field", as Bourdieu would put it, which has its own norms and rules — and forms of capital — that are deeply unfamiliar to many who are outside it. As Cihan Tugal notes, the forms of activism and protest that dominate the left have a clear class character, particularly given how many originate in student politics. On a purely cosmetic level, the self-indulgent speeches, the twee signs, the contrived language, the proceduralism, all of which are normal to the people immersed in the field who have learnt the rules, means that "activism" is culturally and aesthetically a totally different world for many potentially interested working-class outsiders looking in. It is a field in which a working-class (and indeed, petty-bourgeois) habitus would feel like a fish out of water and realise they do not possess the knowledge of the rules of the game to thrive or be taken seriously. That this simple fact, which is evident to anyone on the outside looking in, is not understood, is precisely the problem.

This cultural clash, however, can potentially be overcome. But the problems are much deeper than not wanting to join in, say, a drumming circle. Unlike previous generations of socialists, in which "activism" was banal and rooted in the workplace, activism and socialism now is nearly always something beyond the workplace, a separate field in itself. There is within the left, as Wayne notes, "a neoliberal culture of individualistic entrepreneurialism where the celebrity self is being constantly promoted" through social media. For various reasons, "activism" itself has become a form of identity, and there is a continuous, competitive performance and refinement of the "activist self" within the field. The treatment of socialism and leftist activism as a field in which one can and should build cultural capital and status in order to move up in the field, normally to further a career — either in politics or the media, directly or indirectly — is precisely indicative of the class character of the movement, for it is only the new petty bourgeoisie, with their fixation on getting ahead, with climbing ladders, that would even think of treating socialism and "activism" as a potential career site, a source of social mobility.

Relatedly, central to re-engaging with the working class is, as Wayne notes, "a reckoning with the neoliberal liberalism" that has permeated the left in the West, both in terms of its policy proposals but also the new behaviours and norms that have emerged as an adjunct to liberal identity politics. These are rooted in the liberal individualization of politics, which sees society as a huge web of oppression and discrimination in which we all oppress one another. Not only has this involved the total, wholesale shifting of policy positions towards corporate-friendly issues of representation and identity and away from economic redistribution and class, it also imports increasingly unhinged modes of human interaction, which have sadly moved beyond "online" and into physical leftist spaces, as more and more young people are being socialized into "left" politics through the prism of American-imported identitarian liberalism via social media.

Breaking with these forms must involve the realization that social liberalism and identity politics have a class origin and clear class character. As Walter Benn Michaels, Adolph Reed Jr., Catherine Liu and others have repeatedly pointed out, they are rooted in and animated by the ideology and interests of the professional-managerial classes. As a cadence and set of behavioural norms, it is rooted in the need for aspirational members of the professional-managerial class to gain a competitive advantage in the liberal-professional fields both by building an identity (the pure, righteous individual), and being able to simultaneously discipline or marginalize anyone who might be a threat to your social mobility. It is a new and brilliant weapon for those competitive fields of society where everyone must climb over one another to succeed. Sadly, the reason it has emerged on the left is precisely because the left has been so deeply influenced by the professional-managerial classes, and because "left politics" has become another field in which aspirational people compete for status and upward mobility.

The normalization of these new modes of behaviour — chiefly, a turn to moralizing and scolding — are devastating to attempts to organize internally, but also necessarily preclude the left engaging with "normal people". Identity politics are a fundamentally anti-communitarian development, which dovetail perfectly with the individualist ideology of social mobility, but which are also incompatible with working-class norms of collectivism. These behavioural norms are routine and acceptable to the professional-managerial classes who, in their professional lives, are used to telling others what to do and who are secure and convinced in their own self-righteousness — there is a good chance many of them discipline the working class in their day jobs. But they are totally alien to the overwhelming majority of people. Who would want to join in a movement in which one wrong foot, one slip up, leads to denunciation? How on earth are people meant to build bridges with others if they do not let them speak, let them learn?

The ultimate irony now is that, given the current composition of politics with the working class not engaged, and the union movement being also dominated by the new petty bourgeoisie and the professional-managerial classes, the people who are preaching socialism are often fundamentally individualistic people. Equally, those who they are trying to "convert to socialism", who may dislike the Labour Party or the Democratic Party — they may even vote for the bad guys — and who may not use the progressive language favoured by the new petty bourgeoisie and the professional-managerial classes, often already live collectivist values and are far more instinctively "socialistic" in their values and behaviours than those who are running the left.

Ditching Bureaucracy and Managerialism

All is not lost. It is eminently possible to build cross-class alliances between the petty bourgeoisie and the working class. It is undoubtedly the case that the interests of the petty bourgeoisie and the working class are increasingly objectively aligned and there have been moments, particularly in the Sanders campaign, where the two classes allied for sustained periods of time. The new petty bourgeoisie will continue to be polarized into the working class, and as more and more experience genuine — that is, permanent — downward social mobility, more will be forced into traditional working-class roles. While this will not be nice for the young people who realise that things aren't magically going to get better (join the queue), these shifting sands nonetheless have the potential to create new alliances and new militancy, particularly in the union movement — this is what is happening across America as downwardly mobile graduates lead strikes in the service industry.

We (the new petty bourgeoisie) need to understand why people are angry, what they want, what their values are, what they like and don't like, because these divides are not insurmountable. We do not need to engage in a culture war, but it does mean we need to ask searching questions about what it is that the left are offering people and why it is being rejected. What is it about the left itself that working people — both the working class and the traditional petty bourgeoisie — don't like? What are the actual concrete economic policies — not social policies — that are being put forward that would appeal to people?

Much of the traditional petty bourgeoisie's shift to the right in the modern era has been a reaction against the excesses of capitalist globalization and state interference. The petty bourgeoisie has always been hostile to globalisation and big capital, not because it is innately reactionary or racist, but simply because small producers have always been uniquely marginalized and threatened by these developments in terms of their livelihoods in a way that the professional-managerial classes/new petty bourgeoisie — who have found a base in big capital and the state bureaucracy — simply are not. We need to understand the continuing role of the family among the petty bourgeoisie and why it remains important. Of particular importance, in my view, is understanding and appreciating the deep-seated hatred of bureaucracy that exists among the working class and the old petty bourgeoisie. To think, for example, of the ways in which the bureaucracy — and those who administer it — oppresses and frustrates people.

In *The Centre Blows Itself Up*, David Graeber brilliantly illustrated the appeal of men like Trump and Boris Johnson over bloodless professional-managerial class robots like Starmer, Brown and Blair. One of the main reasons for the appeal of these right-wing demagogues is not because of their policies, but precisely because they are not like bureaucrats or human resources managers, do not *seem* like those who boss us around in work, and indeed, they revel in sticking two fingers up at bureaucratic officiousness. They represent a total break with the interfering, moralizing tenor that has become associated with progressive politics.

This is not just about presentation alone. The actual form of "socialism" that has historically been on offer in the UK has a clear class character that alienates people. In *The Path Not Taken*, the anarchist thinker Colin Ward provides a valuable lesson on "why British socialism consistently fails to win the hearts of the British public". Ward argues that socialism in the UK gradually evolved from a bottom-up, DIY, prefigurative movement, in which working-class people built their own institutions and civic life, to an inflexible, top-down state bureaucracy. He writes that "the political left in this country invested all its fund of social inventiveness in the idea of the state, so that its own traditions of self-help and mutual aid were stifled".

The state itself, rather than working-class emancipation, became fetishized by the cadre of professionals who led the socialist movement and who believed they would be running it. But as Ward notes (echoing Ehrenreich), the professionalization of knowledge in society has been fundamentally disempowering, particularly for the working class, leading people to become hostile towards the plethora of rules that are increasingly imposed on them — by people who presume to know better — without their say. Thus, for Ward, the welfare state — and indeed, "socialism" as we came to know it (i.e., Labourism) — was "a vision of socialism which is governmental, bureaucratic, paternalistic and unloved". This version of socialism was tangibly permeated by the paternalism of the professional-managerial classes.

Subsequently, when Thatcher took aim at this edifice using the language of freedom, large swathes of the working class and the petty bourgeoisie embraced it. Stuart Hall similarly wrote that one of the reasons Thatcherism caught on as a popular movement was precisely because it tapped into a sentiment about the welfare state that was never appreciated by the British left: the state apparatus was something that was done to you, that prods and scolds you, tells you what is good for you.

The millions of people who rejected bureaucratic managerialism and "the tyranny of the townhall" are not nascent fascists as many of the left believed, but just normal folk who did not like being dictated to by those who deigned to know better than everyone. This version of socialism has alienated the working class and the traditional petty bourgeoisie alike.

The left's roots in the state bureaucracy, the professional-managerial classes and its paternalistic moralizing has allowed freedom and liberty become dominated by the right. It has allowed socialism itself to become synonymous with "the state", authoritarianism and paternalism, something which Thatcher exploited effectively to co-opt large swathes of the old petty bourgeoisie and the working class. Yet the left — precisely because it remains dominated by the professional-managerial classes/new petty-bourgeois nexus — is seemingly incapable of breaking with these tendencies. On issues of freedom of speech, the left has become indelibly associated with censoriousness, punishment and telling people what to do and what to think in a way that is utterly alienating. During the COVID-19 pandemic, swathes of the British left fell back on snobbery and authoritarianism, calling for ever stricter lockdowns and wringing their hands at those who did not follow the rules to the letter, leaving sections of the right to lead the critical conversation about the risks to civil liberties posed by indefinite lockdowns and the dominance of the state. In its desperation to oppose nativists like Trump and Farage, the left has become viewed as pro-globalization and, by extension, in favour of the destruction of family and community.

Alliance Between the Petty Bourgeoisie and the Working Class: Abandoning Moderation

The left look at recent petty bourgeois-dominated anti-globalization movements — the *Gilet Jaunes*, etc. — with great unease. These people don't sing songs or carry SWP placards; they are "uneducated", rough, do not concern themselves with identity politics and do not conform to the norms of civility that the left do. Like the petty bourgeoisie throughout history, they liberally use violence. Given that many of these movements have coalesced around fossil fuels and agriculture, they are suspiciously viewed as reactionary, anti-environment "nativists". There is no doubt that this class is volatile, just as it always has been. But we should not continue to think of the traditional petty bourgeoisie as previous Marxists have done — that is, as a class that is innately reactionary, which inevitably supports the status quo or which possesses values that are incompatible with socialism. While the petty bourgeoisie previously helped stabilize capitalism and the status quo, there is no guarantee that they will slavishly support any government: once they experience downward mobility and status anxiety, they spring into action as a potent force. As Chapter 2 demonstrated, it is increasingly proletarianized and the boundaries between it and the working class are blurring. Indeed, because of the heterogeneity of the class and its porous borders with the working class, there is emerging evidence that the self-employed are increasingly voting left.

Despite its potency, the petty bourgeoisie still lack any real formal political representation: the parliaments of the world remain stuffed with representatives of the managerial class and different fractions of capital, not small business. Moreover, the petty bourgeoisie are the only class that acts as a support for the power bloc, but which gains almost no concessions in return. As Chapter 5 demonstrated, housing is arguably the only thing it has gained — its place as a stabilizing pillar of capitalist society is therefore very precarious.

They are, in other words, prime to be won over, and indeed they *have* to be. This fraction needs to be led and given direction, otherwise it will, as throughout history, be co-opted and turn to reaction. And because the petty bourgeoisie and the working class are currently leading the fight against big capital, globalization and state interference, the ruling capitalist class is also far more scared of this fraction of the class than it is the new petty bourgeois and professional-managerial -led left, because for all intents and purposes, the left does not significantly depart from liberal capitalism in any real way in its support for globalization. The modern left, with its focus on the politics of identity and representation, is more easily co-opted and ignored (the issue of housing — the one economic policy that the left seems to care about — being the exception to this). Thus, the new petty bourgeois-led left will be totally incapable of providing leadership or even linking up with this fraction, but the right will be.

What therefore needs to happen urgently is the last vestiges of the organized working-class movement linking up with these emergent traditional petty bourgeois-dominated movements, creating what C Wright Mills called a lower-middle class pressure bloc. However, the professional-managerial-class takeover of the left included large swathes of the trade union movement, which are today, at key positions, regularly staffed by full-time graduates who have not worked in the industry they are representing. The role of the trade union movement in the left's downfall and class dealignment is one which cannot be overstated. As I keep saying, people are not stupid, and the left need to realise that the wholesale working-class rejection of the left is an entirely rational one, rather than the result of brainwashing. They see very well that the majority of trade unions have no fight in them and are often led by charlatans and careerist grifters. People see, in the union bureaucracy and tepid proceduralism, the same things they dislike about the left in general. I have been in a union for my whole adult life and a shop steward for a number of years. As a union rep, the overwhelming majority of reasons given as to why people don't want to join the union is because people know full well the union is weak and will not fight for the workers. What's the point in handing over £20 a month of precious wages for a union that acts as a branch of human resources?

During the COVID crisis, with worker leverage at an all-time high, the trade union leadership in the UK sat on their hands and, I suspect, negotiated a no-strike deal with the government in exchange for concessions on furlough. My own union sent out missives that looked like they had been written by management — trust your bosses, don't kick up a fuss and certainly don't go on strike.

For this reason, and despite recent high-profile union success stories in the UK and the US, union density remains very low, and days lost from strikes are also still incredibly low. As Daniel Zamora perceptively noted recently in the *New Statesman*, many of the current chaotic scenes in key industries are down to people simply walking off the job. Rather than engagement in collective bargaining (worker "voice"), "exit" is the norm. In the absence of the trade union movement, protest has become individualized. As Zamora concludes: "People are revolting, but as individuals rather than as a class."

One of the main arguments used by centrists in the Labour Party is that most people are moderate, therefore the left must make concession after concession in order to not seem "extreme", appealing to some mythical centre-ground. Indeed, the petty bourgeoisie are continuously conflated with this mythical, moderate swing-voter. In fact, the opposite is true. Trotsky makes clear that the petty bourgeoisie rejects socialism precisely because it believes that the left does not take the fight against big capital seriously, whilst fascism and the far-right have historically spoken the uncompromising, anti-establishment language of genuine change, even if this always turns out to be hollow. He argues:

> The despairing petty bourgeois sees in Fascism, above all, a fighting force against big capital, and believes that, unlike the working-class parties which deal only in words, Fascism will use force to establish more "justice"... [Therefore, it] is false, thrice false, to affirm that the present petty bourgeoisie is not going to the working-class parties because it fears "extreme measures". Quite the contrary. The lower petty bourgeoisie, its great masses, only see in the working-class parties parliamentary machines. They do not believe in their strength, nor in their capacity to struggle, nor in their readiness this time to conduct the struggle to the end.

The traditional petty bourgeoisie, desperate for change, can find a leader in the labour movement rather than the far-right. But the main thing that prevented this happening previously was that the petty bourgeoisie saw clearly that the labour movement was weak, reformist and led by cowards. Thus Trotsky concludes:

> And if this is so, is it worth the trouble to replace radicalism by its parliamentary confrères on the left? That is how the

semi-expropriated, ruined and discontented proprietor reasons or feels.

The reason the small petty bourgeoisie supports big capital against their interest, why they have often gone over to the right, is because they know that the labour movement is pathetic, something which is a direct consequence of its dominance by the professional-managerial classes and the new petty bourgeoisie. Thus, as long as this continues, the traditional petty bourgeoisie will not be won over, because they will sense that the left is not serious or capable of bringing about societal change, that it will shit out when the going gets tough, that it is spineless, always seeking compromise rather than confrontation. This awareness of what the left is like extends to the similarly alienated working class.

As Mike Wayne concludes, as long as the left remains dominated by classes outside the working class, particularly the professional-managerial class, "the left will continue to fall under the political and moral leadership of liberalism, and important sections of the working class will be pulled further into the political and cultural orbit of conservatism". As Samir Amin argued, in the absence of progressive alternatives, people under pressure retreat into reactionary ones.

This is mutually exclusive — you cannot integrate the working class or traditional petty bourgeoisie into a movement dominated by the professional-managerial class and its values and policies, not just because the working class dislike the professional-managerial class (they do), but also because the influence of the professional-managerial classes means that economic policies that redistribute wealth or that facilitate the empowerment of the working class will never be countenanced. Thus, if you want to re-engage the working class and the old petty bourgeoisie in "socialist" politics, then the norms, policies and ways of doing politics that have become hegemonic on the left have to go.

What is needed is a total reversal of the split between "the left" and "workers". It is normal now that the left supports the workers but is not of (or led by) the workers (we support *x* strike). This split was completed in the 1990s by Blair with his gentrification of the Labour Party, but the process began in 1968, as the left moved into the universities. Undoing this will not be easy, not least because the professional-managerial class will be loath to give up its power and influence at any level, and because the left has now become the home of the progressive liberal politics that the professional-managerial class advocates.

To achieve it, "politics" must be moved away from parliamentarism and back to workplaces and communities, so workers themselves can lead it rather than professional politicians and leftist celebrities. It therefore has to involve a break with Labourism and electoralism. It will also involve an overdue confrontation with identity politics, the marginalization of the policies of social liberalism and representation, and the foregrounding of populist economic policies, including those which focus on issues of control and autonomy at *work* which can appeal to all the subordinate classes.

There can be no half measures in light of the severity of the situation. Class dealignment is rapidly turning into near-total reversal: as the left's association with educated "progressives" has become taken for granted, the right continue to gain and become the normal choice for the working class and petty bourgeoisie. The way things are being done now has led to the death of the left, so there is no option but to change.

If the working-class movement re-emerges in politics, and is led by strong, working-class leaders rooted in the fighting trade unions, then the traditional petty bourgeoisie and the working class can certainly be won over to the left. It can be done, and change can happen rapidly. Change will have to come from outside the Labour Party, however. As I write this, there have been a wave of railway strikes in the UK, as the RMT — one of the last unions to be run by working-class people, which has wisely disaffiliated from the Labour Party — shows its power and influence, and polls are showing that the public are supportive. Mick Lynch and Eddie Dempsey, the union's leaders, have demonstrated the appeal that can be won when spokespeople for "the left" are not slimy, media-trained careerists.

The Spread of Petty-Bourgeois Ideology and the Need for Optimism

There has not been (to me at least) a real attempt by the left to analyse the rise of conservativism and class dealignment in a sociological way: as something which is related to the changing economy, changing class structure and changing social relations; the new ways in which we live and work and how these changes militate against collectivism. Instead, the left has internalized the liberal principle of the personalization of politics, retreating into catastrophizing and the defeatism of "rainy fascist island". If the Tories win and Labour keep suffering, it's because there are loads of bad people out there. The good people (us, in Labour) are in the minority.

The implication is that people are thick, nasty and that the problem is people rather than structures. This inevitably leads to despair and hopelessness. It manifests itself in laughably misdirected anger at older people, homeowners, boomers or, very often, the petty bourgeoisie.

If we understand that people are encircled by powerful forces beyond their control, that their lives are structured and permeated by ideologies deliberately designed and created to promote individualism — if we understand that ruling classes deploy hegemonic strategies specifically designed to split off the subordinate classes and to incorporate certain classes into the ruling bloc; that our lives are ultimately influenced by what Istvan Meszaros calls "the social power of capital" — things become not just more comprehensible but easier to deal with.

We now live in a society where no work is ever secure, and in which people are constantly having to move between professions and jobs as they desperately try to find a bearable existence. The precarity that once defined the traditional petty bourgeoisie has now become the norm. People now live far more disconnected lives and work in more isolated working environments — indeed, in workplaces where isolation from other workers has been specifically engineered. This does not just apply to workers in the gig economy but to the broader population. As Chapter 2 noted, everyone is increasingly subject to disciplinary metrics and technologies that make us work faster and keep us isolated from and in competition with our colleagues.

We live in isolated communities, in new-builds, in estates that are split off from one another; we are, from a young age, forced to compete with each other in school and are told that we need to get ahead and escape our communities and our friends and have a career (not a job) in order to buy a house. All this naturally produces an individualism and detachment from politics that is entirely rational. If we are permanently looking for other work in order to find some stability, we inevitably internalise an "entrepreneurial subjectivity", which entails building a personal brand and advertising oneself constantly to capital, existing in permanent competition with other people. Under these conditions of competition and insecurity, this behaviour is also rational. If public transport is destroyed, it makes sense to drive a car. If you can't get an appointment with a doctor or be seen in hospital, it makes sense to opt for private healthcare (if you can afford it). People want a house, and get so excited when they buy their new-build, not because they are grasping Tories but because the alternative is so awful; because they now have some security in a society where there is no safety net.

While all this is often simply interpreted as the human condition under neoliberalism, that people are "neoliberal subjects" and so on, as this book has argued, it truly seems to me that what is happening is the experiences, isolated working conditions, and hence individualist ideology of the petty bourgeoisie — was formerly restricted to a tiny percentage of the population working for themselves — is now permeating the wider population even beyond the class itself. Thus, when we ask why individualism, hardness and resentment has permeated the body politic, it is, as this book has shown, because these conditions tend to produce this way of thinking. This is why it is so important to understand the petty bourgeoisie itself.

But just as petty-bourgeois ideology and neoliberalism have been embedded in society through revolutionary right-wing policies such as the right-to-buy, which changed the soul of society and made individualism "rational", these policies can equally be undone. It is eminently possible to enact policies that can encourage a more socialized and collectivist society. Secure work contracts would prevent permanent angst and the drive to compete against one another. Decommodifying housing by mass building council housing would break the hold of the market, as well as providing shelter and security. This removes the incentive for petty landlordism and property fetishization. It has been done before and can be done again. It is also possible to achieve true comprehensivization and the abolition of academies and grammar schools, implementing an education system that breaks down the mental/manual divide and focuses on an integral form of education where all children are taught practical and life skills. The removal of testing, setting and pressure, in turn, removes competition and hierarchies between children, and the awareness that social mobility is not the role of education. Means-testing, another Blairite favourite, encourages competition and resentment between subordinate classes, particularly between the petty bourgeoisie and the working class, whereas universalism can prevent this. The old institutions that facilitated collectivism and have been sold off — sports clubs, community halls, libraries and so on — have to be brought back. Above all, socialism has to come from below, it cannot be led from above, and it cannot be bureaucratic and dominated by a cadre of professionals or managers.

There is a pessimism on much of the left that I cannot understand or comprehend — if I thought people were bad or selfish, I could not get out of bed in the morning, let alone be a socialist. It is a cruel irony that the more time one spends in leftist activism, the more depressed and helpless one will get. It is only when one spends time outside the moralizing and careerism of leftist circles — among normal, decent, often apolitical people — that one feels optimistic about human nature again.

This book is personal to me. The old petty bourgeoisie is the class that I come from and have grown up around. For years I have felt that this experience, which is neither proletarian nor bourgeois, has not been documented or understood at all. I hope this book can go some way towards furthering the understanding of the petty bourgeoisie as a class — its history, formation and evolution; its habits and values; and how its liminal social situation creates its ideology and its political behaviour. As I hope the book makes clear, the petty bourgeoisie is not an inherently reactionary class, and its members are not innately selfish or conservative. I am convinced that most people are good, naturally co-operative and support socialistic policies, and I firmly believe the petty bourgeoisie can be won over to socialism as they have been in the past. The people I have grown up with and the community I come from, and thousands like them, even if they vote the wrong way, are not bad people, and nor should they be written off.

Finally, I have spent most of my adult life and career "on the left" around the new petty bourgeoisie. As I hope I have shown, the aspirations and ideology of this class are not so different from the old petty bourgeoisie at all. What would now be most transformative for the new petty bourgeoise — not just politically but psychologically — would be to abandon social mobility, to dispense with its obsessive focus on climbing the career ladder, to embrace and accept downward social mobility, to realise one can have an identity and meaning without a "career", and that there is nothing wrong with staying rooted and not leaving your small town. This would lead to the gradual erosion of class boundaries between the subordinate classes and help guarantee the formation of broad political alliances, as well as making people a lot happier personally.

TABLES

Figure 1. Class checklist.

	Proletariat	Old Petty Bourgeoisie	New Petty Bourgeoisie	Professional-Managerial Class	Bourgeoisie
Produce value?	Yes	Yes	Yes	Yes	No
Own the means of production ?	No	Yes	No	No	Yes
Autonomy at work?	No	Yes	No	Yes	Yes
Distinct habitus?	Yes	Yes	Unclear	Yes	Yes
Socially mobile? (i.e., do they move up and down the class structure)	No	Yes	Yes	No	No
Positive view of education?	No	No	Yes	Yes	No
Distinct political tendencies?	Yes	Yes	Yes	Yes	Yes
Distinct aesthetics?	Yes	Yes	Unclear	Yes	Yes

Figure 2. Comparisons/checklist: petty bourgeoisie, new petty bourgeoisie, proletariat.

	Old Petty Bourgeoisie	New Petty Bourgeoisie	Proletariat
Economic	Owns own business	Doesn't own own business — has to sell labour like the proletariat	Doesn't own own means of production so has to sell labour (i.e., work) to live
Economic	Rooted in small capital and traditional work	Works in both big and small business and the state bureaucracy	Works in big and small business
Economic/ Social	Historically owns own property (house), which was used to distinguish itself socially from the proletariat.	Split. Some elements outside the cities who have not been proletarianized do, while others- particularly young graduates in the city, do not.	Traditionally did not own their own property but now increasingly does, while a lumpen element is locked out of the housing market.
Social	Precarious — at risk of falling down the class structure and being ruined	Precarious — at risk of falling down the class structure through inevitable deskilling of white collar industries.	Static class — generally does not move up in the class structure

	Old Petty Bourgeoisie	New Petty Bourgeoisie	Proletariat
Social	Isolated form of work	Works in big business but is socially isolated through competition with other workers because of fixation on social mobility	Collective work
Social/ Cultural	Individualistic ideology	Individualistic ideology	Collectivist ideology
Cultural	Distinct culture and aesthetic rooted in the need for distinction vis a vis the working class.	Unclear what the distinct culture or habitus of the class is. Likely that it absorbs cultural elements of the working class and professional-managerial class.	Distinct habitus and aesthetics
Cultural	Negative view of bureaucracy, big capital and globalization.	Lacks the negative view of bureaucracy as it often works in these fields.	Negative view of bureaucracy as it is the most subject to the bureaucracy; the state bureaucracy was created to disempower the proletariat and replace its traditional institutions and forms of knowledge.

	Old Petty Bourgeoisie	New Petty Bourgeoisie	Proletariat
Cultural	Historically a negative view of formal education.	Historically views education very positively as central to facilitating social mobility.	Historically a negative view of formal education, but frequently engages in other forms of self-education.
Cultural	Traditional family unit extremely important for running the business, securing property and reproducing position in the class structure.	Unclear whether family unit retains the same centrality.	Traditional nuclear family unit has traditionally been broken up by work (e.g., both parents have had to work).
Cultural	Geographically rooted.	Often geographically mobile.	Globally mobile but British proletariat *tends* to be geographically rooted.

	Old Petty Bourgeoisie	New Petty Bourgeoisie	Proletariat
Cultural	Has own associational life but these tend to be outside work and viewed in utilitarian ways (i.e., as ways of helping the business, making contacts, arranging marriage to reproduce the business etc). Generally has no *politically* collectivist institutions or distinct intellectual life.	Unclear	Has own institutional and intellectual life.
Political	Distinct political tendencies — chaotic and pulled in both directions; tendency to violence and reformism.	Distinct political tendencies — chaotic and pulled in both directions; tendency to reformism.	Distinct political tendencies — the only revolutionary class.

GLOSSARY OF TERMS

The Proletariat

The working class. A global class which has huge diversity. The class of people who traditionally owned no property, did not own their own means of production and hence had to sell their labour (i.e., work) in order to survive. The class was created by the transition to industrial capitalism. Historically the largest class, and for Marx and Engels was the only revolutionary class. The class has also always tended to have its own intellectual and civic life and culture.

Lumpenproletariat

The underclass. A distinct fraction of the proletariat, defined by worklessness. Marx and Engels took a very dim view of this class, calling them "social scum", claiming that they were venal and prone to criminality, and relatedly that they were politically unreliable, would be (like the petty bourgeoise) easy to manipulate and be turned towards reactionary politics by the bourgeoisie.

Petty Bourgeoisie

The class that was historically defined by its ownership of its own means of production, which historically meant small craftsmen and small farmers. The class occupied an "interstitial" position in the class structure between the working class and the bourgeoisie, distinguished by its autonomy and hence social isolation, which can be compared to the proletariat which worked together collectively in in largescale production. Because of the nature of its business (small handicraft production), Marx felt the class would be made redundant by large-scale manufacturing so branded it a "transitional" class. The petty bourgeoise has evolved and taken on different forms in different epochs, evolving from small farmer and craftsman to shopkeeper, to white-collar clerk, and so on. It has always contained two fractions, an old and a new. The class also had distinct political tendencies throughout history which were rooted in its liminal economic position. Formerly a small class, it has now grown and diversified way beyond the traditional image of the shopkeeper

New Petty Bourgeoisie

A new fraction of the petty bourgeoise created and grown by deindustrialization and the transition to services. Tends to work in "white-collar" industries, is often educated. While culturally often very distinct from the old petty bourgeoise, and economically close to the proletariat because it does not own its own means of production, it is nonetheless socially and ideologically placed in the petty bourgeoise because its mobility — and hence precarity — within the class structure inculcated within it the same individualism, status anxiety and need for distinction as the petty bourgeoise of old.

Traditional or Old Petty Bourgeoisie

The modern version of the "old" fraction of the class. Defined by solo self-employment. A growing class which has changed enormously in the modern era. While historically the class was defined by a distinct habitus, morality and values, its huge size and increasingly blurred boundaries with other classes mean that it is now difficult to speak of a distinct petty bourgeoise habitus. Moreover, the relative autonomy that the petty bourgeoise used to enjoy has now largely been destroyed. It is also no longer rooted in low technology or traditional form of work. Nonetheless, the isolated social conditions and precarity which defined the class throughout history remain intact in the present.

The Professional-Managerial Classes

A new class created by the rise of professionals and managers. First identified and sketched by Barbara and John Ehrenreich in the Seventies, although the idea of a class or caste of intellectuals has been around since Gramsci. Sivanandan also argued that within the broader middle classes, intellectuals and cultural producers now had a disproportionate influence in modern capitalist society within the broader middle classes: "who as purveyors of information, ideas, images, lifestyles find themselves in an unusual position of power to influence the way people think and behave". The class has a distinct taste, aesthetics and culture and also reproduced itself, with the class intermarrying, etc. The class has a distinct ideology which is focused on the supremacy of professional knowledge and education, and has a paternalistic view of the working class that it was created to pacify and manage (outside work) on behalf of the bourgeoisie. Of course, "progressive" fractions of the bourgeoisie had always existed, indeed in the *Communist Manifesto* Marx and Engels argue that this progressive fraction would link up with the working class during periods of revolution. Ehrenreich's concept was distinct and controversial in that she argues the class was more than a fraction (i.e., cultural and social group) of the bourgeoisie, but had become a distinct class with distinct *interests* from the bourgeoisie.

Bourdieu has three key terms which are interrelated:

Habitus

Habitus refers to the habits, dispositions and normal way of behaving that different classes are socialized into. The habitus that we are socialized into structures our entire life: our ways of thinking, acting, behaving, standing, talking, and so on. It is a mental structure which is also *embodied*. It is our second nature. Habitus is a product of a shared history, and typically rooted in the distinct social history and the milieus that different classes experience. Habitus is therefore a very useful companion to understanding class consciousness, for it essentially refers to the ways in which class is lived, embodied and interpreted in everyday life, even if this does not explain how classes are formed in the first instance.

The Forms of Capital — e.g., cultural capital, economic capital, social capital

"Capital" refers to how power operates in everyday life. Any analysis of power cannot focus exclusively on things like money, but on how those with money and power dominate society in different, subtle ways. Capital is an asset that is distributed unevenly among classes, and therefore a form of symbolic power which is used as a tool of the dominant classes to reproduce/perpetuate their control of society. Capital has three forms: economic capital refers to assets which are convertible into money, for example the ownership of property; cultural capital refers to things like educational qualifications, good diction, soft skills such as speaking languages, being able to play sport or a musical instrument; social capital essentially involves things like connections or "who you know". What is often forgotten when discussing capital is that social and cultural capital are contingent upon economic capital. You can learn the aforementioned skills and behaviours if your parents have the money to send you to elocution lessons, or music lessons, and so on; or if your parents can get by on one salary, freeing up another to do these things with you. You similarly develop social capital if you swim in certain social circles, if your dad knows x or y you are better able to get a job in the city, for example.

Field

For Bourdieu, any society is structured and composed of a series of relatively autonomous *fields* (e.g., the economic field, the educational field, the political field, the cultural field — school, university, different employment sectors). Each of these is a structured space with its own laws and power relations independent of the economy or politics, although each field is structured similarly to another, with people at the top and people at the bottom; and in each field there are norms and forms of capital which are valued and specialised, and which people have to be able to deploy to get to the top. The habitus interacts with and can best be understood in relation to the field. Thus someone with a working class habitus feels comfortable and knows the rules of working-class fields and the skills, forms of capital and status and normal ways of being within this field. But when that habitus is transported to another field, the person may feel like "a fish out of water". Thus in *Good Will Hunting*, the eponymous hero feels out of place in the rarefied world of Harvard University, (the field of higher education) and he lacks the requisite forms of cultural capital to allow him to feel comfortable within it.

Distinction

Distinction refers to the way domination and symbolic power in society are reinforced through consumption practices and taste. Bourdieu states that the habitus generates lifestyles and aesthetics — different classes have different tastes and consumption practices: they wear different clothes, shop in different places, eat different food, have different cultural interests, and so on. Distinction is used in everyday life as a shorthand to allow people to understand others, and to understand what we are not, as central to distinction is *distaste*.

"Class *in* itself"

Class which exists "objectively", i.e., a class "on paper". Something that exists, but is not self-aware.

"Class *for* itself"

A class which is self-aware, i.e., possesses class consciousness. Class which exists *subjectively* and which understands its own interests. This is an ideal situation, and takes time and work to achieve.

Class Fraction

Fractions are distinct strata or groups within the same class which can have different interests, different cultures or tastes, but which nonetheless remain part of the same class. For example, the "labour aristocracy" (i.e., skilled members of the working class), were nonetheless part of the working class because they did not own their own means of production. The ruling class today frequently contains competing interests or fractions, so e.g., finance capital, national capital, and so on. They can come into conflict with one another but they remain parts of the same class.

BIBLIOGRAPHY

Adkins, L., Cooper, M., & Konings, M., (2020) *The Asset Economy* Polity

Althusser, L. (1970) *'Ideology and Ideological State Apparatuses'* in *Lenin and Philosophy and Other Essays,* Monthly Review Press available online at: https://www.marxists.org/reference/archive/althusser/1970/ideology.htm

Bano, N., (2021) 'Home Ownership Can't Solve the Housing Crisis' *Tribune* October 2nd https://tribunemag.co.uk/2021/10/home-ownership-cant-solve-the-housing-crisis

Barratt, T., Goods, C., Veen, A. (2020) 'I'm my own boss...': Active intermediation and 'entrepreneurial' worker agency in the Australian gig-economy. *Environment and Planning A: Economy and Space.* 52(8) pp- 1643-1661.

Bechhofer, F., & Elliot, B (1978) 'The Voice of Small Business & The Politics of Survival' *The Sociological Review*, 26 (1) pp. 57-88

Bechhofer, F., & Elliot, B., (1968) 'An approach to a study of small shopkeepers and the class structure' European Journal of Sociology 9 (2) pp. 180-202

Bechhofer, F., & Elliot, B., (1981) *The Petite-Bourgeoisie: Comparative Studies of the Uneasy Stratum* MacMillan

Bechhofer, F., & Elliot, B., (1985) 'The Petite Bourgeoisie in Late Capitalism' *Annual Review of Sociology* , Vol. 11 pp. 181-207

Benn-Michaels, W. (2018) 'The Political Economy of Anti-Racism' Nonsite.org February 11th, 2018 Available online at: https://nonsite.org/the-political-economy-of-anti-racism/

Benn-Michaels, W., & Reed, A., (2020) 'The Trouble with Disparity' Nonsite.org September 10th 2020. (Available online at: https://nonsite.org/the-trouble-with-disparity/)

Birelma, A. (2019) 'Working-class entrepreneurialism: Perceptions, aspirations, and experiences of petty entrepreneurship among male manual workers in Turkey' *New Perspectives on Turkey* Vol.61 pp. 45-70

Blundell, J. (2019) 'Clusters in Uk Self-Employment' *Centre for Economic Performance Occasional Papers*, 48. (Available online at: https://cep.lse.ac.uk/pubs/download/occasional/op048. pdf)

Bourdieu, P. (1984) *Distinction* Routledge

Bourdieu, P. (1987) 'What Makes a Social Class? On The Theoretical and Practical Existence Of Groups' *Berkeley Journal of Sociology* 32, pp. 1-17

Braverman, H. (1974) *Labor and Monopoly Capital: The Degradation of Work in the Twentieth Century* Monthly Review Press: New York

Brenner, R. & Brenner, J., (1981) 'Reagan, the Right and the Working Class' https://www.versobooks.com/blogs/2939-reagan-the-right-and-the-working-class

Burawoy, M. (2009) *The Extended Case Method: Four Decades. Four Great Transformations and One Theoretical Tradition* London: University of California Press

Cant, C. (2020) *Riding for Deliveroo: Resistance in the New Economy* Polity

Carchedi, G. (1990) *Frontiers of Political Economy* Verso

Carter, B. (1995) 'A Growing Divide: Marxist Class Analysis and the Labour Process' *Capital and Class*, 19 (1) pp.33-72

Carter, H. (2012) 'From Slums To Slums In Three Generations; Housing Policy And The Political Economy Of The Welfare State, 1945-2005' *Discussion Papers in Economic and Social History* Number 98,

Chitty, C. (2013) *New Labour and Secondary Education, 1994-2010* Basingstoke: Palgrave Macmillan

Christophers, B. (2020) *Rentier Capitalism: Who Owns the Economy, and Who Pays for It?* Verso

Clarke, S., & Ginsberg, N., (1974) 'The Political Economy Of Housing' *C.S.E. Political Economy Of Housing Group—Papers available online at:* https://homepages.warwick.ac.uk/~syrbe/pubs/ClarkeGinsburg.pdf

Colomb, C. (2007) 'Unpacking new labour's 'Urban Renaissance' agenda:Towards a socially sustainable reurbanization of British cities?', *Planning, practice & research*, 22 (1), pp. 1-24.

Cooper, M. (2022) 'Family Capitalism and the Small Business Insurrection' *Dissent Magazine*, (available online at https://www.dissentmagazine.org/article/family-capitalism-and-the-small-business-insurrection)

Davies, A. R. (2013). 'Right to Buy': The Development of a Conservative Housing Policy, 1945 – 1980. *Contemporary British History*, 27(4), pp. 421-444.

Davis, M. (2005) *Planet of Slums* Verso

Dorling, D., & Thomas, B., (2016) *People and Places: A 21st Century Atlas of the UK* Policy Press

Durose, O. (2022) *Suburban Socialism* Repeater

Eagleton, O. (2021) 'Vicious, Horrible People' *New Left Review 127*

Eaton, G. (2021) 'How Tory dominance is built on home ownership' *New Statesman* 12th May 2021 (available online at: https://www.newstatesman.com/politics/uk-politics/2021/05/how-tory-dominance-built-home-ownership).

Ehrenreich, B., & Ehrenreich, J. (1977) 'The New Left: A Case Study in Professional-Managerial Class Radicalism' *Radical America* Vol 11 (3), pp. 7-22 (available online at https://files.libcom.org/files/Rad%20America%20V11%20I3.pdf.)

Ehrenreich, B., & Ehrenreich, J. (1977) 'The Professional-Managerial Class' *Radical America* Vol 11 (2) pp.7- 32 (available online at https://files.libcom.org/files/Rad%20America%20V11%20I2.pdf)

Engels, F. (1852) *Revolution and Counter-Revolution in Germany* (available online at: https://www.marxists.org/archive/marx/works/1852/germany/index.htm)

Engels, F. (1872) *The Housing Question* (available online at: https://www.marxists.org/archive/marx/works/1872/housing-question/).

Evans, G.,& Tilley, J (2015) 'The new class war: Excluding the working class in 21st-century Britain' *Juncture* 21 (4) https://www.ippr.org/juncture/the-new-class-war-excluding-the-working-class-in-21st-century-britain

Foster, J. (1974) *Class Struggle and the Industrial Revolution* Methuen & Co: London

Gillard, D. (2018) *Education in England: A History* www.educationengland.org.uk/history

Giupponi. G, & Xu, X. (2021) 'What does the rise of self-employment tell us about the UK labour market?' *Institute for Fiscal Studies* Report (available online at: https://ifs.org.uk/uploads/BN-What-does-the-rise-of-self-employment-tell-us-about-the-UK-labour-market-1.pdf)

Gorz, A. (1980) *Farewell To The Working Class: An Essay on Post-Industrial Socialism* Pluto

Graeber, D. (2016) *The Utopia of Rules: On Technology, Stupidity, and the Secret Joys of Bureaucracy* Melville House

Graeber, D. (2018) *Bullshit jobs: A Theory* Allen Lane

Graeber, D., (2020) 'The Center Blows Itself Up: Care and Spite in the 'Brexit Election'' *New York Review of Books*, January 13th, 2020. (Available online at: https://www.nybooks.com/daily/2020/01/13/the-center-blows-itself-up-care-and-spite-in-the-brexit-election/)

Gramsci, A. (1921) 'The Ape People' *L'ordine Nuovo* (available online at: https://www.marxists.org/archive/gramsci/1921/01/ape-people.htm)

Gramsci, A. (1924) 'The Crisis of the Middle Classes' *L'Ordine Nuovo* (available online at: http://marxism.halkcephesi.net/Antonio%20Gramsci/1924/09/italian_crisis.htm)

Hatherley, O. (2011) *A Guide to the New Ruins of Great Britain* Verso

Hatherley, O. (2011) 'Is home ownership really so desirable?' *The Guardian* Tues 31st May (available online at https://www.

theguardian.com/commentisfree/2011/may/31/home-ownership-debt-renting)

Hatherley, O. (2014) 'Here's what a real 'Marxist diatribe' about the UK housing market looks like' The Guardian, Tues 4th Feb (available online at https://www.theguardian.com/commentisfree/2014/feb/04/marxist-diatribe-uk-housing-market)

Heffer, S. (2021) 'The making of Essex Man' Unherd October 18th, 2021 (available online at: https://unherd.com/2021/10/the-making-of-essex-man/)

Henley, A. (2021) The rise of self-employment in the UK: entrepreneurial transmission or declining job quality? *Cambridge Journal of Economics* 45 (3), pp. 457-486

Hill, C (1955) *The English Revolution:1640* Lawrence & Wishart (available online at: https://www.marxists.org/archive/hill-christopher/english-revolution/)

Hobsbawm, E. (1962) *The Age of Revolution: Europe 1789–1848* Weidenfeld & Nicholson

Hobsbawm, E. (1975) *The Age of Capital: 1848-1875* Abacus

Hobsbawm, E. (1987) *The Age of Empire: 1875-1914* Cardinal

Hobsbawm, E. (1994) *The Age of Extremes: The Short Twentieth Century, 1914–1991* Michael Joseph

Hochuli, A., Hoare, G., Cunliffe, P. (2021) *The End of the End of History; Politics in the Twenty-First Century* Zero

Hoggart, R. (1957) *The Uses of Literacy* Penguin

Holloway SL., & Pimlott-Wilson, H., (2021) 'Solo self-employment, entrepreneurial subjectivity and the security–precarity continuum: Evidence from private tutors in the supplementary education industry' *Environment & Planning A: Economy & Space* 53(6) pp. 1547-1564.

Jones, K. (2003) *Education in Britain: 1944 to the present* Cambridge: Polity

Jones, O. (2011) *Chavs: The Demonization of the Working Class* Verso

Kemeny, J. (1980) 'Home ownership and privatization' *International Journal of Urban and Regional Research* 4 (3) pp. 372-388

Kennedy, J. (2018) *Authentocrats* Repeater: London

Kitson, M & Mitchie, J (2014) 'The Deindustrial Revolution: The Rise And Fall Of Uk Manufacturing, 1870-2010' *Centre for Business Research, University of Cambridge Working Paper* No. 459 (available online at: https://michaelkitson.files. wordpress.com/2014/09/wp-459-2014-kitson-and-michie-the-deindustrial-revolution.pdf)

Krylova, A. (2003). Beyond the Spontaneity-Consciousness Paradigm: "Class Instinct" as a Promising Category of Historical Analysis. *Slavic Review*, 62(1), pp. 1–23.

Larson, M. (2013) *The Rise of Professionalism: Monopolies of Competence and Sheltered Markets* Routledge

Lenin, V. (1915) 'On the two lines in the revolution' *Sotsial-Demokrat No. 48* (Available online at: https://www.marxists. org/archive/lenin/works/1915/nov/20.htm)

Lenin, V. (1920) *"Left-Wing" Communism: an Infantile Disorder* (available online at: https://www.marxists.org/archive/lenin/ works/1920/lwc/ch04.htm)

Lenin, V. (1959) *Alliance of the Working Class and the Peasantry* Progress Publishers: Moscow

Liu, C. (2021) *Virtue Hoarders: The Case Against the Professional Managerial Class* University of Minnesota Press

Marx, K. (1852) *The Eighteenth Brumaire of Louis Bonaparte* (available online at: https://www.marxists.org/archive/marx/ works/1852/18th-brumaire/)

Marx, K. and Engels, F., (1848) *Communist Manifesto*. (Available online at https://www.marxists.org/archive/marx/works/ download/pdf/Manifesto.pdf)

Mayer, A. (1975) 'The Lower Middle Class as Historical Problem' *The Journal of Modern History*, Vol. 47 (3) pp. 409- 436

McKibbin, R. (1994) *The Ideologies of Class: Social Relations in Britain 1880-1950* Oxford University Press

Newby, H., Rose, D., Saunders, P., & Bell, C. (1981) 'Farming for Survival: The Small Farmer in the Contemporary Rural Class Structure' in Bechhofer, F., & Elliot, B., *The Petite-Bourgeoisie: Comparative Studies of the Uneasy Stratum* pp. 38-70 MacMillan

Nicolaus, M. (1978) 'Proletariat and Middle Class in Marx: Hegelian Choreography and the Capitalist Dialectic' pp. 230-254 in McQuarie, D. (Ed) Marx: *Sociology, Social Change, Capitalism* Quartet

Peck, J. (1996) *Work-place: The Social Regulation of Labor Markets*. New York: Guilford Press.

Perkin, H. (1996) *The Third Revolution: Professional Elites in the Modern World* Routledge

Pierson, C. (1991) *Beyond the Welfare State: The New Political Economy of Welfare* Polity

Poulantzas, N. (1973) 'On Social Classes' *New Left Review* 78

Poulantzas, N. (1974) *Classes in Contemporary Capitalism* Verso

Poulantzas, N. (1979) 'The New Petty Bourgeoisie' *Insurgent Sociologist*, 9(1) pp. 56-60

Press, A. (2019) 'Forget Your Middle-Class Dreams' *Jacobin* 29th March, *Available online at* https://jacobin.com/2019/03/middle-class-white-collar-unions-kickstarter

Saunders, P. (1978) 'Domestic property and social class' *International Journal of Urban and Regional Research* 2 (1-3) pp. 233-251

Saunders, P. (1984) 'Beyond housing classes: the sociological significance of private property rights in means of consumption' *International Journal of Urban and Regional Research* 8 (2) pp. 202-227

Saunders, P. (1990) *A Nation of Homeowners* Unwin Hyman

Savage, M. Devine, F., Cunningham, N., Taylor, M., Li, Y., Hjelbrekke, J., Le Roux, B., Friedman, S., Miles, A., (2013) 'A New Model of Social Class? Findings from the BBC's Great British Class Survey Experiment' *Sociology* 47 (2) pp. 219-250 (available online at: https://journals.sagepub.com/doi/pdf/10.1177/0038038513481128)

Savage, M., Barker, J., Dickens, P., & Fielding, T. (1995) *Property, Bureaucracy & Culture: Middle Class Formation in Contemporary Britain* Routledge

Scase. R., & Goffee., R. (1981) 'Traditional Petty Bourgeois Attitudes: The Case of Self-Employed Craftsmen' *The Sociological Review* 29 (4) pp. 729-747

Sivanandan, A. (1990) 'All that melts into air is solid: the hokum of New Times', *Race & Class*, Vol 31(3), pp. 1–30.

Stein, S. (2019) *Capital City: Gentrification and the Real Estate State* Verso

Sweezy, P. (1978) 'Karl Marx and the Industrial Revolution' pp. 185-198 in McQuarie, D. (Ed) *Marx: Sociology, Social Change, Capitalism* Quartet

Thier, H. (2020) 'The Working Class Is the Vast Majority of Society' *Jacobin* September 13th, Available online at https://jacobin.com/2020/09/working-class-peoples-guide-capitalism-marxist-economics

Thompson, E.P. (1963) *The Making of The English Working Class* Vintage Books: New York

Trotsky, L (1932) *Germany: The Only Road* (available online at https://www.marxists.org/archive/trotsky/germany/1932/320914.htm)

Tugal, C. (2015) 'Elusive revolt: The contradictory rise of middle-class politics' *Thesis Eleven* 130(1) pp. 74-95

Urry, J., & Abercrombie, N. (1983) *Capital, Labour and the Middle Classes* George Allen & Unwin: London

Waites, B. (1987) *A Class Society at War: England 1914-18* Berg: Leamington Spa

Ward, C. (1987) 'The Path Not Taken' *Raven* No.3. Available online at: https://libcom.org/article/path-not-taken-colin-ward

Wayne, M. (2021) 'Roadmaps After Corbyn: Parties, Classes, Political Cultures' *New Left Review 131*

Weldon, D. (2021) 'Barratt Britain: A Closer Look at The Conservative's Red Wall Seats' IPPR *Progressive Review* PP. 281-285

Willis, P. (1978) *Learning to Labour: How Working Class Kids Get Working Class Jobs* Ashgate

Winant, G. (2021) *The Next Shift: The Fall of Industry and the Rise of Health Care in Rust Belt America* Harvard University Press

Wood, E.M. (1999) *The Retreat from Class: A New 'True' Socialism* Verso

Wood, E.M. (2002) *The Origin of Capitalism: A Longer View* Verso

Woodcock, J. (2019) "The Impact of the Gig Economy" In *Work in the Age of Data*. Madrid: BBVA

Wright, E.O. (1976) 'Class Boundaries in Advanced Capitalist Societies' *New Left Review* (98) pp 3-41 available online at: https://www.ssc.wisc.edu/~wright/Published%20writing/ClassBoundaries.pdf

Wright, E.O. (1985) *Classes* Verso

Wright-Mills, C. (1955) *White Collar: The American Middle Classes Oxford* University Press: New York

Zamora, D. (2022) 'Why your flights keep getting cancelled: Class conflict is back, but without the working class.' *New Statesman* 14th July, 2022. (Available online at: https://www.newstatesman.com/ideas/2022/07/why-flights-keep-getting-cancelled)

Zweig, M. (2011) *The Working Class Majority: America's Best Kept Secret* Cornell University Press

ACKNOWLEDGEMENTS

This book grew out of a short podcast series I did for Repeater Radio in 2020 on the petty bourgeoisie, so thank you to Carl Neville, Rhian E. Jones, Jamie Woodcock, Danny Dorling, Brett Christophers and Alpkan Birelma for their insights on class and for allowing me the space to think and talk about the subject in a deeper way.

I am also extremely grateful to the following people for their help, either through sending me pdfs because I lacked an institutional log in, or taking the time to read through chaotic draft chapters and providing me with feedback: Dai Moon, Mike Harrison, Rob Jones, Sam Parry, Huw Williams, Llywelyn ap Gwilym, Nathan Kusz, Kieron Smith, Steffan Thomas, Ffian Jones, Polly Manning, Jasmine Chorley-Schulz, Owain Hanmer, Bruce Tollafield, Carl Morris, Owain Rhys Lewis, Pete Davies and Paul O Connell. Thank you to my boy Ol and Ash for the cover.

I am also deeply indebted to the good people at Repeater. Thanks to Josh Turner for his tireless organization and production; Matt Colquhoun for copyediting; Christiana Spens for promoting the book. Thanks in particular to both Matteo Mandarini for his thorough engagement with the theoretical material and for helping me see the forest for the trees, and to Tariq Goddard for his patience, encouragement and for keeping faith with the whole thing.

Lastly, writing this book has been a collective endeavour and wouldn't have been possible without the love and support of my friends — too many to mention — and of course my family: thank you Mum and Dad, Luc and Math,

Tim and Sarah, and obviously my wonderful nieces and nephews who inspire and cheer me up every day. Thanks last but not least to Mabli for her patience, love, wisdom and support — cariad gorau.

Repeater Books

is dedicated to the creation of a new reality. The landscape of twenty-first-century arts and letters is faded and inert, riven by fashionable cynicism, egotistical self-reference and a nostalgia for the recent past. Repeater intends to add its voice to those movements that wish to enter history and assert control over its currents, gathering together scattered and isolated voices with those who have already called for an escape from Capitalist Realism. Our desire is to publish in every sphere and genre, combining vigorous dissent and a pragmatic willingness to succeed where messianic abstraction and quiescent co-option have stalled: abstention is not an option: we are alive and we don't agree